BOMBER COMMAND
1939-1945

BOMBER COMMAND
1939-1945

Richard Overy

Foreword by Marshal of the Royal Air Force Sir Michael Beetham GCB, CBE, DFC, AFC, FRAeS

Interviews conducted by Alex Beetham and Sally Lindsay

HarperCollinsPublishers
77-85 Fulham Palace Road
Hammersmith
London W6 8JB

First Published in Great Britain by HarperCollinsPublishers 1997

1 3 5 7 9 10 8 6 4 2

ISBN 0 00 472014 8

Cover painting by Keith Woodcock

Editor: Ian Drury
Design: Mick Sanders and Will Adams
Production Manager: David Lennox
Printed in Italy

Contents

Bomber Command

Reaping the Whirlwind: the film

A Channel 4 documentary film has been produced which accompanies this book. The film, also titled *Bomber Command: Reaping the Whirlwind* assesses the campaign waged by Sir Arthur 'Bomber' Harris, the Commander-in-Chief of Bomber Command against Germany's industrial cities. The programme is made up almost exclusively of unique, never-before-broadcast wartime archive film, including spectacular operational footage. The development of Bomber Command is traced from the brave, but foolhardy early daylight raids to the nightly assaults of awesome power against the Nazi homeland. The film features interviews with RAF bomber aircrews and recently discovered, privately recorded interviews with Sir Arthur Harris himself. For the first time Harris reveals his personal view of the bombing offensive and the political decisions that shaped his military actions, including the controversial raid on Dresden.

The film is a Cinecam Productions documentary, produced and directed by Alex Beetham and now available on video, price £12.99 + £1.50 postage and packing (£2.50 overseas) from the Bomber Command Association, RAF Museum, Grahame Park Way, Hendon, London NW9 5LL, U.K. Telephone (0181) 205 2083.

Also available from the Bomber Command Association is *Bomber Command: Reaping the Whirlwind Part II*. This second film features in greater depth, through fascinating stories and anecdotes, the personal wartime experiences of the aircrew and ground staff of Bomber Command. The video includes rare action footage of the wide range of Bomber Command aircraft at war, operating both on daylight and night raids.

Foreword

by Marshal of the Royal Air Force Sir Michael Beetham, GCB, CBE, DFC, AFC, FRAeS.

If you ask a typical group of 30–40 year olds today what they know about the Bomber Offensive in World War II, they are likely to say 'Oh yes, that was the bombing of German cities when thousands of civilians were killed', and more than likely too Dresden will be mentioned. The Bomber Offensive was, or has become, the most controversial campaign of the war. I say 'has become' because, apart from a few voices, the whole British nation was behind the Offensive at the time. It was a combined Offensive, Bomber Command and the United States 8th Air Force, at least from mid-1942 onwards. From that time, Bomber Command at night and the Americans by day conducted round-the-clock bombing and gave no respite to the Germans.

The seeds of the controversy were sown at the end of the war, when the enormous damage done to German cities and the whole infrastructure of the country became clear. Analysis done immediately after the war by the United States Strategic Bombing Survey and the very much smaller British Bombing Survey Unit, upon which much of the Official History was based, was in parts not uncritical of what the bombing had achieved, particularly in terms of the effects on German industrial production.

It is these documents on which many of the critics of Bomber Command have based their case and have given grist to the mill of those who choose to question whether it was morally right to expose the civilian population to such bombing. Civilians inevitably get caught up in war; many of them were working in factories, or elsewhere, in support of the enemy war effort. These critics choose to ignore the fact that 42,000 Britons were killed during the Blitz. But, importantly, over the years much further information has become available, mostly from German sources, which presents a different picture of what the bombing achieved and now enables a more accurate analysis to be made.

Much of the criticism has been directed at Sir Arthur Harris, the Commander-in-Chief of Bomber Command for the major part of the war, and this came to a head in 1992 when a statue to his memory was erected in London. The impetus for the statue came from those who had served under him in Bomber Command who all felt strongly that he should receive the same public recognition as other great wartime Commanders. The veterans of Bomber Command, who had seen so many of their comrades killed and had been lauded as heroes during the war, have been incensed at what they have always regarded as ill-informed criticism of what both they and their Commander-in-Chief had done. They have always recognised that the criticism has come from a small and vociferous section of the community, and that most of those who lived through the war remain ever appreciative of their achievements and sacrifices. Nevertheless the publicity given to the criticism sticks in the public's mind.

The bomber crews did not enjoy what they had to do. They were very conscious that some innocent civilians unavoidably were being killed in the course of the bombing of industrial cities but they had a job to do and knew that war is a dirty business. Furthermore, they are upset that so much publicity has been given to what was less than half of what they did, and that due public recognition has never been given to the enormous contribution they made to winning the war at sea and on land.

They have been particularly concerned too that, as the years roll by and those who lived through those days pass on, a true picture of what happened should be presented to current generations and recorded for history. In today's world, the first means presentation on television to reach the maximum audience. This was achieved in September 1996 when Channel 4 showed *Bomber Command: Reaping the Whirlwind*, a 50 minute documentary film of the bombing campaign. The object was to portray the facts without bias using archive material and interviews with those who took part. Such has been the success of the film that it was felt a book should also be written to be complementary, not only telling the story of the campaign and the background to it but also analysing it in the knowledge of all the additional data now available more than 50 years on.

I have often been asked, as have most of us who took part, how could we go out night after night to face the formidable German defences – searchlights, AA guns and night fighters – for long periods over enemy territory, normally between 5 and 7 hours? Undoubtedly it could be a daunting prospect and the man who says he was not frightened is still difficult to believe. But we were very young and we were boosted by the tremendous support we were given by everyone on our station and by the general public too. Our groundcrews worked all hours to see our aircraft were in tip top condition and, when we taxied out for take off on a raid, there was always a big crowd to wave us on our way. How could we possibly let them down?

My first three raids were to Berlin, I suppose as tough an introduction as you could imagine. Approaching the target for the first time, I wondered how on earth we could possibly get through the mass of searchlights weaving across the sky to seek us out. 'Wait until they get close and then turn in towards them and not away from them,' I had been told, and it worked. It was comforting that the AA fire bursting like starshells was well below us. Straight and level on the bombing run to the target seemed an eternity and it was a great relief when at last the bombs had gone and we could turn for the long trek home, ever watchful for night fighters until we were crossing the English coast inbound. Back safely from all three raids to a warm welcome, we felt exhilarated and ready to tackle anything.

Our next raid was to Leipzig. This is going to be easy by comparison, I thought. Attacked by a night fighter just after leaving the target, we had a fuel tank holed, our port flaps and ailerons damaged and a badly vibrating port inner engine. We limped home to the first available airfield after crossing the coast. It was a salutary lesson which made us realise what we were up against.

A key factor in our operations was that we were not on our own. We were part of a crew. Each man had his job to do and we completely relied on one another. So, with very few exceptions, we went and, once on the way, we were so busy we hardly had time to think. We lived for the day and we tried not to think about friends and comrades who did not make it back.

Leadership was vitally important, from Harris himself who inspired us all as to the importance of what we were called upon to do and in whom we all had complete faith that he would not hazard us unnecessarily, down to the Squadron and Flight Commanders who were operating with us and set the example. If they were weak and, without question, some were, then there was likely to be a morale problem on that squadron but the overwhelming majority were good and morale was generally, in my experience, very high.

Bomber Command operated from the first day of the war to the last. If there were no operations it was because the weather was too bad, but there were not many occasions when we were completely grounded, for there was a wide spectrum of targets stretching from the Baltic in the North to Italy in the South. Crews got used to flying in bad weather, which could have an adverse effect on bombing accuracy, but the only real weather hazard we worried about was fog back at base. At the end of a long flog over enemy territory, this was something we could do without on return! The blind landing aids of today were not available to us and we hoped the Met men had got their forecast correct.

If the early bombing of Germany was not very effective, what Bomber Command did in the dark days of 1940–42 was to give the British people hope by showing that we were hitting back. When the Command built up its strength and experience and had the resources, Sir Arthur Harris's forecast of 'Reaping the Whirlwind' became a reality. In the following chapters, Professor Richard Overy shows how this came about, by assessing the campaign in a broad context with the benefit of all the information now available, by giving a flavour of the times and by bringing out the human aspect with the recollections of some of those who took part. It is a story that needs telling.

Sir Michael Beetham
Marshal of the Royal Air Force

Bomber Command aircrew being debriefed after a raid. Ever since the war ended the strategic value of their campaign has been the subject of controversy and much ill-informed criticism. Modern research reveals that Bomber Command played a vital role in the Allied victory over Nazi Germany.

Air Chief Marshal Sir Arthur Harris and his family leave for a holiday in Africa after the war. Harris remains one of the most controversial Allied commanders of the Second World War. Post-war critics usually overlook the fact that the orders to bomb cities such as Dresden were given to him by the Air Ministry. His blunt, robust defence of Bomber Command continued until his death in 1983.

Preface

Few campaigns have generated more heated argument than the bombing of Germany by the Allies between 1940 and 1945. A great many distortions and illusions litter the popular view of the part RAF Bomber Command played in that campaign. Not the least of these is the view that all Bomber Command ever did was hammer away at German cities regardless of morality or military good sense. Bomber Command did a great deal more than this, and in the process contributed in a variety of ways to the Allied war effort. The narrative here is intended to show the whole record, and to make it clear who was responsible for taking the decisions that affected Bomber Command.

No one can tell what it was like to serve and fight in the Command better than the veterans of themselves. The larger part of what follows is devoted to these recollections. They are the fruit of a series of taped interviews carried out for the documentary film, *Bomber Command: Reaping the Whirlwind*, first shown on Channel 4 television in September 1996. I have been given generous access to these interviews by the film's producer, Alex Beetham, without whose assistance this book would not have been possible. The interviews were transcribed verbatim, complete with pauses and asides. I have edited them where it was obviously necessary and sensible to do so, but they are as close to the original as possible. I am very grateful to all those veterans who have allowed their interviews, and in some cases their private memoirs and photograph collections, to be used in making the book.

Many other kindnesses have been done along the way. Marshal Harris's daughter, Jackie Assheton, has allowed us to reproduce photographs from her father's private collection. The RAF Museum at Hendon has been more than helpful in supplying both pictures and captions. Thanks are due to Robin Parker, for bringing all the parties together in the first place, to Sally Lindsey for her success in getting veterans to talk candidly about their experiences; and to Roy Irons, who did sterling work in the Public Record Office hunting down documents. The Bomber Command Association deserves special mention for its work in commissioning and developing the film, and their keen support of the subsequent book. Ian Drury has been a patient and painstaking editor: a well-merited thanks.

Richard Overy
London
April 1997

Chapter 1
Building the force, 1936-40

Bomber Command was born on Bastille Day. On July 14th 1936 the Air Defence of Great Britain, the umbrella organisation of Britain's air forces, was replaced by a system of four separate commands, organised according to function: Fighter Command, Bomber Command, Coastal Command and Training Command. Bomber forces were placed under Air Chief Marshal Sir John Steel, with headquarters at Langley, Buckinghamshire. The change was made in order to encourage greater specialisation within the Royal Air Force (RAF), with the object of making each branch better able to perform the role assigned to it. The division promoted the development of a distinct sense of identity for each command built around different training schemes and very different technologies. Bomber Command's function was to bomb. The formal organisational change in 1936 gave the Command a more distinct strategic role than it had enjoyed hitherto. Naming the force helped to define the doctrine it was to pursue.

British bombing policy was shaped by the experience of infant air power in the Great War. Bombing at, or just behind, the front line was commonplace by 1918. What separated British policy on air power from that of her allies and enemies alike was the growing conviction among air enthusiasts both military and civil that long-range air attacks against targets deep in enemy territory could prove strategically useful. Any moral or legal scruples that the British authorities might have had disappeared with German raids on British cities, first with Zeppelin airships, then in the summer of 1917 with heavy bombers. The first reaction to these attacks was the creation of the Royal Air Force as a separate service. Then in June 1918 an Independent Air Force was established in France as part of the RAF to carry out a bombing campaign against German industrial cities under the command of General Hugh Trenchard. The new bombing force was the direct ancestor of Bomber Command.

Trenchard was a former commander of the Royal Flying Corps, the army air force that disappeared with the creation of the RAF. He had been a critic of the policy of independent bombing before he assumed command of the Independent Force and, despite his later reputation, remained sceptical of its effects. He was instructed by the Air Staff to attack the 'root industries' of the enemy and 'the moral [sic] of his nation'. Both were to be found in 'densely populated industrial centres'. Enthusiasm ran high. The Air Staff considered long-range bombing important enough to determine the eventual outcome of the war. Trenchard nonetheless experienced the greatest difficulty in obtaining the machines and trained men to perform the grand task he had been set. Even when he had the necessary equipment, much of the Force's effort was devoted to tactical missions in support of the army. A survey carried out shortly before the Armistice revealed that 49 per cent of the Independent Force sorties had been carried out against enemy aerodromes, and only 7 per cent against iron and steel works and 8 per cent against chemical factories. At its peak the Force consisted of no more than 120 aircraft, and it dropped a total of only 540 tons of bombs, mostly on military targets, the rest on a small number of Rhenish cities that could be reached from French bases. Great plans were laid for an Inter-Allied Force to mount a combined bombing offensive against German industry in 1919, but the coming of peace on November 11th 1918 brought the project to an abrupt end.

The first independent bombing campaign was a failure. In 1919 a bombing survey team arrived in Germany to judge the value of the Independent Force. Its conclusions were largely negative. Angry German house-owners petitioned the British Government for compensation, but the damage done had been slight. The survey made much of the panic widely reported in the cities that had been bombed, and drew from this the conclusion, strongly maintained by Trenchard throughout the 1920s, that the moral impact of bombing was much greater than any material damage. The ratio, Trenchard suggested, was of the order of 20:1.

The Boulton-Paul P.75 Overstrand medium bomber was developed in 1934 from the Boulton-Paul Sidestrand, first flown in 1926. Seen here on display at an Empire Air Day, the type was flown by 101 Squadron at Bicester, but was phased out in 1938.

A flight of Boulton-Paul P.29 Sidestrands seen in 1936. Designed as a day bomber in 1925, the Mark III was developed in 1929. It could carry over 1,000 pounds of bombs and had a range of 520 miles, but only 18 were built before it was replaced after 1936.

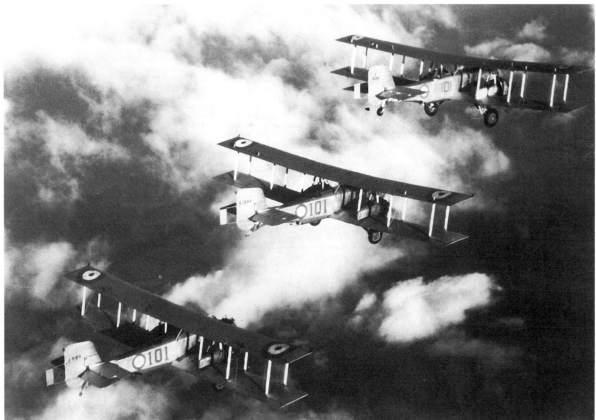

Above: The Fairey Battle squadrons sent to France suffered catastrophic losses during the Battle for France in 1940. Battle pilots attacking a bridge over the Meuse won the RAF's first VCs of the war on 12 May. Two of the aircraft seen here were lost over France: K9325 did not return from attacking German ground troops at St Vith on May 11th 1940, while K9353 was shot down by flak (all crew killed) near Bouillon the following day. K9324 survived and was sent to the RAAF.

Left: A Handley-Page Heyford Mk 1 under mock attack by a Hawker Fury. The Heyford first flew in 1930 and was in service by 1933. Fifteen Mk 1s were built; they had a maximum speed of 154 mph and a range of 930 miles. Many Bomber Command pilots began their careers flying Heyfords, which were used until the outbreak of war.

The lessons of the Great War were ambiguous. German and French air strategists persisted with the view that air power, including bombing, was most effective at the fighting front where it could be brought to bear against enemy forces. In Britain, which had been both a victim of city bombing and the architect of the first coherent bombing campaign, the RAF stuck by the view that some form of independent bombing against what were called the 'nerve centres' of the enemy was a more cost-effective and speedier way of fighting modern war. The RAF War Manual produced in 1936, the year in which Bomber Command was first established, proclaimed that 'the bomb is the chief weapon of an air force'. Thus the new Command was established in a service that had remained consistently committed to the concept of independent bombing from its inception in 1918.

Much less thought had gone into developing the practical means to carry out a bombing campaign. The Government was primarily interested in a bomber force as a form of deterrent, and it was in general hostile to the idea of bombing anything other than military targets. The bombing of the Spanish city of Guernica by German forces helping Franco shocked British opinion. It also shaped the Government's reaction to the growing threat of Germany, which had begun to arm in the air from the year Hitler came to power, in 1933. The British Government assumed that in any war with the new Germany the indiscriminate attack of British cities from the air would be a central part of the German war plan. The bombing 'striking force', as it was known, was therefore developed to counter the specific German threat. However, the record now shows that the German Air Force had no such plan. The German air service was built up in the 1930s as a tactical force. Plans for long-range bombers capable of attacks on the enemy economy were still in their infancy in 1939. But the British Government could not know this – it expected the worst of the Third Reich and prepared accordingly.

The creation of Bomber Command in 1936 was part of a general drive to expand the air force in all directions. There was a great deal of work to be done. Bomber technology was no match for the strategy of long-range attack it was supposed to fulfil. The current generation of bomber aircraft were little better than the models that had armed the Independent Force. They were mainly light bombers, biplanes with limited range and negligible striking power. The larger Handley Page Heyford carried only 1,500 pounds of bombs and could fly only 740 miles, there and back, at a speed of 137 mph. In 1936 a new generation of heavier bombers was already in the pipeline – Wellingtons,

A younger Arthur Harris (seated centre) on a tour of duty in East Africa in 1932 as commander of a flying boat squadron. He later described it as 'the most enjoyable year I had in service'. He returned from Africa to a job in the Air Ministry.

Life as a regular

'Ever since I was a boy I wanted to fly, just to get my feet off the ground. I wasn't well-educated enough to go in as a pilot so I had to start at the bottom and work my way up. I was an aircraft hand on general duties until they started training me and my training went on right through my life in the air force. I qualified as a rigger looking after the air frame, but they asked for volunteers and I qualified as an air gunner. I went for an aircrew interview and it was pointed out that most of the people who got their feet off the ground were the other side, the blue bloods. Most of the pilots in those days were ex-public school and it was only in 1937 and 1938 that they started bringing in observers who had been through apprentice school as a fitter or rigger.

I was never one of the elite. I had to go the long way round. You applied and you did some training on your own aerodrome or you went away and did it. Someone shot a cow when I was at Scampton. We had loose guns with a round pan, and he didn't know much about what he was doing. He fired his gun from 500 feet and a cow collapsed on the farm below. The Irishman put it on his cart and took it to the aerodrome to ask about compensation. One night the IRA came and smashed our place up.'

Harry Jones, Bomber Command gunner

Hampdens and Whitleys – all of which were metal monoplanes capable of much further range and larger bombloads. The Wellington, the brainchild of the Vickers designer Barnes Wallis, could carry 4,500 pounds of bombs a distance of 1,200 miles at a speed of 235 mph. But even at the outbreak of war in September 1939 there were only six squadrons of Wellingtons operational. There were many other deficiencies: far too little attention had been paid to navigation; the bomb sights were inherited from the Great War; stocks of bombs were tiny and of small calibre; and for a force long committed to bombing there was remarkably little emphasis on training men to bomb.

The Air Ministry and Air Staff knew this. In 1936 began the search for a new generation of heavy multi-engined bombers that could be equal to the task of what became known as 'strategic bombing'. A key figure in drawing up the specifications for the new heavy bomber force was a young Deputy Director of Plans, Group Captain Arthur Harris. Against the objections of more senior colleagues, who favoured a large number of medium bombers, Harris argued that only the heavy bomber promised the long range and great lifting power that would give Bomber Command real offensive potential. He won the argument and shaped the future course of Bomber Command.

The new specification for a bomber capable of flying 3,000 miles with 8,000 pounds of bombs at a height of 28,000 feet revolutionised aircraft design in Britain. The result was the Short Stirling, by no means the most successful or popular of the new generation of four-engined bombers, which came into service during 1941. Despite continued political pressure to opt for cheaper medium bombers, the Air Staff persisted with the heavy bomber programme. In 1938 they issued the specification for what they called the 'Ideal Bomber'. It was to have all the current advances in military aircraft design, much heavier armament to cope with the expected threat from the new generation of fast fighter aircraft, and a speed of 300 mph carrying 12,000 pounds of bombs. Interrupted by the outbreak of war, the development of the Ideal Bomber was saved by converting designs for heavy two-engined bombers into four-engined craft. The results here were the much more successful Halifax and Lancaster bombers, which became the mainstay of Bomber Command after 1942.

The next requirement was the men to run the new service and fly the planes. The RAF had 30,000 men in 1934 with 11,000 reservists in the Auxiliary Air Force. There existed a total of 42 squadrons, many under-strength and poorly armed. Under the expansion schemes for the RAF begun in 1934, and accelerated in 1936, it was planned to produce first 41 medium bomber squadrons, then in the final pre-war programme (Scheme M) a total of 85 heavy bomber squadrons by March of 1941. The programme placed demands on the British aircraft industry that could not be met from current resources, and a good deal of rearmament money was spent on expanding basic industrial capacity. Expansion at this rate also strained the existing programmes of recruitment and training. In 1937 the RAF Volunteer Reserve was set up with the object of training 800 additional pilots a year. The response was literally overwhelming. In three years the scheme turned out over 5,000 pilots. Volunteers poured in from all over the British Empire, and by 1939 the RAF had 118,000 regulars and a reserve of 68,000.

Dressing down

'When I came back in 1935 I was horrified at the state of the RAF. I'd left a very pleasant RAF and I found things quite different. People answered back. I remember an occasion when this Warrant Officer stopped me. He was probably the chairman of the mess. He tore me off the most terrible strip. Where did you get that uniform? Where did you get those shoes? My socks were knitted, my shirt was just a shade the wrong colour, my tie was even a crocheted tie. Then along the path came what I assumed was the squadron postman, delivering letters to the mess. He was in a terrible pickle. His tunic was undone all the way down, he had a civilian shirt, he was wearing plimsolls, his hair was in a terrible state, he needed a shave and he looked an absolute dead loss compared with a rather spic and span Sergeant, with a uniform to fit and tailor-made shoes. And he left me for a moment and started off on this fellow and he started from his shoes.

"What's happened to your regular boots? Only sergeants wear shoes and wear them outside."

And so it went on, all the way up until he got to this patch over his eye. He stopped for breath and said, "What's the matter with the eye?"

And this guy just shifted his letters and said, "It's full of bullshit," and walked on.

I've never been so staggered in my life. That was the new air force.'

Hamish Mahaddie, Bomber Command pilot

Seen here in 1936, the Hawker Hind light day bomber was the most widely used aircraft in Bomber Command before the war, a total of 527 being built. Powered by a Rolls Royce Kestrel engine, the Hind could reach a maximum speed of 185 mph and carried 510 pounds of bombs under the wings. Regarded more as an operational training aircraft than a front-line bomber, it was withdrawn from active service in December 1939.

Flying or bust

'I'd have been bored to tears as a soldier or a sailor. Flying was the life for me – I knew that. First of all I was a flight mechanic and then I took a flight engineer's course for eight weeks. I concentrated on the air frame side of it because I thought I knew all about engines. I failed the engine exam and passed the air frame exam. They gave me one week to clue up on it and I passed the second time. Now at a young age I had had an operation for varicose veins and I did not want to fail the air crew medical examinations. So I signed my own medical chits before I left Gosport. I didn't do anything really bad – I didn't sign myself "doctor". I believe I left that blank. I just signed the chit. Halfway through the course they caught up with me and said I had to report to the medical centre and that was the longest walk of my life. I thought now I'm for 80 days in the glasshouse. But they merely said I had not had a medical. I had to go past four doctors and the last one told me to strip off. He was in a very bad mood. He told me to lie on the bench, and I said, "Which way up?"

He said, "On your back, you bloody fool."

I stretched myself out and he started tapping me with a little hammer. "You have varicose veins," he said.

I wouldn't answer him. He asked me what the scars on my leg were, and I said cuts. He told me I had got varicose veins. I was sent to a panel of doctors. They said that I had a choice of returning to my old unit or having an operation. I took another operation, was passed fit and was back on the course.'

Maurice Manser,
Bomber Command flight engineer

A Canadian in Bomber Command

'As a youngster I was a navigation fan. I read Flight magazine, Aeroplane and so on in our book stores all the time. I saw a little advertisement by the Air Ministry saying join the RAF on a short service commission, become a pilot. I finally decided to write to them to see if I would qualify as a Canadian with a Canadian standard of education, and they said yes, apply through the Royal Canadian Air Force. I went through my medicals and was accepted and came over in 1938 under a scheme in which the RCAF interviewed me, did all my medicals and so on and paid my way across.

I entered under the condition of doing four years service as a short-service commissioned officer in the RAF. At the completion of that the RCAF would have paid my way back to Canada and I would have served six years on the active reserve of the RCAF. If all had gone well I had a very good shot at becoming an airline captain. But at the same time you could see the writing on the wall. If this war did come I certainly wanted to be in the air force and not slogging it out on the ground. I'd already spent two years in an Army reserve regiment and it didn't appeal to me. I launched into flying and I'm happy that I did.'

**Wilfred John 'Mike' Lewis,
Bomber Command pilot**

A Heyford Mk 1 in service with 99 Squadron at Mildenhall in Suffolk, where it arrived in 1934. Designated a heavy bomber, it carried 2,500 pounds of bombs as its normal load, but could carry up to 3,500 pounds. Note the retractable 'dustbin' gun turret under the fuselage.

The Volunteer Reservist

'I had no ambition whatsoever to be in the army. I didn't want to be in the trenches I'd seen at the cinema and in the newspapers. Horrible scenes of trench warfare – people being gassed, butchered with bayonets. I thought if I'm going to die I may as well die quickly in the air and be done with it.

I had always wanted to fly, but I couldn't afford to go to flying school. Then they opened up a Volunteer Reserve centre in Manchester where I was living, and here was my opportunity. I applied to join and started to fly in 1939 in Tiger Moths at weekends. We got £25 per annum retainer and a shilling an hour flying pay and payment for attendance at lectures. It was like a club and I was lucky to get in. Sometimes you wouldn't fly for three weekends because the weather was so bad so I didn't break any records. It took me 17 hours to go solo. By the time war broke out in September I had just about finished my military flying training and expected to go off to the service flying school. But they took the aeroplanes away, put a balloon barrage up over the aerodrome and we were sent home for 12 weeks not knowing what we were going to do.

Eventually I was sent to Cambridge University, to Emmanuel College. We spent most of the time drilling and square bashing and route marching and had lectures on navigation and theory of flight and armaments. After six weeks I'm sure we could have outdrilled the brigade of guards. We were so fed up with it; we wanted to fly again. Out of the blue I was posted to Rhodesia and finished my training there.'

John Gee, Bomber Command pilot

John Gee, a pilot with Bomber Command during the war, began flying in 1939 on Tiger Moths. 'I was very fearful there was going to be a war… I thought if I'm going to die then I may as well die quickly in the air and be done with it!'

Joining the WAAFS

'I saw WAAFs driving in convoy one morning. You didn't see many women drivers in those days, so it seemed very exciting to me. I thought I'd like to have a go at driving heavy lorries. I put my age on a bit. I was getting on for 17, but when I first thought about joining I was 15. I don't know if it was easy for most girls to get in under age but I managed it. I liked wearing uniform, apart from the hat. I was on a few charges for not wearing a hat.

All kinds joined. There was a chorus girl, one was a farmer's daughter… The first day we arrived there were hundreds of girls with suitcases and civilian clothes. They sent trucks to pick us up and we all paraded in a hall. Then one of the WAAF officers came in and said we all had to strip. Then we all paraded and someone looked for nits in your hair. That was the worst thing. It shocked most of us… The first night we were all in beds which had to be stacked in threes in the morning. I could hear some of the girls in the night crying.'

Eileen Richards, WAAF in Bomber Command

A New Zealand recruit

'In 1937 I had already joined the 1st Battalion of the Wellington Regiment, and so by 1939 I was a well-trained heavy machine-gunner. When the war started I had no desire to carry a 47 pound machine-gun with me wherever I went. My friends in the Territorials were very keen for me to join the first echelon of the New Zealand Division, but I thought it would be a much more comfortable war sitting down rather than carrying a heavy machine-gun. I had to wait until the RNZAF announced its recruiting scheme, an intake of 20 pilots, 20 observers and 20 air gunners every month. That morning I went into one door of the bank in which I worked, the Bank of New Zealand, signed in the attendance book and ran out of the other door of the bank to the Air Department to sign on. I found that I would have to wait a whole year before

I could become a pilot, but a friend in the Air Department said that if I was prepared to sign on as an observer he would put my file on the top. I was in in a month.

The instructors were well-trained experienced officers, mainly from the RAF, but they had so little equipment. We flew for bombing and gunnery in Vickers Vincents, which were really nothing much better than animated box kites. We flew for navigation in the small airliners of Union Airways, DH 86s and 89s, and when I left New Zealand as a fully trained observer I'd done a total of 52 hours flying. Four of them were at night over New Zealand with lights on, and yet I was destined for Bomber Command. Had I known what was coming I think I would have died of heart failure before I'd even left the Dominion.'

Sam Hall, Bomber Command navigator

A Westland Lysander Mk IIIA converted for special duties with Bomber Command for work with the Special Operations Executive (SOE), which undertook resistance work in occupied Europe during the war. Bombs could be carried on the Lysander, fitted to small racks protruding from the wheel spats. The type first saw service in 1938.

Early days

'I was soon integrated. There were squadron and station duties which we all had to perform besides our normal squadron flying and servicing tasks. One of these duties was that of Duty Signaller, which a squadron wireless operator had to do, by roster, whenever night-flying was on the agenda. On such occasions the Duty Pilot and the Duty Signaller were the essential flying control organisation. There were no runways and a flarepath had to be laid out using goose-neck flares fed by paraffin. A large flare known as the Money Flare, about 3 feet high and 4 feet in diameter, made of cotton waste held together in a stout wire basket and soaked with paraffin, was placed at the approach end of the flarepath.

The Duty Signaller had two Aldis Lamps, one with a green lens, the other with a red lens; he and the Duty Pilot were stationed by the Money Flare on to which paraffin was poured whenever an aircraft was about to land. The procedure was for a pilot taxiing his aircraft to the flarepath to flash the identification letter on his upper and lower ident lights using a keying device in the cockpit. Seeing this the Duty Signaller would call out, for example, "S for Sugar on the ground, sir". If all was clear the D/P would reply, "S for Sugar on the ground a Green", and the D/S would then flash "S" with the green lamp sighted on the aircraft. A pilot wishing to land would likewise flash his letter, but this time the D/S would call out "L for London in the air, sir", and would be instructed to flash a red or green depending on the state of the circuit.

Although Duty Signaller could be a rather cold stint at times, even when wearing an Irvin jacket, also very smelly due to the burning paraffin, I quite enjoyed it. One station duty that I hated, though, arose in that winter of 1938/39 through the activities of the IRA who had planted several small explosive devices in GPO pillar-boxes; there was also some concern for the security of military installations. We therefore had to mount standing patrols day and night covering the working areas of the station. It was a two hours on, four hours off job during a 24-hour stint starting at 0800 hours. Initially we were armed only with a police truncheon and patrolled singly. Later we carried rifles at night – but no ammunition – and patrolled in pairs; the object of the rifle was to go through the loading motion hoping that the challenge of "Halt who goes there?" to the sound of the bolt action might serve to bring any intruder to a state of submission. What a miserable duty that was, particularly on a cold windy night with the hangar doors clanging eerily.'

Life in Bomber Command in the spring of 1939, from a memoir by Squadron-Leader W. Jacobs

A squadron of Hawker Hart light bombers seen in 1936, operated by the Auxiliary Air Force. Designed by Sir Sidney Camm, the Hart was the mainstay of British light bomber squadrons between the wars. A total of 992 were built, starting with the prototype in 1927. When it first flew it could out-pace RAF fighters with its top speed of 185 mph.

The German War Minister, General Werner von Blomberg (fourth from left), on an official visit to Britain for the Coronation of King George VI, visits an RAF base. Behind him is a Handley Page Harrow heavy bomber, introduced in 1937 but phased out at the end of 1939 in favour of the Wellington.

A production line of Fairey Battle light bombers at the Heaton Chapel factory in Stockport. The Battle was an up-to-date light bomber when the specification was issued in 1932, but by the time it entered service in 1937 it was too slow for the new generation of fighters and proved a disaster in combat during 1940.

The new Bomber Command expanded geographically to cope with the additional manpower and aircraft. It was organised in six Groups, the sixth of which was an Operational Training Unit. On the eve of war an Air Striking Force was set up to accompany the army to the Continent, composed of ten squadrons of Fairey Battle light bombers considered unsuitable for longer-range operations. The most pressing need was for airfields capable of coping with heavier bomber aircraft, which needed longer and stronger runways and substantial facilities for storage and maintenance. By 1939 Britain had three times the number of air stations existing in 1934. Bomber Command had 27 airfields in southern and eastern England, divided between four operational groups and a reserve group, with headquarters at Wyton, Grantham, Mildenhall, Linton-on-Ouse and Abingdon. The headquarters of the Command was at Richings Park, Langley, in Buckinghamshire (the wartime headquarters at High Wycombe was not occupied until 1940), and from here the Commander-in-Chief was able to organise the movement of Britain's entire bomber forces.

The main issue faced by Bomber Command was the precise nature of the role it was to perform in the event of war. For much of the inter-war period the function of Britain's bomber forces was never clearly defined. There was of course no real threat until the emergence of a rapidly rearming Germany in the mid-1930s. The Air Staff assumed that bombing would pick up where it had finished in 1918, attacking the industrial centres of the enemy to deprive him of the sinews of war and to demoralise his population. But the rather vague formula arrived at in

discussions between the three armed services in 1928 talked only of the air force helping to 'break down the enemy's resistance' by attacks on 'objectives calculated to achieve this end'. When the Chiefs of Staff drew up more precise guidelines during the early rearmament phase, the role of bombing was more narrowly defined. Bomber forces were to help in the defence of Britain by attacking enemy air power; they were to assist the Royal Navy and, if necessary, the army; attacks on the enemy economy were relegated to the end of the list, to be made only under circumstances in which the Government deemed an attack on enemy civilians to be justified. Little was left of the RAF conception of strategic bombing until it was revived by Winston Churchill in the summer of 1940.

Nonetheless the RAF was left with the task of deciding what kinds of targets it should attack if it were ever asked to attack an enemy's economic and military system. At the end of 1937 the opportunity was handed to them. The Government decided that Germany was now a very real threat, and that detailed plans should be made for air action in case the worst happened. In October 1937 the Air Ministry drew up the so-called Western Air Plans, a list of 13 objectives for the RAF in the event of war. The most important were contained in Group I, Plans 1 to 5. Three of these applied directly to Bomber Command: first, the attack on the enemy air striking force; second, direct support of military operations by disabling German communications behind the battle front; and third, and from the Command's view the most significant, an attack on 'German War Industry', and in particular the oil and heavy industry of the Ruhr area, Germany's industrial heartland.

Hawker Hinds of No 21 Squadron, Bomber Command, stationed at Lympne in Kent, on an air exercise in August 1937. By the end of that year 21 squadrons were equipped with Hinds, as well as six squadrons of the Auxiliary Air Force.

The Fairey Hendon Mk II, which saw service briefly with Bomber Command in No 38 Squadron from December 1936 to January 1939. The design was a radical answer to a night-bomber specification in 1927, but by the time it was finally ordered by the Air Ministry in 1934, it was already obsolescent. Only 14 examples of the Mk II were built.

The Western Air Plans, 1937

Group I

W.1   Plans for attack on the German Air Striking Force, and its maintenance organisation.

W.2   Plans for reconnaissance in co-operation with the Navy in Home Waters and the Eastern Atlantic.

W.3   Plans for close co-operation with the Navy in convoy protection in Home waters and the Eastern Atlantic.

W.4   Plans for attacking the concentration areas of the German Army, and the interruption of its communications in an advance into Belgium, Holland and France.

W.5   Plans for attacking enemy's manufacturing resources in the Ruhr, Rhineland and Saar.

Group II

W.6   Plans for attacking enemy's air manufacturing resources in Germany.

W.7   Plans for counter-offensive action in defence of seaborne trade in co-operation with the Navy.

Group III

W.8   Plans for the attack on specially important depots or accumulations of warlike stores other than air, in enemy country.

W.9   Plans for putting the Kiel Canal out of action.

W.10   Plans for the destruction of enemy shipping and facilities in German mercantile ports – precedence to be given to the Baltic.

Group IV

W.11   Plans for attacking the enemy's manufacturing resources in areas other than the Ruhr, Rhineland and Saar.

W.12   Plans for attacking the German Fleet or a section thereof by air in concert with the Navy either in harbour or at sea.

W.13   Plans for attack on enemy's headquarter and administrative offices in Berlin and elsewhere.

Air Staff, December 9th 1937 (PRO AIR 14/225)

Above: The Bristol Blenheim Mk I began life as a private venture before its high speed attracted the interest of the Air Ministry in 1935. The first batch was delivered to No 114 Squadron in March 1937, but the very first plane crashed on landing. It began to replace the Hind from 1938.

Right: This Fairey Battle of No 63 Squadron was supplied to the Royal Australian Air Force for training in 1940. In total 739 Battles were sent to Canada and 364 to Australia, where they were used mainly for training. Its top speed of 257 mph was 50 mph slower than that of the Messerschmitt Bf 109.

Bomber Command under a new Commander-in-Chief, Sir Edgar Ludlow-Hewitt, appointed in September 1937, was most enthusiastic about the last of these. It was widely agreed among RAF leaders that an enemy air force was difficult to destroy by bombing. Targets were widely dispersed, small, easily repaired and for the most part beyond the range of existing bombing aircraft. Little or no preparation was made for a counter-force strategy. Much the same argument could be made for attacks on road and rail. When, after the outbreak of war, the RAF was pressed to say what its bomber force in France was capable of, it had to admit that a week of intensive bombing was likely to cut only three German railway lines, and that only temporarily. The view of Bomber Command was that attacks on German industry were both more strategically useful and operationally realistic.

In December 1937 Bomber Command was ordered to draw up a list of priority targets. This was done by Air Intelligence and the Air Targets Sub-Committee, a branch of the Industrial Intelligence Centre set up in 1934. Discussions occasioned a good deal of argument about what was and was not decisive in the operation of a complex industrial system. The end result was a compromise. Bomber Command favoured the electric power system; the civilian planners argued for attacks on the Ruhr dams and canal and rail transport. Ludlow-Hewitt thought that Bomber Command could cripple the German electric power system in the Ruhr in 'about a fortnight'. The canal and rail lobby thought that 3,000 sorties would bring the whole of Ruhr industry grinding to a halt in a matter of days.

Even the Air Staff thought these estimates wildly optimistic. The Chiefs of Staff, whose job it was to make the final decision, were unimpressed. Bomber Command was told to confine its operations to attacks on the enemy air force and the defence of British shipping, and was ordered only to attack clearly identifiable military targets. The British and French staffs, meeting together in April 1938, formally agreed to avoid the intentional bombing of civilians. Though Bomber Command chafed at the bit, it was compelled to accept this very limited directive down to the outbreak of war and beyond.

In truth Ludlow-Hewitt knew that his force was not capable of a great deal. The conversion from older bomber types to the new generation was much slower than had been anticipated. The light bombers, the Battle and Blenheim, were clearly unsuitable for long-distance heavy bombing, though 16 out of 33 operational squadrons in September 1939 were equipped with them. Even the heavier aircraft, the Hampdens, Whitleys and Wellingtons, when fully loaded, could go little further from British bases than the Ruhr. Operational preparation was still in its

infancy. Only in 1937 did Bomber Command concede that a pilot could not simultaneously fly and navigate the aircraft. A second pilot was introduced on bomber aircraft in 1938, but where there was room for only one crewman in the cockpit the observer/gunner was given a short course in navigation. Not until 1939 was it recognised that bombers needed a specially trained navigator. Even then navigation relied on simple methods. In daylight or strong

Making a will

'I came back after training in Rhodesia in summer skies on single-engined aircraft. I got posted in the winter in total blackout to a heavy bomber Operational Training Unit. I was scared stiff. We used to taxi around, particularly at night time, literally praying that we hadn't forgotten some essential part of the cockpit. There was no real system of instruction: take off, go round and land, and the same thing again and again. In the three or four weeks I was at that OTU 22 Wellingtons crashed due to the inexperience of the pilots and engine failure. If you passed through the OTU training you were bound to get through operations.

I arrived on 99 Squadron at Waterbeach. I met the commanding officer and my flight commander. They were quizzing me about how much flying I'd done. I had a total of 230 hours flying, of which only 50 were on twin-engined aircraft. That was all on the Wellington. I hadn't flown any other twin-engined aircraft before, and only 15 hours had been done at night, and here I was posted on to a heavy bomber night squadron. I could see the look on their faces and I wasn't a bit surprised when we left their offices and the adjutant said to me, "John, have you made your will?"

I said that I hadn't, and he said, "Right, we'll soon sort that out for you."

He sent for one of the pilots who was a solicitor by profession and within 10 minutes we made my will. I think my estate consisted of one bicycle and a cricket bat, so it didn't take long to do. But they thought my chances of getting through were virtually nil.'

John Gee, Bomber Command pilot

A tough training

'Since we were destined for Bomber Command, night flying practices began early in the training programme. On our first night detail we had just turned into wind on the flare-dotted grass runway when Bob Whitehead, who was acting as first pilot, gave a horrified shout. At the far end of the runway there was an intense burst of flames. The aircraft that had taken off ahead of us had crashed on take-off. We were instructed by Flying Control to abort the sortie and return to dispersal.

When events were pieced together it appeared that the trainee pilot of the crashed Wellington, who was short of stature, may have put down the aircraft's nose as he stretched down for the lever that retracted the undercarriage. He also caused the aircraft to swerve when only a few feet from the ground and it hit another aircraft dispersed on the airfield boundary. When the Wellington crashed and burst into flames the fuselage ruptured on one side allowing one member of the crew who was sitting at the rest-bed position to escape. But the remainder were incinerated, and I had witnessed the end of the first member of our New Zealand course to become a casualty.

It was the gentle and happy Maori, 19-year-old Doug Rewa.

As the war progressed and training casualties mounted, funerals became commonplace, but I can recall accompanying Doug's bier along the road to the cemetery on the outskirts of Bassingbourn village. His coffin on its carriage was piled high with wreaths and, in the warmth of a summer's afternoon, the pervasive scent of the flowers accompanied the sad procession for the length of the journey. He was the third serviceman to be buried there, but now there are six long rows of graves, all with the neat headstones provided by the Imperial War Graves Commission, to indicate mutely the toll exacted during final training.

Finally we were detached to Jurby in the Isle of Man for air-gunnery and bombing training. On our last night there we strolled to the smoky local inn for a final visit. There was little laughter on that occasion and a tendency to stare into our beer with a contemplative look for, without a word on the subject being said, we knew that the time was imminent for all our training to be put to the acid test.'

Memoir of a young New Zealander in Bomber Command, 1939

moonlight it was difficult to find the target. In cloud it was impossible. Numerous aircraft were lost in training before the war through navigational error. Training in night-flying was even more rudimentary. In 1938 only 10 per cent of all hours flown were at night. By the outbreak of war night-flying training was routine only for the pilots of the Whitley, the slowest and most vulnerable of the new generation of bomber aircraft. Bombing accuracy had also been woefully neglected for a force asked to attack communications and airfields. Bombing trials in September 1938 showed that even at 2,500 feet against undefended targets an accuracy of 15 per cent was all that could be achieved. High-level bombing trials showed that only three bombs out of a hundred hit the target.

The weakness of Bomber Command played its part in the Munich crisis of 1938. A few weeks before Prime Minister Neville Chamberlain made his first flight in an aeroplane to see Hitler, Ludlow-Hewitt wrote to the Air Ministry that Bomber Command was virtually powerless; it could reach only the fringes of north-west Germany and faced unacceptably high losses against German defences. He suggested that Britain rely on the North Sea and its air

defences to counter any German air campaign. To commit Bomber Command in its current state of unreadiness was to invite 'major disaster'. This was an extraordinary indictment of his own force, given the emphasis for so long placed on bombing strategy in British air thinking. But it was a realistic one. Even after a further year of preparation, in September 1939 Bomber Command was still a small force in the early stages of serious operational development. For much too long the practical efficacy of strategic bombing was, in the words of John Slessor, one of the most influential thinkers in the pre-war RAF, a 'matter of faith'.

When war broke out on September 3rd 1939 there was an almost universal expectation that fleets of German bombers would appear over London dropping bombs or gas. Air raid warnings sounded in the capital almost immediately, sending the population scurrying for trenches and shelters. It was a false alarm, a misidentified British aircraft. Bomber Command stood by. Its instructions were clear. British and French staffs agreed that bomber aircraft should be used only to assist the battle on land. Until that battle began, Bomber Command was

Night flying

'My total night flying training was one solo circuit in an Oxford. Six months later at Upwood I had to night-fly a Blenheim with no dual. I was told to take a Blenheim up with my air-gunner and take off at dusk and keep going round and round until it was dark. I had to do this on the basis of one solo circuit. You are in a completely strange and alien environment, doing everything entirely by instruments. Your whole technique of approach and landing is entirely different with a flarepath.

The next night my entire crew were sent off round England at night time. We had to do two cross-countries, come back to a beacon and then do another one. We were up for about 2 hours and then the instructions were that we circled, found a flashing beacon and then flew 2 minutes on a certain course before we saw the flarepath. I did this and it was just black after 2 minutes. Back to the beacon and try again. When I'd done this about six times I was getting quite desperate. I thought I'd gone mad or I must be doing something wrong. Then suddenly the flarepath came on. They had been telling us from the ground what was happening but we were not receiving it. There were German intruders and that was why they had put the flarepath out.

I got down and landed, immensely relieved, and so were my crew because they were stuck with this pupil pilot who'd never done any night flying before. The one after came in and crashed on the flarepath and burst into flames. That caused panic and uproar. The ones that were still up were told to go and circle the beacon and wait for further instructions. At the end of the night, out of the six of us who'd gone flying that night, three were written off and one of the other three, who'd been told to go and circle the beacon after the crash, was forgotten about in the panic and he went round and round the beacon till he ran out of petrol and killed himself. Of the 21 crews on our OTU course, six were written off before we even got on a squadron.'

Sir Lewis Hodges, Bomber Command pilot

'War with Germany': air plans in the Munich Crisis

Most Secret

It is impossible to define in any detail, in advance of the event, the course of action that will have to be adopted by the air striking force at the outset of a war with Germany. It must depend to a very great extent on the action that is taken by the German air forces, partly because they have the initiative owing to their superior strength, and partly owing to the policy of His Majesty's Government that we should not initiate air action which may cause heavy loss to the civil population.

We must conserve our resources, owing to our shortage of reserves, and that for this and a variety of other reasons we cannot hope for quick or impressive results in the initial stages… Taking the above factors into account it is considered that it would be unwise to begin by retaliation on the Ruhr until we are in a position to do so effectively. Sporadic and inaccurate bombing of the Ruhr by a few squadrons at night only, would be ineffective and generally undesirable. When we attack we must do so effectively, and it is essential that we should be able to destroy the generating stations and coking plants which have been selected as the first and most vital objectives.

It is during this early period when our offensive action is invariably limited, that effective use might be made of dropping propaganda from the air… To begin with, therefore, attacks on Germany direct from the United Kingdom must be directed against objectives on the coast and in the extreme North of Germany, with the objects:

(a) of the destruction and dislocation of really important objectives, which will seriously affect the German capacity to carry on the war, and

(b) of forcing the enemy to disperse his active fighter defences between the North of Germany, the French Front and the Czechoslovak front.

Air Staff, September 27th 1938 (PRO AIR 14/225)

The coming of war

'In that August of 1939 I was on leave with my family in Wales, and I received a telegram from the squadron instructing me to report back to the station forthwith because it looked as if war was imminent. I remember entering the living quarters there and everything had been transformed. All the electric light bulbs had been removed and blue light bulbs had been installed, which gave it a ghostly atmosphere. No blackout had been installed in those early days.

At the outbreak of war on September 3rd 1939 I was in the hangars at Finningley with other members of the squadron listening to the broadcast by Neville Chamberlain that a state of war now existed between our country and the Germans. I remember this dramatic moment very clearly. We rushed out of the hangars on to the tarmac and looked out towards the east coast expecting to see German bombers coming over immediately.

There was a feeling of the unknown. We were not sure what was going to happen. We were fully occupied because we had just received new equipment. Hampden bombers had arrived and we were geared up to a big training programme, particularly night flying. The first time I flew a Hampden at night it was a great shock, because on take-off one was used to seeing the lights of Doncaster in the distance. But on this occasion it was pitch dark, no horizon, not a light to be seen.

Sir Lewis Hodges, Bomber Command pilot

directed to confine itself to reconnaissance, propaganda flights and attacks on German naval targets in the North Sea. 'Unrestricted air warfare', according to the Air Ministry instructions, 'is not in the interests of Great Britain'. British air forces remained subject to Chamberlain's formal proscription of any attacks that posed a risk to civilian lives, a ban that was only lifted the following May, when Chamberlain was no longer Prime Minister.

The bomber force at Britain's disposal in 1939 was larger and better equipped than it had been at the time of Munich, but it was still a force of very limited capability. Ten squadrons of light bombers were sent to France at once. Other squadrons were placed in reserve. The striking force that was left consisted of just 23 front-line squadrons, equipped with 280 bombers, one group of Blenheims, one of Hampdens, one of Whitleys and one of Wellingtons. These aircraft formed the core of Bomber Command's

equipment until 1942, when heavier bombers at last became available in quantity.

The limitations of the force were fully exposed when operations began against German naval targets. Though the range was short the operations were fraught with difficulty. The weather during the winter months was the main obstacle. Aircraft flew in atrocious conditions, which made the location and identification of naval targets particularly difficult. The instruction to avoid any civilian casualties limited what could be attacked on the German coast. Finally German defences were strong around naval targets, in anticipation of British attacks. Losses proved exceptionally high in daylight raids, and the damage inflicted minimal.

One of the worst raids occurred on December 18th 1939, when 24 Wellingtons were sent out on an armed reconnaissance of the German port of Wilhelmshaven and surrounding waters. Two aircraft were forced to turn home,

Military objectives

Our policy in respect of air bombardment at the outset of a war was agreed with the French in the course of the Staff Conversations in London in April this year in the following terms. 'The Allies would not initiate air action against any but purely "military" objectives in the narrowest sense of the term, ie Naval, Army and Air Forces and establishments, and as far as possible would confine it to objectives on which attack would not involve loss of civil life.'

Action against objectives will be subject to the following general principles:

(a) The intentional bombardment of civil populations is illegal.

(b) It must be possible to distinguish and identify the objective in question.

(c) Bombardment must be carried out in such a way that there is a reasonable expectation that damage will be confined to the objective and that civilian populations in the neighbourhood are not bombarded through negligence.

Air Ministry, 'Instructions Governing Naval and Air Bombardment', August 22nd 1939 (PRO AIR 8/283)

but the remaining 22 flew into the waiting fighters already alerted by German radar. They photographed the area but dropped no bombs because of the risk of civilian deaths. Ten aircraft were shot down, two more were lost on the way home, and three were so badly damaged that they could not regain their home base. Only seven aircraft from the original force returned. From that date on, Bomber Command was forced to accept that its bombers could not operate by day. The faster Blenheims were sent out in ones and twos to reconnoitre, but larger attacks were abandoned. The Wellingtons and Hampdens followed the example of the Whitleys and began to bomb mainly at night, if at all. The anti-shipping campaign fizzled out. In all, 861 sorties were flown, only 61 tons of bombs were dropped, and one German submarine and a minesweeper sunk. Bomber Command lost 40 bombers.

While the Command learned harsh lessons over the North Sea, the Whitleys were reserved for a propaganda war against the German population. On the very first night of war ten aircraft dropped leaflets over northern Germany. The campaign continued, with interruptions caused largely by the winter weather, until the following April. The Whitleys flew at night and at a height that helped them to avoid both flak and night-fighter threats, but also increased the severe risk of icing. The crews were subjected to intense cold for which they were inadequately prepared. Effective oxygen supply was lacking and heating rudimentary or non-existent. Crews wore layers of clothing to avoid freezing to death. Hands froze to the equipment and the

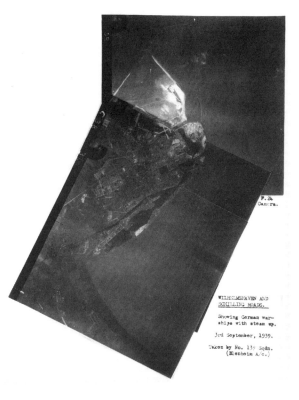

Bomber Command's first operational photographs of the war: two frames of the German port of Wilhelmshaven. Bomber Command aircraft played a key role in long-range reconnaissance in addition to their offensive function.

Fighting the cold

'Freezing! The aircraft used to ice up. We had leaflets to drop and if you cut the pack and touched the knife to your skin it would stick. You tried to put as much clothing on as you could because you couldn't get a lot of movement in the aircraft, you can't jump up and down to keep warm. One of the things I remember about the winter of 1939/40 was the absolute cold. If I could get a pair of silk stockings I'd wear those, then woollen socks and then flying boots, which were fur-lined, then an inner jacket like a teddy bear with a canvas coating, then a leather jacket with fur, three pairs of gloves – a silk pair, wool and then leather gauntlets. Sheer cold is one of the worst things. You had to sit there and try to think warm.'

Greg Gregson, Bomber Command WOP/AG

Bomber Command WOP/AG (Wireless Operator/Air Gunner) Greg Gregson, who began the war dropping leaflets over Germany, and was transferred late in 1940 to the Middle East: '...you had to keep going, no matter what happened.'

Leaflets, not bombs

'The morning of Monday 4th September brought great activity in the Flights of both 77 and 102, and it soon became apparent that we were to do our first show tonight. Details of aircraft and crews were posted in the Flight Authorisation Book during the afternoon: "Raid DM82 Whitley K8958 Crew P/O Bisset, P/O Kierstead, Sgt W. Less (Obs), LAC W. Jacobs (WOp/AG), LAC C. Killingley (Rear Gunner). ETD 2359."

The fuselage forward of the door was crammed with large parcels of leaflets wrapped in coarse brown paper tied with thick twine. Access, normally difficult enough because of the retracted ventral turret, was now extremely difficult through the narrow alley between the parcels on either side both fore and aft of the turret. At the evening briefing we were acquainted with the purpose of the mission and the reader will understand our feelings at not being called upon to deliver anything more damaging than a good supply of paper and stout rubber bands on Germany's industrial heartland. However, maintaining strict wireless silence, except in emergency, until clear of enemy territory, we were to enter German airspace north of Holland and, avoiding neutral territory, fly southward distributing our leaflets down the Ruhr valley, into France and home across the English Channel.

By the time we crossed the enemy coast we were at 15,000 feet breathing oxygen. Visibility was good but ground features were obscured and navigation was by dead reckoning assisted by wireless bearings obtained by the direction-finding loop aerial. Shortly before we commenced leaflet dropping we observed a beam of light apparently aimed in our direction from a point slightly below and to the right of our nose. We judged it to be airborne and Bill Lees gave it a burst from the front gun; it went out immediately and we concluded that we had been the object of an attempted night-fighter interception.

The lot of dropping the leaflets fell to P/O Kierstead and myself, and what a wearisome task it was. At 15,000 feet the outside temperature was about 15 degrees below freezing on the Fahrenheit scale. We had to disconnect ourselves from the oxygen supply and we were soon bathed in sweat from the effort. The parcels nearest the flarechute were discharged first to clear the surrounding area. Soon the thick brown paper and string became a problem until space was cleared into which it could be condensed out of the way. The parcels could only be moved with difficulty over the raised turret, and to reduce the effort of moving them to the flarechute we had to partially lower the turret with consequent effect on airspeed and flying characteristics. The whole process seemed interminable and we were quite exhausted by the effort at that height. We then found that the turret would not fully retract due to frozen hydraulics.

I have read several accounts of leaflet dropping written by those not directly involved and these, together with photographs showing individual bundles of leaflets being loaded, tend to create a false impression of what was entailed. I am not aware that individual bundles were ever loaded into aircraft, as to do so would have created a very unstable load. The leaflets measured 8 7/16 x 5 3/8 inches when folded to produce a four-page leaflet of that size. Five leaflets were placed inside each other, and bundles of these, about 4 inches thick, were secured by a stout rubber band located 2 inches from one of the narrow ends. The secured end of the bundle was fed into the flarechute so that on emerging into the slipstream the loose end was presented to the full force causing the bundle to separate and scatter immediately. The 18, perhaps 24, bundles and these large cumbersome parcels had to be opened progressively as the drop proceeded.

With the dawn we found ourselves above complete cloud cover. At about 0640 hours, having had only occasional loop aerial bearings to check our dead reckoning, and believing ourselves to be well clear of enemy territory, I broke wireless silence and obtained bearings from our own direction-finding system and these, when plotted, placed us close to Dieppe. Being anxious about our fuel state we decided to break cloud and found ourselves over water with Dieppe behind us. P/O Bisset decided to land immediately on a small aerodrome that seemed to be inactive but the only one we could see. On final approach we thought it judicious to unload the guns, of which I was responsible for the two in the ventral turret, which had to be lowered to bring the breeches *to the unloading position. I found the turret still difficult to move and was still wrestling with it when we touched down.*

Looking aft through the small slit windows in the fuselage I saw a blue-clad figure being thrown off the leading edge of the port tailplane. Apparently this gallant French sentry had thrown himself on to the tailplane in an attempt to arrest our speed. Although somewhat foolhardy he seemed to be unhurt and by the time we came to rest, with the nose almost in the boundary hedge, he was some distance away strolling nonchalantly with his rifle in the slung position. We had been airborne for 6 hours and 55 minutes, our longest flight so far.

Refuelling from small cans by hand was a lengthy business. We were on the ground for 3 hours and 35 minutes, being airborne again at 1030 hours. The turret had thawed out while we were on the ground and I was able to unload the guns, but due to atmospheric phenomena I was unable to contact Driffield until we were halfway home, and I had to request Abingdon to relay my messages. We arrived at base at 1255 hours after a combined flight of 9 hours and 20 minutes. Thus ended our first operational flight.'

From a memoir by Squadron-Leader W. Jacobs, Bomber Command

effort of dispatching bundles of leaflets through tubes in the underside of the aircraft produced giddiness and nausea. Endurance flights were made as far as Vienna and Warsaw, but on these operations losses were regular and wear and tear on aircraft and crew scarcely worth the effort. British propaganda seems to have made no observable impact, except to remind the German population that Allied aircraft were capable of operating deep into German airspace. The lessons for the RAF were obvious. The leaflet raids alerted the force to the need to improve navigation skills and conditions inside the aircraft.

In May 1940 Bomber Command found itself able at last to fulfil its primary objective, that of supporting military operations on land. Bomber Command had certainly not had a phoney war since September, but its actions had lacked any clear strategic objective. The invasion of the Low Countries and France launched by Hitler on May 10th transformed the war. Bomber Command wanted to meet that emergency by attacks on the Ruhr to disrupt German industry. Its new Commander-in-Chief appointed in April, Sir Charles Portal, was more favourable to this idea than his predecessor, and very much more than either the British or French general staffs. The Allied leaders wanted Bomber Command to help the land campaign by attacks on the supplies and rear communications of the German armies, and against German air force targets. The Battles and Blenheims of the Advanced Air Striking Force suffered debilitating losses in daylight raids on German positions. Heavier bombers were called in from British bases to supplement these attacks, again with heavy loss. During the retreat to Dunkirk, Bomber Command attacked German troop concentrations and reinforcements.

The shift to attacks on German targets coincided with the appointment of Winston Churchill as Prime Minister on May 10th. He had long been an enthusiast for air power.

In the First World War, as First Lord of the Admiralty, he had organised attacks by naval aviators against German airship bases in Germany, and had been instrumental in securing the survival of the RAF as a separate service in 1919. Since the outbreak of war in September 1939, again as First Lord of the Admiralty, he had pressed Bomber Command to adopt more aggressive tactics against the German navy. He had fewer scruples about bombing than Chamberlain. When German aircraft attacked and destroyed a large part of the Dutch city of Rotterdam on May 14th, Churchill shared the view of his War Cabinet that the nine-month truce on bombing civilians was over. The following day Bomber Command was authorised to begin attacks on German targets east of the Rhine.

The new directive revived the pre-war arguments about what to bomb. Portal was told that 'indiscriminate action' was still prohibited. Oil and communications, already selected before the war, were regarded as primary targets. But the main objective became the German air force. It was expected that any pressure Bomber Command could bring to bear on Germany's oil supplies, aircraft industry and air installations would ease the plight of French forces still fighting a desperate rearguard action against German armies. At the most it might mean the diversion of fighter aircraft back to the Reich and away from the fighting front. On May 30th Bomber Command received the directive to concentrate bombing against transport and air power targets in north-eastern Germany on clear nights, with reasonable visibility.

The first attack had already been carried out on the date that the bombing ban was lifted, when 99 bombers were sent to attack industrial targets over a wide area of the Ruhr. The night-time raid was carried out for the loss of only one Wellington. Although the damage done was slight, the raid marked the starting point of the campaign against German industry planned since 1937.

On the brink

'We had finished training and were being driven to the Operational Training Unit where you are put together as a crew. It was in the coach as we were approaching – I can remember the very road, I can remember the trees – when suddenly I realised good God, I might get killed. All those boyish dreams and ventures went and we teamed as a crew, we did circuits, we flew round England, and six weeks afterwards we were sent to number 10 squadron.

I had a feeling of unease in my stomach the whole time. I can remember the first operation. I used to like Dickens and I can remember sitting in the operations room with the flying suit on ready to go out. Just before I put the suit on I was reading "Pickwick Papers", and I kept reading the same page over and over again. Nothing was absorbed, nothing went in. There was a confusion in my mind, a kind of inner alienation from my usual calm. But we were good actors. We all pretended that everything was well.'

Harold Nash, Bomber Command navigator

A medium bomber designed to meet a 1932 specification, the Handley Page Hampden was tested in June 1936 and delivered to squadrons from August 1938. With a maximum speed of 254 mph, it could carry 4,000 pounds of bombs some 1,200 miles. This example was delivered to No 7 Squadron early in 1939. Hampdens saw regular service in the first two years of the war.

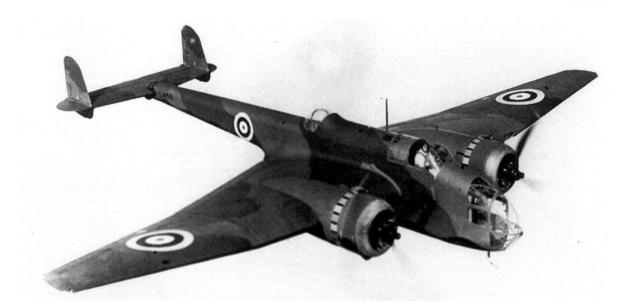

The Fairey Battle formed the core of the light bomber force deployed to France in September 1939 to form the Advanced Striking Force. It carried four 250-pound bombs in wing cells and could be modified to carry two more externally.

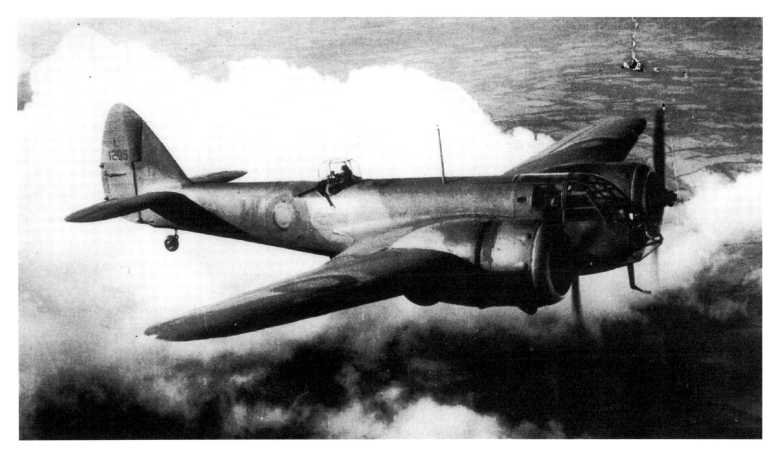

An early raid

'I pedalled into the aerodrome and they said, "Hurry up, you're flying."

This was 8 o'clock in the morning. There was not a cloud in the sky, it was unreal. Wellingtons were scattered all over the sky. You thought the flak was going to hit you straight between the eyes and then it veered off. We went through a huge barrage and you couldn't see anything except big puffs of black smoke. As we came through the barrage there were the Messerschmitts waiting for us. We hadn't got any guns at all. All our gadgets had packed in so we had no front gun, no rear gun or anything. We discovered afterwards that they used the wrong oil in our hydraulic system.

During one of these attacks I was hit in the back and then through the ankle. I rang up the skipper and said, "I've been hit and it bloody well hurts."

He told me to come to the front and get it dressed. I staggered to the front of the aircraft. The wireless operator saw my ankle and got a hypodermic syringe and bunged this stuff through my flying trousers into my leg, which killed some of the pain. He was hit and killed immediately. He went a funny sort of grey and purple and died. A Messerschmitt sat on our tail and shot right through the aeroplane, through the rear turret and out through the front of the aircraft. I was sitting on the bed behind the wireless operator's area watching the blood coming out of my foot. The second pilot had to stand with his legs astride and the bullets going between his legs. Then a bullet hit him in the thigh.

I heard the skipper say he had got to go down. We had caught fire. We were over an island off the German coast and he found a bit of beach to land on. We were burning by now. I got to the hatch at the top and pulled myself up but I got stuck and I could feel the flames burning my rear end. They pulled me out and carried me to the sand dunes.'

Harry Jones, Bomber Command rear gunner

This early wartime publicity photograph taken in 1939 shows a Blenheim I of No 107 Squadron. 'The rear gunner is ready to deal with any adversary,' says the caption, although operational experience revealed that the type's defensive armament was inadequate for daylight bombing missions.

Swinging a transfer

'While I was at Lyneham an aeroplane came in and landed and stopped its engines, a twin-engined aeroplane, and the pilot came out through the roof, and I thought it was the most charismatic and glamorous thing I'd ever seen and I asked what it was and they said it was a Mark IV Blenheim. I decided from that moment that that's what I was going to fly, and while I finished my intermediate training on twin-engined Oxfords at Brize Norton and got my wings I'd been pestering my instructor all the way through to get me on to Blenheims…

Of course, when the time came I found I was posted to Kinloss up in the north of Scotland to a Whitley operational training unit. My heart sank at the news, but when I actually saw them in action I was appalled. I'd never seen such a dreadful, boring looking thing, nose down, going at what looked like about 50 miles an hour. As soon as I arrived at the OTU I had an interview with the Wing Commander. I said could he get me posted away on to Blenheims, and he said no… So I started to fly this Whitley and I found that flying it was exactly what I'd dreaded; it was slow and cumbersome and heavy and unresponsive. And then, after having had one or two dual[-control] circuits, I hit upon a wonderful scheme. I'd fly it around all right, do the approach all right and then when I got to about 50 or 100 feet above the ground I'd suddenly go all helpless and say it was all too big and heavy and I couldn't pull the stick back properly or use the rudders properly. The instructor at first thought it was quite genuine and tried to get it right, then he got very angry and told me to bloody well get on with it. He had a talk with the Wing Commander and said this chap is a menace. The Wing Commander said to me, "Well, you're to be posted to a Blenheim OTU and leave the Station as quickly as possible. You're quite mad," he said. "You realise that they operate in daylight and have horrendous casualties?"

My overriding wish and desire to fly Blenheims took precedence over everything and I was delighted… The moment I got in a Blenheim with the instructor and he told me to take off and I opened the throttles and felt this surge of power, and the taking off, the lightness, I knew it was for me, absolutely my plane.'

Charles Patterson, Bomber Command pilot

Below: Fairey Battles delivered to No 63 Squadron at Upwood in Huntingdonshire in May 1937. The squadron was turned into a training unit when war broke out. The last Battles were withdrawn from combat service in July 1941.

Below right: Charles Patterson, Bomber Command pilot. 'I couldn't see myself in the army, marching about and sleeping in the dirt and dust and carrying a rifle. As a soldier I'd have been hopeless … the only way I wanted to fight was as a pilot.'

A Percival Proctor used by Bomber Command for communications duties. Percival Aircraft Ltd was based in Gravesend, founded by the designer and air race enthusiast Edgar Percival. During the war Proctors were used in England by No 8 Group, the 'Pathfinders'.

The Vickers Type 246/281 Wellesley, designed as a private venture by Vickers's designer Barnes Wallis, was taken on by the Air Ministry in 1935 as a medium bomber. It first joined squadrons in April 1937, but was phased out from 1939. The model seen here was used by the Long Range Development Unit. It had a standard range of 1,100 miles, but its endurance record was 7,162 miles.

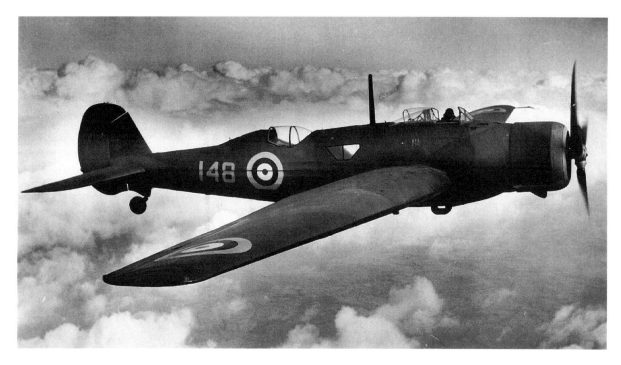

The Wellington's robust construction enabled many a crew to get back to Britain despite heavy damage. Remarkably this Wellington BII of No 12 Squadron survived even this, returning to serve with No 158 Squadron. Its luck ran out on 13 April 1942 when it went missing during an attack on Essen.

The 7 squadrons of 2 Group were equipped with Blenheim Mk IVs by 1939. The Blenheim was produced in much larger numbers than the other pre-war bomber designs, with 4,430 built in Britain, including 1,134 of the Mk I.

Right: Hampdens on delivery to RAF Radlett in 1939. Handley Page invited the press to watch the aircraft flight tests before delivery to the RAF to show the modernisation of the force. In the background is an Avro Anson, one of the most widely used trainers in Bomber Command.

Below: No 37 Squadron assembled for a group photograph in 1938. The squadron was stationed at Feltwell in Norfolk and was equipped with Handley-Page Harrow II heavy bombers, one of which is seen here. The Harrow equipped five Bomber Command squadrons and could carry 3,000 pounds of bombs. It later served as a troop transport.

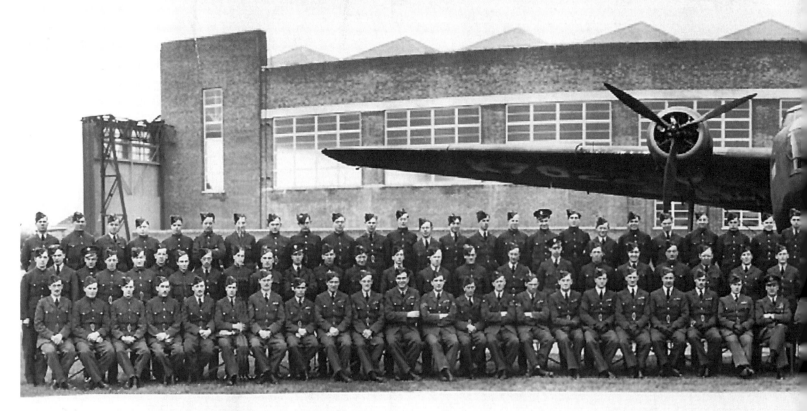

No. 37 (BOMBER) SQU...
FELTWELL

A Blenheim Mk IV in flight. Blenheims were the first British aircraft to bomb a German target, 15 aircraft making a low level attack on German warships off Wilhelmshaven on 4th September 1939. They hit the 'pocket battleship' Admiral Scheer but 4 were shot down, one crashing into the cruiser Emden.

N. ROYAL AIR FORCE.

EMBER 1938.

Right: An early example of the Avro Manchester, a twin-engined heavy night bomber, developed from an Air Ministry specification in 1936 for a fast, versatile, heavily defended bomber, capable of carrying 8,000 pounds of bombs. The first prototype flew in July 1939 and it reached operational squadrons in early 1941 only to prove a technical failure.

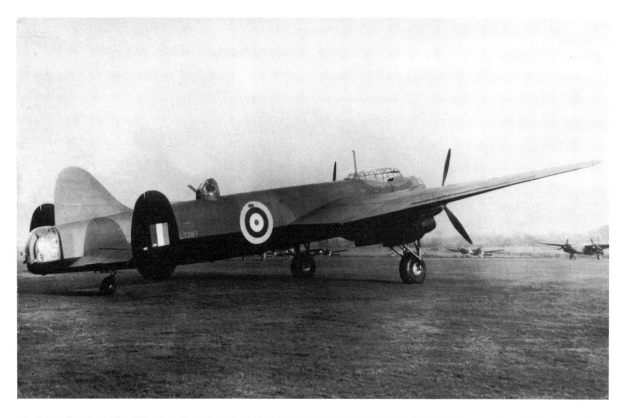

This group photograph gives an idea of the size of the twin engine Whitley. Few crews thought well of the type, many citing the arctic chill of its draughty interior, but a number of dissenters praised its robust construction.

A fruitless search

'We were told quite early on December 23rd that we would be required for ops. A covering of snow lay on the ground as we prepared for take-off. It was a Saturday and some of the tradesmen had been stood down, so my room mate gave me a hand getting into the turret. He gave me the thumbs up as the Whitley squelched through the slush-covered grass. We were airborne at 1130 hours and climbed away from the airfield. The saving grace of this sortie was that it would be at low level where the temperatures were not too bad, but cold enough in my draughty turret. We crossed the coast at Flamborough Head, our usual place of departure, at 2,000 feet and were able to see quite well despite the slight drizzle. How bloody cold and uninviting the North Sea looked.

The pilot gave Fletch and I permission to test our guns and soon tracers and incendiaries burned their way down as we let go. We passed to the north of Heligoland and began our "creeping line ahead" search pattern. Bick, the pilot, exhorted us to keep our eyes skinned and I diligently scanned behind while the rest of the crew searched ahead. After about 30 minutes in the area north west of Sylt we were alerted to a ship.

"Ship off the starboard bow, heading north."

The adrenalin began to surge again as Bick turned the aircraft towards it. As we neared the ship it was recognised as a merchantman, and up at the sharp end [the crew] were endeavouring to identify the flag flying from its stern. Our feelings were mixed when Enery called, "It's Swedish, neutral".

Leaving the ship unmolested we continued our search, but there were no further sightings. We reached our PLE (Prudent Limit of Endurance) and set course for home.'

Larry Donnelly, Bomber Command WOP/AG

The first raid on Germany

'Later that day, March 19th, we discovered that we were going to take part in the first bombing raid against a German land target, namely the seaplane base at Hornum on the Friesian Islands. The change in bombing policy was a retaliation for the raid by the Luftwaffe on Scapa Flow in the Orkney Islands on March 16th, during which a civilian was killed. The retaliatory raid was to be a "one off"; we would attack no further land targets until the Germans invaded Scandinavia and the Low Countries.

We were called to briefing early in the evening, during which we were given the gen on the impending raid. The force of 50 aircraft would be the greatest number of RAF bombers to concentrate on a single German target to date. The atmosphere during briefing was charged with anticipation and excitement at the prospect that we were going to drop bombs instead of those "bloody leaflets".

The flight over the North Sea went smoothly, but the excitement mounted when "Nipper" announced over the intercom that we would soon be near the island and the target. He went to the bomb-aiming position in the nose of the aircraft to prepare for the bomb-run from 4,000 feet. The adrenalin flow increased when he reported that he had identified the target and called "Bomb door open!".

We started the bomb-run and the litany commenced: "Left, left, steady … ri-ght, steady" as we ran the gauntlet of the flak and searchlight defences. The Whitley lurched as the bombs dropped away. We were now receiving the attentions of the defences, but the skipper kept the aircraft straight and level to enable "Nipper" to plot the bursts. Some of the flak got uncomfortably close to the tail and I was blinded by the searchlights, so I opened fire down the beams.

We got away unscathed from our first bombing sortie. Although the bomb-run had lasted only a few minutes it had seemed much longer. Fletch came on the intercom, reporting that one of our bombers had just transmitted an "X" signal to base, which, when decoded, read "The natives are hostile".'

Larry Donnelly, Bomber Command WOP/AG (both extracts from *The Whitley Boys: 4 Group Bomber Operations 1939-1940*, Air Research Publications, New Malden, 1991, pp 77-78)

Until the poor winter weather set in later in 1940, Bomber Command carried out intermittent raids on German industrial and military targets in the belief, soon to be disabused, that designated installations could be identified correctly and hit with accuracy.

Portal himself was highly sceptical of the policy he was asked to fulfil. He did not believe that his current force had the capability to knock out German industries or seriously to disrupt the operation of the air force, a view confirmed by photo reconnaissance of the areas attacked. Moreover Bomber Command was asked to divide its operations between a wide number of targets, and this dispersal of effort reduced what little impact the force could make. Portal wanted fewer targets and concentrated attacks. He favoured attacking communication centres, but he believed that fewer and heavier attacks would have a strong moral impact on the German population as well. His views played an important part in shaping the campaign Bomber Command waged in Germany over the next four years.

By the middle of June the strategic picture had altered dramatically. On June 17th France sued for an armistice and the first phase of the war on land abruptly ended. Britain was isolated in Europe. Hitler hoped that she would seek peace on German terms, but Churchill rejected any thought of capitulation, though aware of just how vulnerable Britain's position was. The Royal Navy could defend Britain and its trade routes with difficulty; it could not take the war to Germany. The only force that could be brought to bear directly on the enemy was Bomber Command. From being an auxiliary of the land campaign, the Command therefore found itself by default in the vanguard of the British war effort. Churchill became an enthusiast for bombing in the absence of any other means of attack. In July he wrote to his friend Lord Beaverbrook: 'When I look round to see how we can win this war I see that there is only one sure path ... and that is an absolutely devastating, exterminating attack by very heavy bombers from this country upon the Nazi homeland.'

Early days

'After the war broke out we were placed on standby to attack German naval units if they ventured out into the North Sea and that's as far as we could go. We could not drop bombs on land. Most times we didn't find anything at all. It heated up in the Norwegian campaign, which resulted in a disastrous attack on a cruiser and destroyers in Kristiansund in April 1940. 44 Squadron went out with 12 aircraft to attack the cruiser and the Richthofen squadron was sitting right alongside. Out of the 12 that went out only seven came back. It was an error in the Group operational headquarters in not transmitting Bomber Command's operational directive that we should not approach within 50 miles of the Norwegian coast unless we had cloud cover.

We went in under an absolutely cloudless sky. We were literally over the harbour when the next thing people started reporting that fighters were climbing up. The German pilots had obviously been briefed on the ability of the Hampden to defend itself because we couldn't traverse our guns to reach them. They turned in and just sat blasting away at us and blowing us out of the sky until eventually they ran out of gas and had to go home themselves. If there had been more gasoline I think none of us would have reached our home. We were sitting ducks. It was terrifying.'

**Wilfred John 'Mike' Lewis,
Bomber Command pilot**

Flying over Rotterdam

'When the invasion of Holland took place I was recalled from leave and went on my first operation on 15th May 1940 against mainland Germany. Our target was Dortmund and on the way back we were routed via Rotterdam. The German Air Force had bombed Rotterdam the day before and it was still in flames. I realised then only too well that the phoney war was over and that this was for real. By that time the fire services had extinguished a number of fires, but they were still dotted around the whole city. This was the first time I'd ever seen devastation by fires on this scale. We went right over the southern outskirts of Rotterdam at about 6,000 or 7,000 feet, and you could actually smell the smoke from the fires burning on the ground. I was shocked seeing a city in flames like that. Devastation on a scale I had never experienced.'

Wilf Burnett, Bomber Command pilot

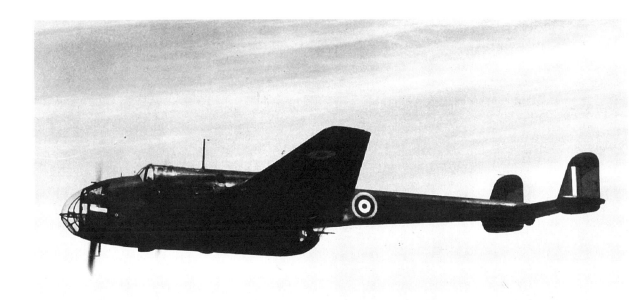

Left: The Handley Page Hereford was a sister aircraft to the Hampden, employing Napier instead of Bristol engines. First flown in October 1938, the aircraft was plagued with engine trouble and never saw active service. The 150 examples built at Short and Harland were used for training and at the bombing and gunnery schools.

With only two .303 machine guns, the Blenheim I had neither the firepower nor the performance to escape German fighters in 1939. The Mk IV, entering service that year, had three more guns but they would make little difference.

Hampden medium bombers were used for armed reconnaissance, and from May 1940, after the ban on bombing Germany was lifted, they attacked rail and oil targets in the Ruhr. They were last used for an attack on Wilhelmshaven in September 1942.

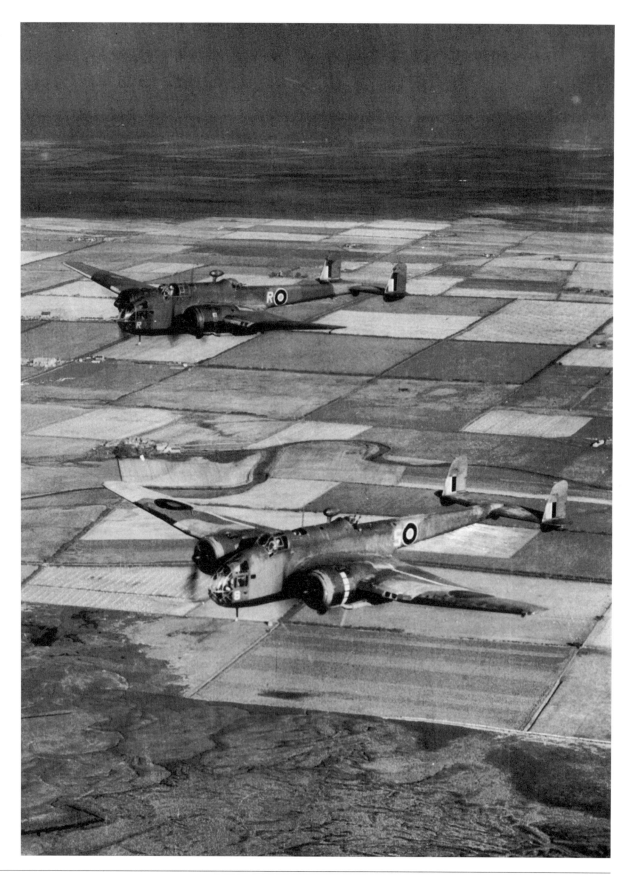

Above: The Hampden was 'a beautiful aeroplane to fly', recalled one pilot, 'terrible to fly in, cramped, no heat, no facilities where you could relieve yourself … but a joy to fly. I could have gone on for ever with the Hampden.'

Left: A line of Blenheims belonging to No 114 Squadron, based at Wyton in Huntingdonshire. The core of the light bomber force before the war, they were being used as night fighters by the autumn of 1940 because of their vulnerability in a daylight bombing role.

Right: A Blenheim IV that has crashed in training in 1941. 'The instructors at the Blenheim OTU,' recalled a veteran pilot, 'were a very few survivors of the appalling casualties of the Battle of France when daylight Blenheims were shot down like flies…'

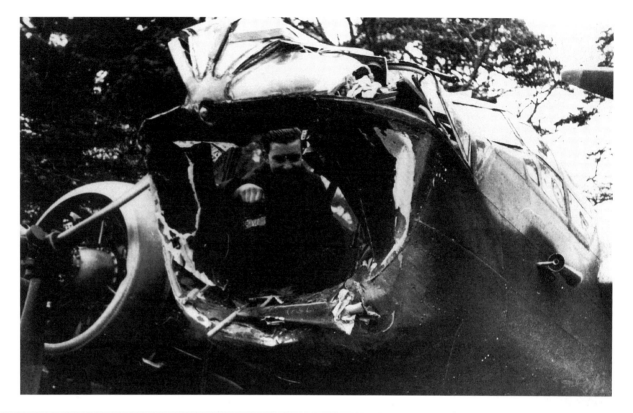

Below: The Armstrong Whitworth Whitley Mk I was the first of the new generation of RAF heavy bombers. Developed from 1934, the prototype flew in 1936 and it entered squadron service the next year, replacing ageing biplane bombers. The Mk I was removed from service in 1939.

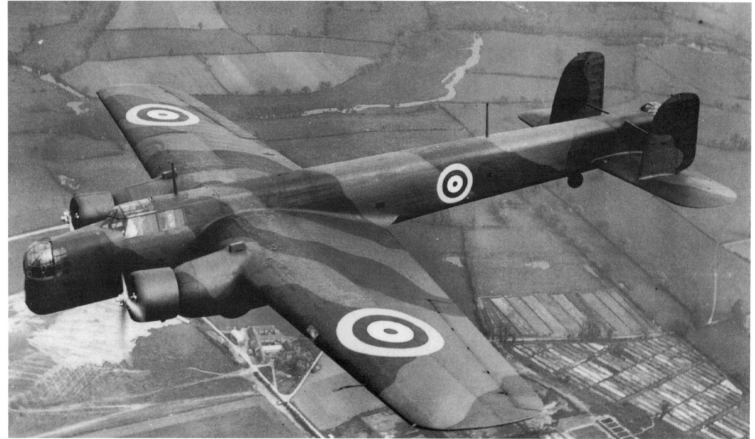

BUILDING THE FORCE, 1936-40

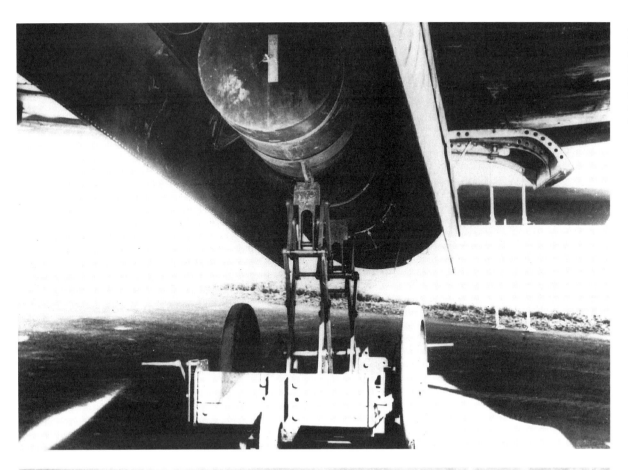

A mine is loaded on to a Hampden medium bomber. The Hampdens undertook many of the mining operations from the earliest days of the war. During 1939-41 approximately 2,000 mines were dropped from the air, around 4 per cent of Britain's wartime total.

A Bristol Blenheim in a steep dive. Dive-bombing trials were carried out during the 'Phoney War' period, but the results were meagre. The Advanced Air Striking Force trained only seven pilots and dropped only 56 bombs in practice runs.

Above: The Mark V was the standard Whitley bomber, of which some 1,445 were produced, seeing active service until December 1942. An unattractive aircraft to look at, the Whitley was unpopular with crews. 'If you went through a shower of rain,' recalled a veteran, 'you got wet.' They saw regular service over Germany until the advent of the four-engined bombers.

Right: The Vickers Wellington twin-engined night heavy bomber first flew in 1936, but it proved to be a revolutionary design and was still in service at the end of the war. With a range of 3,200 miles and a maximum bomb load of 4,500 pounds, it was the RAF's standard heavy bomber until 1941.

Chapter 2

Bomber Command at war

Throughout the war Bomber Command was a multi-role force. Churchill's private view that the bombing of Germany was the only way out of Britain's critical position in 1940 had the effect, and continues to have the effect, of focusing attention on just one of the things that RAF bombers did during the war. The attack on Germany was unarguably the single most significant thing that Bomber Command did, but it was only a fraction of the whole. Throughout the war, British bombers continued to support naval and land forces with tactical bombing of enemy forces, bases and supplies. At intervals during the war a large part of Bomber Command's operations was concentrated on a major objective other than German targets – the campaign in support of the OVERLORD invasion, for example, or the CROSSBOW offensive against the V-weapons. Men and equipment were diverted regularly to the Mediterranean theatre, or to the Far East after 1941, where they became part of the local campaign, subject to the control of theatre commanders, though they were recruited and trained by Bomber Command. The figures on Bomber Command activity in Europe compiled at the end of the war give a clear indication of the many differing functions the force was asked to perform. In the first two years of war Bomber Command concentrated its efforts on a wide variety of targets connected in the main with the land campaign in 1940 and the subsequent efforts to avert invasion and blunt German air and naval power. Only 22 per cent of bomb tonnage was devoted to German industrial cities; 43 per cent was dropped on military targets (invasion ports, airfields, military stores and communications, etc) and 13 per cent on communications serving German forces in north-east Europe. Between February 1942, when Air Marshal Arthur Harris became Commander-in-Chief, and May 1945, some 43 per cent of Bomber Command bomb tonnage was directed at industrial cities in Germany, while over 40 per cent was devoted to support for land operations, long range reconnaissance, mining, supporting resistance operations, attacks on communications and airfields and the war at sea. Bomber Command was never simply a force to assault Germany's economic system.

The famous Boeing B-17 'Flying Fortress' in RAF colours. The B-17 Mk 1 served with No 90 Squadron, Bomber Command, at Boscombe Down. First developed in 1934, it became the mainstay of the American bomber forces in Europe from 1942.

Anti-invasion bombing

'Having joined 97 squadron at Coningsby in Lincolnshire, we had to wait a while until a few Manchesters were delivered to us. We did some training flights and came the night of our first operation. At the time the invasion of Britain was very much on the cards and Hitler was assembling lots of large motorised barges in the Channel ports. My first raid was to bomb the docks at Calais. I carried about 15 1,000-pound bombs in the Manchester. It was an easy navigational trip because it was only 20 miles across the Channel. Leaving from Beachy Head I steered a course for about 20 minutes and sure enough up came the coast.

It was a moonlit night; we could even see the fingers of the docks. I said, "This is too good a chance to miss. Let's get some of those barges. We'll drop just one bomb at a time."

The bomb aimer went down to his bomb sight and lined up some of the barges. We were bombing from about 15,000 feet, and with a bit of "left, left, steady and right and steady", I felt a little leap of the aeroplane and number one bomb went. I proceeded inland and did what was called a procedure turn: 45 degrees to one side for about a minute and a half and then a turn back and you come over your old track. On the way out we did "left, left, steady, steady, bomb gone", and that was two bombs. There were 13 to go.

I began to notice in the perspex of the cockpit little flashes, like someone lighting a cigarette down behind me, and I asked the rear gunner, "Can you tell me what that light is behind us?"

He said, "There's some flak behind us, Captain, but it's well behind us."

We did three or four more runs and all the time these flashes were getting brighter and brighter and I was beginning to hear a crump each time. I became suspicious and said, "Jack, are you sure that flak is safe?"

He replied, "Oh yes, skipper, it's a good 25 yards off yet!"

On that run I said "Drop the lot", and off we went back across the North Sea.

We were so inexperienced. I had at least 1,000 hours as a pilot, and I was just lost. I didn't know what I was doing. I was sent the next night to Calais again as a punishment for

being so stupid. This time the weather wasn't so kind. From the English coast you could see underneath a layer of cloud the lights of Calais and the searchlights, but as you approached you came into the cloud and the target was hidden. I realised we weren't going to be able to bomb visually and unless you could see the actual target you had to take your bombs back to base, which was a dangerous thing. I said to the crew, "We're not going to be able to drop these on the barges at Calais. Let's go home."

I turned north, got the coffee thermos, and the smell of forbidden cigarettes began to waft up the fuselage from the back. I lost a bit of height and said to the navigator, "What time do you think we'll reach the English coast?"

With a tone of utter surprise, he said, "Have you left the French coast then?"

"Yes," I said, "I told you we were giving it up."

"How long ago was it?" he asked.

I couldn't imagine – half an hour, quarter of an hour. I told him 20 minutes.

"Right," he said, "we should be coming up to the coast in about 5 minutes' time."

I'd lost height from 15,000 down to about 8,000 feet by then and sure enough a coastline came up dark velvet against the silvery sea. I didn't recognise the huge river mouth, with large islands. Panic hit me then, because we simply didn't know where we were. It was certainly not England. I didn't realise that in losing height the scale of everything had gone up and that the mouth of the river I saw looked like the Emden or the Rhine. The navigator came up to look at the coastline with me and as we came in over it to my horror guns started firing at us and searchlights waved around in front of us.

I turned out to sea to give a bit more thought to this. I asked to have any maps passed up to me and I looked at the coastline from Scotland to the bay of Biscay trying to find this river mouth. We used to have an emergency frequency on the radio which was called "D for Darkie", which you could call for help. I pressed the button and called "Hello Darkie, this is Lifebuoy A for apple calling, do you read?" and a voice came back, "Allo, Lifebuoy A apple, zis eez——, vill you land pleeze?" This proved they were hostile down there – there was no question of an RAF character talking like that. We were utterly lost and in German territory.

The end came when my gunner called, "Skipper, I think I can see a beacon."

There were networks of beacons flashing all over the country at night, and we had been given a code on a sheet to identify them. I set a course north from there and much to my pleasure our own home beacon came into view and we were able to land. Now my Wing Commander was very unhappy about this whole procedure because he'd had to wait up for 6 hours unable to go to bed because he had a missing aircraft. He tore me off a strip.

I said, "But sir, Darkie, I'm sure it was a teutonic accent."

"Yes," he said, "there's a Polish squadron down there." So that explained that.'

Rod Rodley, Bomber Command pilot

The Handley Page Harrow II served with No 115 Squadron at Marham in Norfolk. This bomber/transport equipped five squadrons before the war, but was quickly transferred to operational training and transport duties. This example served until 1945.

The story of the campaign against Germany is the subject of the next chapter. What follows is the story of the many other things the Command was asked to do to contribute to Britain's wider war effort. It is a long list, and it begins with the desperate efforts made in the aftermath of French defeat and the retreat from Dunkirk to avert the danger of German invasion and blunt the efforts of the German air force in the Battle of Britain. On July 4th 1940 the Air Staff directed Bomber Command to make attacks on enemy ports and shipping 'a first priority'. Then, when German air activity began to increase, the top priority went to any targets calculated to reduce the immediate threat of German air attack – air bases, oil supplies and any aircraft factories within striking distance. By September, when German preparations were well advanced for Operation Sealion, the invasion of southern England, the force was switched back again to an anti-invasion role. Its orders were to attack the concentrations of barges and transport vessels in the invasion ports, including Rotterdam, Le Havre and Antwerp, and the Command continued to do so until the threat of invasion disappeared with the bad weather of October.

On the night of September 7/8th the first direct attack on the invasion fleet took place; 92 bombers, a mixture of light and medium aircraft, were sent against the Channel ports. For the first time they could be used to full effect. The short distance meant that a full bomb-load could be carried, and the coastal targets were easy to find and identify clearly. Repeated attacks by almost the whole force reduced the German fleet by 12 per cent and hampered the organisation and assembly of troops and equipment. The German Navy reported to Hitler that the air situation made invasion too dangerous; on September 17th he finally postponed Sealion indefinitely.

Bomber Command continued to play a part in the war at sea after the invasion scare was past. Much of the responsibility for attacks on German shipping and the protection of British trade fell to Coastal Command, but Bomber Command played a two-fold role: to provide attacks on submarine bases and construction to reduce the submarine threat, and to contribute to the mining campaign. The Command was first directed to attack submarine construction and shore bases on September 21st 1940, but opportunities for attack were few. By the spring of 1941 Churchill was so anxious about merchant ship losses and the threat to British supplies that on 9th March Bomber Command was instructed that for the following four months it should devote its energies to the submarine.

Although at first the Admiralty accepted the RAF belief that the best way of blunting the German submarine threat was to attack it at source, in the docks where submarines

Bombing the barges

'The Station Commander gathered all officers together one morning in August or September 1940 and told us that it appeared invasion was imminent and that we should be prepared for it. I remember the silence that followed. We left the room and I don't think anyone spoke, but we were all the more determined to make certain that we did everything possible to deter the Germans from launching their invasion.

At the time we were bombing the invasion barges in the Channel ports, undertaking operations almost every other night. I remember one operation in particular against the invasion barges. We had part moonlight, which was very helpful because navigation in those days depended entirely on visual identification. We flew to the north of our target so that we could get a better outline of the coast. We followed the coast down towards our target, letting down to about 4,000 feet so that we could get a better view of what was below, and to increase the accuracy of the bombing. At that height light anti-aircraft fire was pretty heavy and fairly accurate so we didn't hang around after dropping our bombs. This was done repeatedly over a period of time until the invasion was called off.'

Wilf Burnett, Bomber Command pilot

were constructed, pressure was brought on the RAF to release bombers for the direct attack on bases, on larger naval units, even for long-range operations deep over the ocean, for which Bomber Command pilots had not been trained. Bomber Command complied without enthusiasm. In March 1941 the battle-cruisers *Scharnhorst* and *Gneisenau*, based in the French port of Brest after a successful assault on merchant shipping, were attacked repeatedly by Bomber Command aircraft. In all 829 tons were dropped, but only four bombs actually scored a direct hit, enough, it turned out, to make it impossible for the two ships to join the formidable *Bismarck* when she sailed for the Atlantic in the middle of May.

In July 1941 Bomber Command was given responsibility for anti-shipping operations from Cherbourg to Wilhelmshaven to supplement the work of Coastal Command, but Sir Richard Peirse, who had

Left: The Lockheed Ventura Mk I light bomber was another useful import from the USA. It served with several squadrons in 2 Group, Bomber Command, including an Australian and New Zealand squadron.

Below: Handley Page Halifax bombers seen over the French port of Brest, where the German battle-cruisers Scharnhorst *and* Gneisnau *and the heavy cruiser* Prinz Eugen *were berthed . The intensity of Bomber Command's raids on Brest led the three warships to make their celebrated 'Channel Dash' back to Germany in 1942.*

The phonetic alphabet

The radio call-signs used in the war of 1914-18 were revived at the start of the Second World War.

A	ACK	N	NUTS
B	BEER	O	ORANGE
C	CHARLIE	P	PIP
D	DON	Q	QUEEN
E	EDWARD	R	ROBERT
F	FREDDIE	S	SUGAR
G	GEORGE	T	TOC
H	HARRY	U	UNCLE
I	INK	V	VIC
J	JOHNNIE	W	WILLIAM
K	KING	X	X-RAY
L	LONDON	Y	YORKER
M	MONKEY	Z	ZEBRA

could give in the sea war was more indirect than direct. Bombers hit the great German naval base at Kiel regularly, and with some success. Other naval ports were attacked, and Bremen, close to English bases and home to the Focke-Wulf aircraft factories, was hit repeatedly, forcing the company to move away from the bomb zone. But on balance the damage done was not decisive. Bomber Command still lacked the necessary equipment to hit targets heavily enough or with sufficient accuracy to do serious damage. The collaboration with the naval war simply diluted a force still far from effective strength.

More success was gained from Bomber Command participation in the mining campaign, in which it played a significant part from the spring of 1940 onwards. The mining operations were carried out by the aircraft of No 5 Group, which was commanded in 1940 by Arthur Harris. It was a particularly hazardous operation, for minelaying involved long overseas flights, as far as the Baltic Sea, and mines had to be dropped from a very low height, at times almost touching the surface of the sea. Intermittent flak attack from shore-based and seaborne anti-aircraft guns added to the dangers of the weather over the North Sea. Losses of bomber aircraft on mining operations reached 408 aircraft by the end of the war, with three-quarters of those losses occurring before the end of 1943.

succeeded Portal as Commander-in-Chief of Bomber Command on October 5th 1940, made every effort to escape from the obligation and in late November 1941 Coastal Command took back responsibility for the Channel. In the opinion of the Command the support they

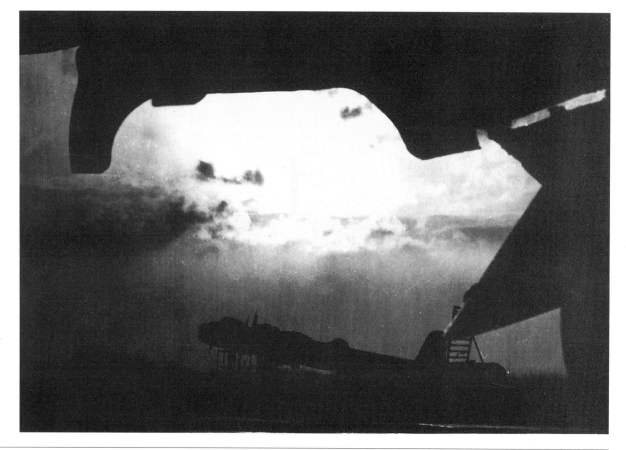

Short Stirling Mk I heavy bombers of No 218 Squadron seen at Downham Market, Norfolk. The Stirling was the first of the new generation of four-engined bombers, designed to a specification in 1936 for a bomber with a massively increased bomb load. Stirlings entered operational service in August 1940 and flew their first mission in February 1941 against Rotterdam.

The prodigious quantity of bombs delivered by Bomber Command were brought to collecting points on a daily basis. Local depot trains connected with the railway network, storage and distribution being co-ordinated by No 42 Group Maintenance Command.

With a bomb load of 14,000 pounds, the Short Stirling provided a dramatic increase in Bomber Command's offensive power. However, only two years after its introduction the type was withdrawn from the Main Force after suffering disproportionate losses to flak and night fighters.

Above: The Avro Lancaster became the most famous of Bomber Command's aircraft. The Mark BVII, one of the last variants to be produced, is seen here painted in Far Eastern colours for the so-called 'Tiger Force'. The bombers were sent to India for use in the Pacific war, but Japan surrendered before the force became operational.

Right: A crew prepares to embark in a Wellington. The type remained part of the Main Force until 1943 and continued to serve elsewhere until 1945. A total of 11,460 Wellingtons were built at Weybridge, Chester and Blackpool.

The second of the heavy bombers to be developed in the 1930s, the Halifax began life as a twin-engined aircraft powered by Vulture engines, but was transformed in 1937 into a four-engined model using Rolls Royce Merlin X engines. The first prototype flew in October 1939, and it entered service in December 1940.

Short Stirling Mk IIIs of No 199 Squadron ready for inspection at Marham in Norfolk. The Mk III entered service in 1943, but casualties were heavy as it was unable to reach the same altitude as the accompanying Halifaxes and Lancasters.

Dropping a mine

'Mining was a major role, particularly for the Hampden squadrons of No 5 Group. The magnetic mines that were used fitted very neatly into the bomb bay of the Hampden, and they carried out the majority of the early mining operations. These magnetic mines, which were relatively new, were dropped by parachute at low altitude, about 1,000 feet. They came down on to the surface of the sea by parachute, and then the effect of sea water on a soluble plug enabled the parachute to be released. The parachute floated away and the mine itself became active and sank to the seabed, where it rested until a ship passed over the top.

The laying of these mines was critical. They had to be dropped in fairly shallow water in order to be activated. So navigation was a problem, as these operations were carried out mainly by night. They were carried out to the Baltic in great numbers, along the sea lanes of the Friesian Islands, the north German coast, the entrance to the Kiel Canal. We had to fly low over the North Sea, which was not pleasant, particularly when you had low cloud, and rain and static. You very often got thunderstorms. You got the effect of static electricity building up on the aeroplane, which caused what was called St Elmo's fire, like a blue flame flashing on the windscreen. It was not dangerous, but disconcerting. Then in bumpy conditions you had to find the enemy coastline, assess your position and then do a run to find the actual spot in the sea where the mine had to be actually dropped. We did a great number of these mining operations in the years 1940 to 1942.'

Sir Lewis Hodges, Bomber Command pilot

Crewmen examine flash photographs taken after bomb release. The 'flash' was a cylinder 3 feet long, weighing 20 pounds and containing 9 pounds of explosive. It was detonated in a single burst after control signals were activated when the bomb firing key was pressed.

The mining campaign had limited results in the first two years. But from 1942 onwards, when Harris took over the Command, minelaying became a permanent thorn in the side of the German navy. He ordered all suitable bombers to be converted so that they could carry mines. In agreement with the Admiralty, orders were placed for a great increase in mine production. The new generation of acoustic and magnetic mines proved much more effective.

From 1942 to 1945 Bomber Command dropped an average of 1,113 mines per month, accounting for an estimated 490 ships sunk and 410 damaged. Mines were laid from Bordeaux to the Baltic, on the shore line and in the main rivers, estuaries and canals.

In 1944, as part of the campaign against German oil supplies, Lancasters dropped mines on the Danube river to slow down the flow of Romanian oil. With

A minelaying disaster

'It was a minelaying trip off the Friesians, exactly the same trip as I had done on my first operation about six months before. This time I was the first pilot. On the whole, minelaying was regarded as a piece of cake. You then had to lay mines from a very low height, about 400 feet with the magnetic mines.

We came down to 400 feet and the navigator said, "I can't understand what's happening. We should be there but the sea has stopped and I can't see a coastline shape at all."

We flew around a bit, no one firing at us. We realised what had happened. The sea had frozen over – it was very cold in February – so that the outlines for the land were indecipherable anyway. Whether we were over the right island we couldn't tell. Finally it turned out we were over the next-door one, so we were in the right lane for laying the mines. We thought we would lay them there because it was obviously an island, and obviously a bit of sea.

And then I can't really say what happened. I remember suddenly searchlights were on us and a total feeling of chaos. I remember seeing some tracer, but I don't remember any feeling of being hit. I do remember very strongly the feeling that the engine had no power. We were in a spin at 400 feet. I had been told by my instructor that the only hope in a Hampden in a spin is to push the nose down as hard as you can, which I did even though the ground was very close. The next thing that I remembered was the shattering of everything and thinking, "This is it!"

The navigator and I were saved by the fact that the aircraft must have been just regaining flying speed. We slithered along the ice with minimum friction. We were in the forward, uptilted part of the aircraft and survived. The two gunners were both killed in the crash. They were smashed to bits at the back of the aircraft. After the crash I was able to pull the navigator, who was unconscious, some of the way away from the wreckage in case the 2,000-pound magnetic mine went off. I then made off over the dunes, just trying to get away from the possibility of capture.

Eventually a rather frightened German soldier appeared over the dunes shouting at me. I said what I had learned to say from films of the First World War. When you were taken prisoner you said "Kamerad". He took me into his dugout where there was a very polite and friendly naval officer – it was a naval flak unit – who spoke excellent English and had been at Oxford in the 'twenties. It became very unreal. I heard him reporting over the telephone: "We shot one down by flak!"

I spent the night there, and the next morning a small Fieseler Storch aircraft came over from Holland. I remember thinking – a slightly romantic notion one had of being an RAF pilot – that now I must try and escape. There had been one case of a Hampden pilot who had managed to get control of what was probably a Storch, and killed the German pilot and flown it back to Britain. I thought that I would get into the aircraft and hit the pilot over the head and try to fly it. Now it seems absolutely ludicrous, because actually when we got into the thing there was another Luftwaffe officer with us who immediately produced a revolver and sat facing me. It was a tiny little aircraft and I was squashed in the back and he sat facing me throughout. I had to drop that romantic notion. At the same time I was by then beginning to feel extremely relieved to be still alive. Then I heard the phrase that I was to hear over and over again for the next few days: "For you the war is over". And indeed it was.'

Robert Kee, Bomber Command pilot

improvements in mine technology and bombing accuracy, the low-level tactics of the early years of war were replaced by attacks from 12,000 to 15,000 feet. The mine campaign not only cost a substantial quantity of Axis shipping, it also forced the German navy to divert resources to minesweeping and anti-aircraft defences. By the end of the war some 40 per cent of the German navy's effort was devoted to clearing the mines laid by Bomber Command, and the major sea routes from Scandinavia to the Baltic ports had become severely disrupted. In the Mediterranean the mining of Axis sea routes from the air contributed substantially to the interruption of supplies to Italian and German armies in North Africa and to the exceptionally high losses of the Italian merchant marine, which by 1943 reached two-thirds of all Italian shipping.

But much of this success lay in the future. In 1941 Bomber Command found itself pulled in a great many directions, without achieving decisive results in any of them. Apart from the demands from the Navy and Coastal Command for help in the sea war, Bomber Command found crews and equipment diverted to the struggle in the Middle East and, after the Japanese attack of December 7th 1941, to the Far East as well. Crews from the Command flew Blenheims, Wellingtons and, from 1941, Stirlings and Halifaxes too, down to the Mediterranean. Experienced officers were pulled away from the Command into training units and combat overseas.

At home Bomber Command was asked to take part in what became known as 'Circus' attacks to try to bring the German fighter force into action in areas of north-western Europe within range of British fighters. In the first half of 1941 Bomber Command mounted 190 sorties, heavily escorted by fighters. After the German invasion of the Soviet Union on June 22nd 1941, the British War Cabinet looked for ways to relieve the pressure on the new ally. The 'Circuses', which had achieved little, were given a new lease of life and Bomber Command found itself forced to undertake the kind of daylight raids on northern Europe that the Luftwaffe abandoned in 1940 as too costly. Despite fighter escort the slow and poorly armed bombers took high casualties. The rate of loss rose from 3.9 per cent in May to 7.7 per cent in August. Bomber Command was ordered to reduce the pressure on crews and the 'Circus' attacks subsided.

These many diversions left Bomber Command with a thin line of forces to continue the attacks on German military and industrial targets that it had been directed to undertake from the summer of 1940. More damaging to its cause was the growing evidence from photo-reconnaissance and intelligence sources in Europe that a very great proportion of bombs failed to reach within miles of the target. Churchill's close confidant and scientific adviser, Lord Cherwell, initiated a detailed operational

Arthur Harris began his military career as a bugler in the Rhodesia Regiment in 1914 but rose to command a fighter squadron of the Royal Flying Corps during the First World War.

Middle East posting

'We were on a raid into Tobruk, laying mines. We moved up to an advance base, and I met this rear gunner who flew with us sitting on a concrete block outside the mess.

"Don't sit there," I said. "You'll get piles."

He replied, "Oh, I'll be on a cold slab before the morning anyway."

"Don't be so daft," I said.

"You can do one of these raids," he said, "but you can't do two."

I went over to him and said, "Look, go sick. It's a night raid – go sick and you won't be missed."

"We'll go," he said.

We were laying mines low level and we had to drop them in precise positions because the Navy were going in with high-speed launches. It meant several runs over the target. On the first run there was a terrific bang outside the rear turret. The intercom went. We sent somebody down to have a look and he was splattered. We didn't take him out of the turret, we scraped him out. He knew it was coming. How, I don't know.'

Greg Gregson, Bomber Command WOP/AG

survey in August 1941 carried out by a member of the Cabinet secretariat, D. M. Butt. He examined photographs and operational reports from approximately 10 per cent of Bomber Command sorties in June and July and concluded that only one-third got within 5 miles of the target; for the easier attacks on targets in France the proportion was two-thirds. The effect of the report was to undermine confidence at the highest level in the whole bombing strategy.

Churchill felt the criticism of bombing keenly. From his high hopes of bombing in the summer of 1940, which he expressed without any clear idea of the nature or limitations of bombing operations, he moved to profound disillusionment. Half-mockingly, he compared Bomber Command operations to the Charge of the Light Brigade. In September 1941 he minuted that bombing could not be more than a 'heavy … and increasing annoyance' to the enemy. In November Peirse was summoned to Chequers, where the Prime Minister ordered him to conserve his aircraft and crews until he had a sufficient force to inflict serious damage. The Navy and Army began to press for the diversion of bombers to meet urgent needs in the Atlantic and the Mediterranean. Bomber Command had, by the end of 1941, reached a point of crisis. In January Peirse himself became the victim of the constant haemorrhage of Bomber Command resources to other tasks when he was posted to India. For a month the commander of No 3 Group, Air Vice-Marshal Baldwin, stood in as an emergency commander-in-chief.

The man chosen to take over Bomber Command was Air Marshal Arthur Travers Harris. A career airman, Harris was born in 1892 into a family of civil servants and soldiers. He moved from England to Rhodesia in 1910 and in 1914 volunteered for the First Rhodesia Regiment as a bugler. After seeing action in the conquest of German West Africa, he engineered a posting to the Royal Flying Corps where he commanded a fighter squadron. He stayed on in the new RAF and saw action in Afghanistan, Iraq and Palestine. He was in the Middle East when war broke out in 1939, but returned to Britain as commander of No 5 Group Bomber Command, based at Grantham. In 1940 he was recruited by Portal as Deputy Chief of Air Staff at the Air Ministry, and in May 1941 he was sent as head of an RAF delegation to Washington. It was here that he learned of his new appointment. In February he returned to England and on the 23rd was formally appointed Commander-in-Chief, Bomber Command.

Harris was a man of strong views, which bordered at times on sheer prejudice. He disliked army life and had scant regard for the commanders of either of the other services. He spoke his mind with a degree of candour that made him unpopular in many places and gave him

Blenheims at war

'2 Group from 1940 into 1942 was the light bomber group in Bomber Command, and was used for a wide variety of things that the medium bombers, the Wellingtons, Whitleys and Stirlings, didn't do. In my tour in the Blenheim we started doing medium-level night bombing, we then did low-level anti-shipping anywhere down the coast from Denmark to Western France. We then did some night low-level on specific targets, mostly ports, canals close to the coast. Then we did the "Circuses" where we had the fighter escort. We attacked targets usually near the coast because British fighters at that time were relatively short-range. We occasionally pulled up the enemy and were attacked once or twice by Me-109s.

We did hit the sea one night in a Blenheim, off the entrance to the Kiel Canal. It was a misty, foggy night. We were looking for a ship that was reputedly in the Canal, and as we turned away from this very flat country we hit the water and bounced off. It transpired later we'd lost one propeller blade and we'd bent back the other five. We came back with the aeroplane vibrating badly, and we set off to fly down along the Friesian Islands, really expecting that we would have to make a landing or ditching. The guns were too active, so we said we would risk the North Sea. We set off for home. I had plotted a position in the middle of the sea, and I said, "If we get past there, we'll ditch and Air Sea Rescue can pick us up in the morning."

But we came all the way back. We got to the airfield, but because we were making such a strange noise they turned all the lights out. The RT we had at the time, the old TR9, was notoriously inefficient, and it took us some time to persuade them to put the lights on. Eventually we got them and landed back at base successfully.'

Ted Sismore, Bomber Command navigator

a reputation for unapproachability that he had no interest in disabusing. Nevertheless he made close friends and inspired loyalty. He was terse, businesslike, immensely hard-working, and single-minded to a degree.

Flying low

'The great thing about low flying was that it was always the aim to be as low as you could with safety, because it protected you from the guns, and from radar. It was exciting to be down among the trees, but the pilot had to be looking a long way ahead to see what he had to do next. Over Holland and the North German plain you could get very low indeed. Further inland, with the hills, not quite so low. You did see everything that was going on. We were navigating then with a map. Church steeples were great navigation aids at low level. If you had a map with churches on, the easiest way to navigate was by steeple. You could also see people – you could see cars, trucks, horses and carts. In hilly country we literally flew past someone's front door, and as we flew past I looked across over the wing tip and a man opened the door. I was looking him straight in the eye at about 40 feet. On one occasion in the flat country of Northern Germany we were flying very low across some open fields with very few trees, and there was a farmer with his horse and cart coming towards us. We were down deliberately low; I doubt if 10 or 20 feet would be an exaggeration. As we got close the horse reared up and threw the man off the cart before we went over. We were that close to people.

Low flying in itself was not dangerous. We were flying in a Blenheim, cruising at 180 mph. That's slow – you've got time to see trees, even high-tension cables. I've known people clip the target by being a few feet too low, but that was unusual. Occasionally somebody came back with a piece of tree.

Now night low level was different. That really was dangerous if you got a bit too low, and people sometimes did. We had one night when we were attacking shipping in the Channel at full moon. One Blenheim came back and landed and the pilot asked us to come and look at it.

"What happened?' we said.

"Well, I saw a ship so I bombed it and hit it," he said. "I pulled up over the mast and I dropped down the other side. There was another ship there I hadn't seen, so I went through his mast."

When we got out to the aeroplane we found that the propeller hadn't hit the mast, but the engine had collected a piece of wood that was burning gently against the cylinders.'

Ted Sismore, Bomber Command navigator

Flying Officer Leonard Cheshire and crew beside a Handley Page Halifax Mk I of No 35 Squadron. Cheshire became one of the legends of Bomber Command, surviving the war despite flying tour after tour. 'I loved flying,' he wrote. 'I found the dangers of battle exciting and exhilarating, so that war came easily to me.'

Joining the 'circus'

'I was seconded to 408 RCAF Squadron as a Flight Commander at one stage in 1941 and shortly after we had completed our formation we were detailed to do daylight operations. This was very unusual, but at that time Fighter Command was having a fairly flat time, the Russian offensive was on and so they were doing a mass of sweeps over France to try and encourage the German fighters to come up and do battle, quite unsuccessfully. They thought it might be helpful if they could put up a few bombers as decoys and they gave us a very close and heavy fighter support. We did a few operations over France but the Germans soon realised that six Hampdens didn't pose a very great threat. They were not prepared to sacrifice their fighters against a massive number of fighters escorting us, so they stayed on the ground and left us to the anti-aircraft gunners. We got quite a hammering from anti-aircraft fire because at 10,000 feet, 145 mph, you are pretty much a sitting target. We did that for about five or six sorties, then we reverted to night operations, to our great relief.'

Wilf Burnett, Bomber Command pilot

A Vickers Wellington Mk IA of No 215 Squadron undergoing repairs at Stradishall. The repair and maintenance organisation was a vital dimension of the bombing effort. Thousands of bombers were returned to service within days of sustaining serious damage.

The Driffield raid

The broken tail of a bomber destroyed on the ground at Driffield in Yorkshire by a German air raid in March 1941, the second major attack on the air station in six months.

'Have you ever heard of the raid on Driffield? We had been to Italy on 13th March 1941, the first raid on Italy from this country. We came back up to Driffield on the 15th, we had lunch, we were in the anteroom. People were still pretty tired after the flight and the air raid siren went and we thought "another bloody raid". Then all of a sudden the bombs began to drop and there was a mad exodus out of the mess to the air raid shelter. We had to go along one of the wings of the mess to reach the shelter and one of the bombs hit the mess. One chap was blown down the entrance to the shelter with a windowframe wrapped round him. Quite a number of aircraft were hit and there was a fair bit of damage to the station. As a result we were taken off flying for Bomber Command and were sent to Prestwick flying Ansons on Atlantic patrols protecting shipping…'

Jim Verran, Bomber Command pilot

Above: A Whitley Mk V damaged by the first German attack on Driffield on August 15th 1940 at the height of the Battle of Britain.

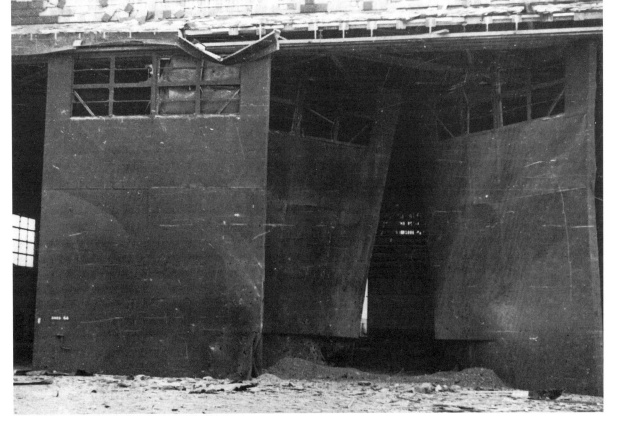

Left: Damage from the same attack on Driffield: the raid caused serious damage to the hangars and staff buildings, and cratered the runway.

Officers of No 99 Squadron at Waterbeach in Cambridgeshire in October 1941. By the end of the war two of these men were dead, four were missing presumed dead and four were prisoners of war.

Beating the weather

'Icing was always a big problem in the winter weather. You would take off and climb through a bank of cloud. The aircraft would be slow climbing and you could see the ice forming on the wings. It was not only the weight of ice that affected the aircraft, but it changed the shape of the wings and the thing became almost uncontrollable. Ice would also get on the propellers, but more insidiously it would get into the carburettors of the engine. You could operate the hot air control incorrectly and create a situation in which it was making ice. The critical range was from about -4 degrees to +4 degrees. The cooling effect of the petrol going through the carburettor caused ice to form, so that from just above freezing the temperature of the carburettor could be actually below freezing. You had to bring in your hot air control to bring the temperature up, but make sure you knocked it out again quickly as you went up because as the temperature dropped again you fell back into that dangerous zone. Then you wanted cold air. I'm sure a lot of young pilots who had been butchers and bakers and all sorts of things, and then flown in America or South Africa, didn't understand this and got iced up.

We had a terrible raid on Berlin in about October or November in 1941 and lost about 45 aeroplanes, the highest loss of the war up to that point. I'm sure most of the aeroplanes went down due to bad weather and I doubt if any of them found the target. If we got iced up on the way there we just had to come back. We'd get down below and get the engine running again, try to bomb something like an aerodrome in Holland and come back to base. I remember the wing commander saying the next day, "Well, thank God you're back because we lost three aeroplanes last night." Sir Richard Peirse was C-in-C Bomber Command at that time, and Churchill sent him a message saying, "It's all right bombing the Germans, but don't try and beat the weather."'

John Gee, Bomber Command pilot

Meeting the C-in-C

'Sir Richard Peirse, that was, the morning after the Berlin raid. The officer aircrew, 18 pilots and one navigator, were assembled in the operations room to meet the great man. You've got to remember that over the previous few months the highest ranking officer I'd seen was a Group Captain, and here was the first time I was going to see an Air Marshal. There didn't seem to be any gold braid left in the world for anybody else.

He was introduced to us, and when he came to me he said, "When did you do your last operation?"

I said, "Last night, sir."

He said, "Good, good. Where did you go?"

I thought to myself, well surely you know because you sent me there, but all I said was, "Berlin, sir."

He replied, "Good, good. What did you think of it?"

I thought this is no time to say that I was frightened stiff, so all I said was, "Very interesting, sir."

He said, "Good, good. How many raids have you done?"

Very proudly I said, "Four, sir."

Immediately he turned to the squadron commander and said, "I'd like to speak to somebody with a bit of experience." My moment in the limelight had gone.'

Sam Hall, Bomber Command navigator

On a great many things Harris proved clear-sighted. His defence of the big bomber against the medium bomber in the debates about air rearmament made possible the pursuit of an offensive air strategy later in the war. He was dismissive of the effects of propaganda raids and of the diversion of Bomber Command effort to the many small and indecisive operations demanded by the army and navy. He was convinced that bombing would be effective only when the technology had greatly improved and when air forces were concentrated in mass, and it was on these two preconditions that he focused the early part of his tenure in office. Above all he carried with him the conviction that no single target on the enemy side held the answer to German defeat. He remained hostile to what he dubbed 'panacea' targets, not because they were difficult to hit – and the accuracy of Bomber Command operations increased remarkably over the war – but because he realised that an enemy economy and social structure could not be

dislocated by an attack on just one of its many elements with the prospect of forcing a decision. Bombing was a blunt instrument in the Second World War, and Harris pursued a strategy that he believed would use that instrument to best effect.

The force Harris inherited in February 1942 was little larger than it had been in 1939. On the day he assumed command there were 378 serviceable aircraft with crews, of which 50 were light bombers and only 69 of them the new generation of heavy bombers, the Stirling, Halifax and Manchester, which had reached the force during 1941. On average Bomber Command could put no more than 250 medium and heavy bombers in the air on a day-by-day basis. The performance of the force improved very slowly during 1942 because of the transition from the medium bomber to the heavies. The Command had 47 squadrons in January 1942, and 52 at the end of the year, with three

An airman's airman

'I went to No 44 Squadron at the beginning of August 1939, and Harris became our AOC on 1 September 1939, two days before the war started. I got to know him very rapidly because he was a man who insisted on knowing his people. He was always coming down to the station even before the hot war started to see how we were doing and to meet the aircrews, to lead from the front as much as he could. Slowly we came to know him and to like him. I admired his attitude, the whole business of trying to do everything for us that would improve our operating capability. He did that, certainly, while he was our AOC, and I think he did that as long as he was C-in-C, Bomber Command. He was an airman's airman. Fortunately I was able to get to know him a little better. Through some kindness on his part, he invited me to his home for Christmas 1939, and I spent Christmas with him and Mrs Harris as their guest. Harris had a bit of a brusque manner, but this didn't detract from his personality. You liked the person, there was warmth there. When he left in September 1940 there was certainly a drop in that personal contact with the new AOC, and it was a noticeable drop.'

**Wilfrid John 'Mike' Lewis,
Bomber Command pilot**

Before the Lancs

'I did my first flight and first tour on Hampdens. A beautiful aeroplane to fly, terrible to fly in – cramped, no heat, no facilities where you could relieve yourself. You got in there and you were stuck there. The aeroplane was like a fighter. It was only 3 feet wide on the outside of the fuselage and the pilot was a very busy person. There were 111 items for the pilot to take care of because on the original aircraft he had not only to find the instruments, the engine and all that, but also he had all the bomb switches to hold the bombs.

I loved the Hampden, two tremendously reliable engines. I was one of the six original pilots to have flown with the first Manchester squadron. That was a disaster. The aircraft itself, the air frame, had many shortcomings in equipment in the beginning, but as we found out Avro were excellent in doing modifications and re-equipping the aeroplane. The engines never were and never did become reliable. They did not give enough power for the aeroplane, so we ended up with two extremely unreliable 1,750 hp engines and having to haul a 50,000-pound aircraft. We should really have had 2,500 hp engines. If you felt that you'd lost one, that was it, you weren't coming home. It didn't matter if you feathered the propeller or not, there was only one way you went and that was down. I have seen an aircraft doing a run up on the ground and had two pistons come right out through the side of the engine. The original bearings were made without any silver as an economy measure, so they weren't hard enough. The bearings would collapse the connecting rod and the piston would fling out through the side of the engine and bang!, your engine just destroyed itself.

I finished my second tour on Manchesters, except for one month in July 1941 when they had to ground them and put new engines in them. We went back to Hampdens for a month, but I finished my tour on Manchesters. I had my tour leave of a very generous one week for the end of a second tour, came back and was to be posted to No 44 squadron, which was the first Lancaster squadron. My old squadron commander came along and asked me to do one last trip because they didn't have a captain to fly it. My 61st operation ended with my becoming a prisoner-of-war. I was climbing at the time because we were early and still trying to get altitude. There was silence and then the rear-gunner shouting "Fighter!". Tremendous bursts of cannon fire into the port engine. My reaction was to slam the stick hard forward to drop the nose and pick up speed, and the second burst came just over the top of our heads with the gunners all firing. I broke left and he broke left and the only sound was a momentary one of the aeroplane going back off into the darkness. That was the last we saw of him. The battle was over in about 10 seconds.

The only evidence of anger was a lot of holes in the engine cowling and the wing and a great stream of gasoline coming out of the main port gas tank. None of the crew was damaged, no shot actually entered the fuselage. Probably one bullet went through the radiator and shortly thereafter the engine temperature suddenly started to go and bang!, it ceased and that was it. We feathered the engine and I started back home, but we were just slowly losing height. I crash-landed the aircraft on the beach of the Dutch Friesian island of Ameland about 1.00 am. I was fortunate. The whole crew survived. No injuries other than a broken bone in one hand of the tail gunner, and one who hit the windshield and had concussion. Very short, nothing dramatic except for that 10 seconds and it's all over. That was being shot down.'

Wilfrid John 'Mike' Lewis,
Bomber Command pilot

on loan to Coastal Command for the sea war. Although 19 new squadrons were formed in 1942, 13 of them were posted to overseas theatres or transferred to other commands. There was, however, a very real change in the nature of Bomber Command equipment. During the summer of 1942 Blenheims and Whitleys were withdrawn from operations. The Manchester, which was plagued with technical problems, was withdrawn in June, and the Hampdens were finally phased out in September. By the end of 1942 Bomber Command had 36 heavy-bomber squadrons equipped or equipping with Lancasters, Halifaxes and Stirlings.

Harris's arrival coincided with other changes. The great strength of German defences, organised in the so-called Kammhuber Line across northern Germany, made up of radar stations, night-fighters, anti-aircraft artillery and searchlights, made it necessary to improve bombing tactics. A new navigational aid, codenamed *Gee* (Ground electronics engineering), was introduced early in 1942 to allow bombing on non-moonlit nights, and new radar aids were in the pipeline. Improvements in training were at last bearing fruit, while the range and calibre of bombs was also greatly improved.

Nevertheless there was a great deal of ground to be made up. Harris had absorbed the lessons of the Butt Report. 'It was glaringly obvious,' he later wrote, 'that the average crew in average weather could not find their way to the target.' Between February and August 1942 an effort was made to rectify this through the development of a specialised target-finding and target-marking force, which came to be known as the Pathfinders. The new group, which was activated on August 15th 1942, transformed the performance of a bomber force that was dropping almost half its bombs in 1941 on open countryside. But for much of 1942 Harris was aware that the force he inherited was not yet equal to any of the tasks it had been asked to carry out.

Above: Short Stirlings lined up at the Central Navigation School at Shawbury in Shropshire in September 1944. Navigation was initially a part of routine training, and was carried out by the pilot or other crew member. A central school was established in 1940, and the navigator became a specialist operator in every bomber crew.

Left: A Halifax Mk II of No 10 Squadron landing at Melbourne in Yorkshire after a raid on Stettin in April 1943. The Mk II was powered by four Rolls Royce Merlin XX engines and entered service in 1941.

This Whitley Mk V of No 102 Squadron crashed at Topcliffe in December 1940. 'They used to call it the flying coffin,' recalled one veteran.

A Halifax Mk II of No 51 Squadron damaged after a raid on Frankfurt in December 1943. By this time, German anti-aircraft guns were deployed in vast numbers and could deliver rapid fire to targets at up to 30,000 feet. One survivor remembered 'anti-aircraft fire so thick you could have lowered your undercarriage and landed on it'.

Air Marshal Harris (centre, with glasses) inspecting the famous blue books that carried detailed maps of the bomb damage done to enemy targets. To the right is Air Marshal Robert Saundby, who was Harris's senior staff officer. 'I relied enormously on his experience,' Harris later wrote.

Constructed from wood, the De Havilland Mosquito medium bomber was one of the most remarkable technical developments of the war. Designed in 1940 and entering service only a year later, it was able to fly fast enough and high enough to be all but immune from interception. The Mk B IX seen here served in Pathfinder squadrons formed in 1942.

The standard photo-electric cell night camera with ancillary equipment. In July 1940 the first order was given for 200 cameras to be carried by bombers on raids to record the impact of the bombs. The F24 camera had a flash cylinder capable of generating 170 million candle-power at the point of detonation.

Learning by experience

'The one failing of the whole training system was that we weren't told more of what to expect. We just learned it strictly from experience, except for the pilot who had done two trips as a rule before he took his own crew. He didn't tell us much about what to expect; in fact I don't remember the pilot telling us anything.

I was a tail gunner in a Halifax and away we went. One night we got attacked by two fighters. I shot down the one that came in from the rear, a Ju-88, and the mid-gunner spotted the one underneath and the pilot was able to take violent evasive action. Unfortunately the bomb aimer was mortally wounded and died after we went back to England. Within a few hours everybody was shook up. The wireless operator got hit in the rear end with a fragment of cannon shell and the aircraft was just shattered. The bomb aimer was standing in the astrodome and he was hit in the head. The attack hit the top of the aircraft. The flaps came down and the undercarriage came down; the bomb doors fell open; we had no hydraulics; the wireless set blew up and we had to fly another 2 hours or more to get back to England. We landed at a fighterdrome in the south of England. We didn't crash, we landed wheels down.

We had some leave to go to the bomb aimer's funeral and then went back on ops. From then on you were pretty apprehensive. I'm not going to say strict discipline because it wasn't a matter of strictness, it was a matter of strong discipline. There was no chatter, no unnecessary banter on the intercom. There was silence. When somebody switched that mike on everybody knew it and everybody was listening. You'd hear them breathing, and if they'd nothing to say the pilot would ask who was on the mike. You were apprehensive.

After my original crew got shot down I flew with various crews. One crew I went with on their first trip and that was at the time [I'd done] 20/21 trips. That was an unforgettable experience because they just chattered the whole time: "Look at the lights", "Look at that", "Do you see that?". Finally I was such a nervous wreck that I had to tell them to keep quiet and they did. It was not a happy trip, but we got home fine. They unfortunately went missing a couple of trips later. They never did get any experience.'

Wilkie Wanless, Bomber Command rear gunner

Bombing in the dark

'If I look back at the diary record I made of all my trips by the end of 1941, it reads pretty depressingly in terms of successful operations. I find Brest, but I could see nothing but flak and patchy cloud. The bombs probably fell into the bay. We were trying to hit the Scharnhorst and Gneisenau at the time. Here is an attempt to bomb Brunswick, hopelessly dark. Dropped some incendiaries at what we hoped was Hannover. Düsseldorf also hopeless, bombed searchlight concentration. Kiel, three in succession. Hopeless again, very bad weather, brought a 2,000-pound bomb back. Mannheim, too much cloud. A great number were like that. There were one or two successes. Here's Hamm, a very good trip, moonlight. Bombed four big fires along the edge of the marshalling yards, flew back at nought feet. But that was rare. When I read about only 5 per cent of aircraft getting within 15 miles of their targets, that did not surprise me. Most people who read it were shocked, but I don't think it would have surprised anyone who was bombing in 1941.'

Robert Kee, Bomber Command pilot

A poster explaining to crews how night photography worked. The aircraft had a circuit that linked the camera and flash with the bomb-firing key so the picture was taken automatically. Crews were encouraged to take a second picture after bombing, although not all were prepared to linger over the target area.

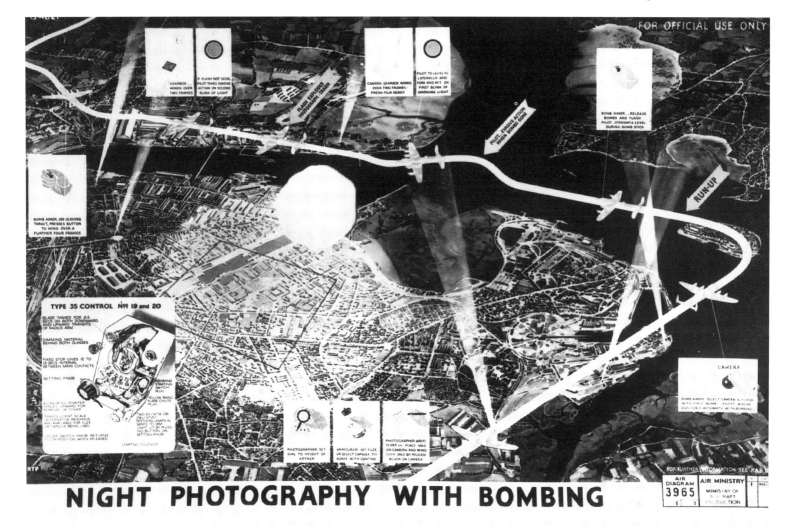

NIGHT PHOTOGRAPHY WITH BOMBING

Right: Night photography was not entirely reliable. Here the brightness of the German searchlights has produced a picture before the flash cylinder has ignited.

Below: Light generated by fires on the ground also degraded the quality of night photography. This picture was taken over Magdeburg during a raid on the night of 16/17th January 1945; the 'fogging' effect obscures the ground image entirely.

Reforming the Command

'I don't think we realised at the time that our equipment wasn't really up to it. They'd forgotten to design or produce any navigation equipment, so the Wellington bomber, which was intended to be a day bomber, had to operate at night because it was so vulnerable during the day. It had virtually the same equipment that the Tiger Moth had, with one exception – the Wellington had a loop aerial. Here we were flying 500 or 600 miles over enemy territory, trying to locate a target in total blackout, often with cloud below us and a lot of industrial haze. It's not surprising that our bombers were 5, 10 miles away. There was no bomber stream. We were largely on our own, perhaps 10 or 14 aircraft at intervals. Bomber Command was pretty ineffective, but we didn't realise it at the time. We thought we were finding the target and doing a good job, otherwise our morale would have been really zero.

When the Butt report was produced, we didn't know about it at all. It was kept very secret indeed. It wasn't until Sir Arthur Harris took over in 1942 that things began to change. By that time I had done my first tour of operations and been fortunate enough to be sent to central flying school to do a flying instructor's course. I spent two and a half years instructing before I went back on operations and during that time the whole thing had changed completely. The navigation equipment was highly organised with radar navigation. We had the benefit of the bomber stream, and the Pathfinders marking the target, and of course an enormous weight of aircraft. To fly in a stream of 500 aircraft out over Beachy Head with all the navigation lights on! Soon they were all switched off, and you couldn't see any of them. But they were all still there, a wonderful feeling of power.'

John Gee, Bomber Command pilot

The Bristol Blenheim IV carried a crew of three: pilot, observer/ navigator and gunner. Here the observer takes the F24 camera on board.

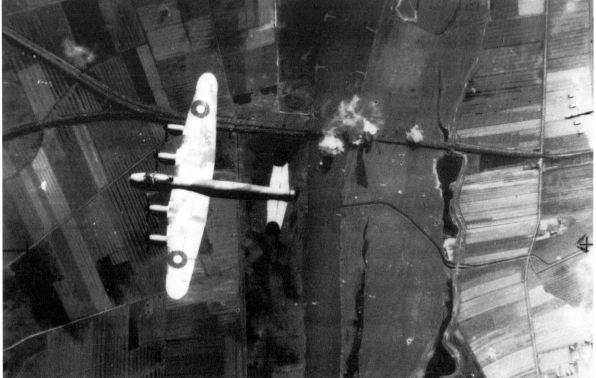

By 1945 the Allied air forces had achieved air superiority over Germany, and Bomber Command delivered some attacks in daylight. Here a Lancaster scores a direct hit with a 22,000-pound 'Grand Slam' bomb, the most powerful conventional weapon of the war.

Target markers strike the Pauillac oil refinery at the mouth of the Gironde river in western France on August 4th 1944. During that summer the USAAF and Bomber Command concentrated on attacking German oil resources with considerable effect on the enemy war effort.

Five minutes after the target markers were released, Bomber Command Lancasters struck the target from 10,000 feet. Here the concentration of bombs obliterates the refinery.

Shortly before Harris took over the Command, an effort had been made to clarify exactly what the role of the bomber force was supposed to be. This followed more than six months of argument from the time of the Butt report about the kind of targets that bombing, under current circumstances, could realistically damage. The final directive, No 22, was issued on February 14th 1942, ten days before Harris took up his appointment. The most important decision concerned the nature of the attack on Germany. Until then, first oil, then communications had been singled out as the primary target, though neither had been attacked with any consistency or effort. The new directive followed a line that had been strongly urged by the Chief of the Air Staff, Sir Charles Portal, since the late summer of 1940. The primary objective was now to be 'the morale of the enemy civil population and in particular, of the industrial workers'. Attacks were to take the form of large raids on Germany's major industrial cities.

Directive Number 22

'Air Ministry to Air Marshal Baldwin, Feb 14th 1942

You are authorised to employ your effort without restriction, until further notice, in accordance with the following directions.

It has been decided that the primary object of your operations should now be focused on the morale of the enemy civil population and in particular, of the industrial workers. With this aim in view, a list of selected area targets is attached… You will note that Berlin has been included amongst the targets. In this case your operations should be of a harassing nature, the object being to maintain fear of attack over the city and to impose A.R.P. measures… Essen is the most important of the selected primary targets. I am to suggest that this should be selected as your initial target… Finally, I am to say that, although every effort will be made to confine your operations to your primary offensive, you should recognise that it will on occasions be necessary to call upon you for diversionary attacks on objectives, the destruction of which is of immediate importance in the light of the current strategical situation. In particular, important naval units and the submarine building yards and bases may have to be attacked periodically, especially when this can be done without missing good opportunities of bombing your primary targets.'

C. Webster & N. Frankland, *The Strategic Air Offensive against Germany* **(HMSO, 4 vols, 1961); Vol iv, Appendix 8**

Harris was not the author of this directive, nor had he exercised any influence upon the discussions that had given rise to it. Although he accepted the directive, he had a poor regard for the strategy of 'morale-breaking' as such. There was little that the civilian population could have done to stop the war, he later recalled, 'with the Gestapo standing by' and 'the concentration camp around the corner'. He saw as his task first and foremost the destruction of Germany's capacity to wage war by attacking the major industrial cities. Demoralisation was a by-product of that strategy, but Harris saw his chief objective in the war economy, not the civil population. This was essentially the campaign he waged over the next three years against targets in Germany when bombers were not required for other tasks.

This was in reality seldom the case. Although Harris and the Air Ministry wanted to concentrate the bomber force on a single campaign to maximise its effect, the demands of co-operation with the other services proved irresistible even for so intractable a personality as Harris. For at least a year after he joined Bomber Command the Battle of the Atlantic continued to be a top strategic priority, and naval targets remained high on the list of bombing objectives. Directive 22 stipulated that the force should always be prepared to abandon its primary targets to collaborate with the Royal Navy and, when required, with the Army. Harris complied unwillingly, but he could not flout the Chiefs of Staff. Thus Bomber Command remained a multi-role force throughout the war.

The improvements in training and equipment certainly served to make Bomber Command's contribution to the naval war more effective. During 1942 the number of mines sown increased more than ninefold over 1941. In 1944 the Command dropped over 16,000 mines, compared with 1,000 in 1941. Three squadrons of bombers were loaned to Coastal Command for anti-submarine patrols. Harris resisted sending more, and in this case his judgement was almost certainly at fault. When very-long-range aircraft were finally made available to Coastal Command in April and May 1943 they plugged the 'Atlantic Gap' – the area of ocean that conventional aircraft could not reach – with just 37 converted bombers. At the same time the Command kept up the attack on the submarine bases on the French coast at Brest and Lorient, and attacks on the submarine industry on the German north coast, which in 1942 absorbed 26 per cent of the whole bombing effort. The extent to which these attacks dented submarine production has never been very precisely calculated, but it was almost certainly less than the expectations of the campaign. Attacks on the submarine pens achieved little except the progressive destruction of the towns surrounding them. Until 12,000-pound bombs capable of penetrating deep concrete were available in 1944, the submarine pens remained secure.

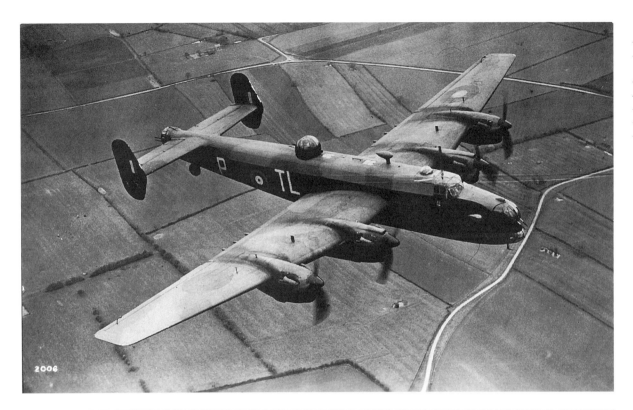

Thirty Bomber Command squadrons were equipped with the Handley Page Halifax, including 15 of the Royal Canadian Air Force and three of the Royal Australian Air Force stationed in Britain. This Halifax Mk II is from No 35 Squadron, flying from Graveley in Huntingdonshire in May 1942.

In addition to its bombing and pathfinder roles, the Mosquito became a very effective night intruder, attacking enemy night fighters over their homeland. This Mk XIX served with No 68 Squadron.

The submarine battle over Augsburg, April 17th 1942

'When the curtain drew back at the briefing there was a roar of laughter instead of the gasp of horror. No one believed that the air force would be so stupid as to send 12 of its newest four-engined bombers all that distance inside Germany in daylight. We sat back and waited calmly for someone to say, "Now the real target is this". Unfortunately it was the real target, a factory near Munich that was a major manufacturer of diesel engines for submarines.

At that time it was touch and go in the North Atlantic between Britain having enough to eat and not having enough to eat. The crews were determined that these diesels should not go forth in submarines. The route took us low, at about 100 feet, down to the south coast, across the Channel. We were to join 44 Squadron at the south coast, six aircraft from each squadron, and we were to go as a formation of 12 the rest of the way. We saw 44 Squadron slightly ahead of us, but we realised that they were drifting to port, and we continued in the direction we should have been going.

Our six aircraft pressed on very, very low across the Channel so that we were underneath the radar. I could see the sandbanks of France coming up ahead of us. We had no opposition at all crossing the defended coast and proceeded south of Paris where I saw the second enemy aircraft I saw during the whole war. It was probably a courier, a Heinkel 111. It approached and, recognising us, did a 90-degree bank turn back towards Paris. We continued on flying at 100 feet.

Factories across occupied Europe were used by the Germans to sustain their war effort, and Bomber Command attacked them regularly. The Philips factories at Eindhoven, a key source of radio equipment, were attacked by 93 aircraft of 2 Group including 47 of the newly arrived Lockheed Venturas on December 6th 1942. Full production did not resume for six months, but 148 Dutch civilians lost their lives.

Occasionally you would see some Frenchmen take a second look and wave their berets or their shovels. A bunch of German soldiers doing PT in their singlets broke hurriedly for their shelters as we roared over. The next opposition was a German officer on one of the steamers on Lake Constanz firing a revolver at us. I could see him quite clearly, defending the ladies with his Luger against 48 Browning machine guns.

Our route took us from the north end of Lake Constanz across another lake, where we turned north towards the target. We hadn't seen a thing on the way of the German Air Force. We were belting at full throttle at about 100 feet towards the targets. I dropped the bombs along the side wall. We flashed across the target and down the other side to about 50 feet, because flak was quite heavy. As we went away I could see light flak shells overtaking us, green balls flowing away on our right and hitting the ground ahead of us. Leaving the target I looked down at our leader's aircraft and saw that there was a little wisp of steam trailing back from it. The white steam turned to black smoke, with fire in the wing. I was slightly above him. In the top of the Lancaster there was a little wooden hatch for getting out if you had to land at sea. I realised that this wooden hatch had burned away and I could look down into the fuselage. It looked like a blow lamp with the petrol swilling around the wings and the centre section, igniting the fuselage and the slipstream blowing it down. Just like a blow lamp.

He dropped back and I asked our gunner to keep an eye on him. Suddenly he said, "Oh God, Skip, he's gone. He looks like a chrysanthemum of fire."

One other of our aircraft caught fire just short of the target, but kept on, dropped the bombs and then crashed. The raid was suicidal. Four from 97 Squadron got back, but only one from 44. Five out of twelve.'

Rod Rodley, Bomber Command pilot

Below left: The aftermath of a precision-bombing attack on Amiens prison by six Mosquitoes from No 21 and No 464 Squadrons on February 18th 1944. The attack was carried out to free French resistance fighters imprisoned there by the Germans.

Below: A Messerschmitt Bf 109 seen taking off from Heraldo airfield during an attack by No 114 Squadron on November 27th 1941. Bomb hits are indicated by small plumes of smoke.

German defences continued to inflict casualties to the end of the war. Here a bomber breaks in two during a daylight attack on the Frisian Islands on April 25th 1945.

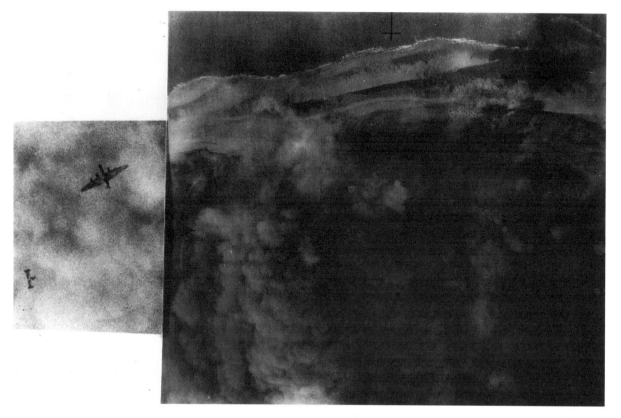

Many Bomber Command squadrons served overseas, directly supporting army operations. In January 1944 there were 16 bomber squadrons in the Mediterranean theatre and a further 10 in India and Sri Lanka. This Lancaster Mk III of No 61 Squadron made a wheels-up landing at Blida, northern Algeria, in July 1943.

More obvious success was achieved against German surface vessels. The *Scharnhorst* and *Gneisenau* were damaged by mines laid by the Command as they retreated to Keil in February 1942. The *Gneisenau* was so severely damaged in subsequent attacks that she was broken up; the *Scharnhorst* was repaired only a year later. The remaining units of the German fleet were picked off by bombers one by one: the *Scheer* and *Lutzow* in April 1945; the *Admiral Hipper* in dry dock in the same month; the *Schlesien, Köln* and *Emden* were all severely damaged. The largest German ship after the loss of the *Bismarck* was the battleship *Tirpitz*. Bottled up by the British blockade, the ship was attacked on September 15th 1944 by Bomber Command from Soviet bases in Alten Fjord. Damage to the bows forced the ship to withdraw to Tromsö, where on November 12th it was attacked by 30 Lancasters from Lossiemouth in Scotland, carrying the 12,000-pound 'Tallboy' bomb. The bombers attacked in clear weather, but the fighters assigned to protect the vessel scrambled too late. Two bombs hit the *Tirpitz*; she blew up, rolled over and sank. One Lancaster was hit by flak and was forced to land in Sweden, but the others returned safely. Bomber Command successfully neutralised any threat the German surface fleet might have posed in the last year of war.

Collaboration with the Army gradually overshadowed Air-Navy co-operation as the Western Allies first reversed the tide of Axis successes in North Africa, then took the war to Italy in 1943, and to France the following year. The directive of February 1942 kept open the question of when and in what form Bomber Command should assist the land war, but the relative failure of bombing in 1940 did not blunt the Army's enthusiasm for direct air support. The bomber component of the tactical air forces in the Middle East played a significant part in the campaign, its role being to attack shipping, supply lines, stores and troop concentrations. Before the invasion of Sicily in July 1943 the bombers played the role of long-range artillery. Wellington bombers worked with American Flying Fortresses and Liberators to attack airfields, communications and port facilities. RAF bombers joined in the attack on the island of Pantelleria, lying between Tunisia and Sicily across the route of Allied attack, which proved to be a classic example of the moral impact of heavy bombing vastly outweighing the degree of physical destruction. Only 200 of 11,000 Italian forces on the island were killed, but the massive bombardment produced an almost immediate surrender.

When Italy was invaded on September 3rd 1943

A Consolidated B-24 Liberator heavy bomber serving with the RAF in Italy in 1943 is seen on fire after a mid-air collision. The B-24 was primarily used by the US 8th Air Force in Britain and the US 15th Air Force in the Mediterranean.

bomber forces continued to attack tactical targets deep in enemy territory, while Bomber Command flew across Europe to attack the industrial cities of the north in the hope of speeding up the surrender of Italy. Italian targets had been hit intermittently ever since Mussolini brought Italy into the war on the German side on June 10th 1940. The very first raid against Italy was undertaken on the night of June 11/12th by 36 Whitleys. After flying from their bases in Yorkshire, the bombers refuelled in the Channel Islands before making the long flight to Genoa and Turin. Twenty-three aircraft were forced back by the freezing conditions experienced over the Alps, and only nine bombed Turin and two Genoa. Both cities were fully illuminated as the aircraft approached. Little damage was done, but two Whitleys crashed on their return to France. Although the weight of attack directed at Italy was tiny compared with the German campaign, the poorer state of Italian preparations produced lower battle casualties and a disproportionate impact on the bombed populations. Italian war production in 1943 was reduced, according to

one recent estimate, by as much as two-thirds, thanks to the mass exodus of workers from the bombed cities. Fear of continued bombing did play a part in the decision of the Italian Government to surrender on September 8th, but only a part.

Many lessons were learned from the role of airpower in the Mediterranean theatre. Bombing in direct support of the ground forces was largely ineffective against fleeting and concealed targets and this work was confined to cannon and rocket-firing fighters and fighter bombers in the campaign in Normandy, which opened on June 6th 1944. Attacks on communications had mixed success in Italy, partly as a result of the division between American and British air forces and the lack of any clear plan for the assault. When preparations began in earnest for a Western Allies invasion of France in the last months of 1943, the Allied Combined Chiefs of Staff recognised the need to create a unity of air command and to use the heavy bombers for tasks for which they were more clearly suited. This decision had unexpected implications. In the

The first raids on Italy

'On 11th June [1940] about midday, still heavy with sleep, I was roused by someone, obviously in great haste, and told to report to the crew room immediately. It transpired that Italy had entered the conflict and we were to proceed to Jersey as a means of getting closer to Turin where, that night, we were to bomb the Fiat Works. What a glorious summer day it was as we left Driffield at 1430 hours thinking somewhat disgruntledly what we could have been doing at Bridlington on a well-deserved day off.

In N1471 we left Jersey at 2010 hours for Turin. About two and a half hours out, still climbing to clear the Alps, we entered cloud and soon encountered severe turbulence. Electrical disturbance was the worst I had experienced and the noise in my headphones was unbearable. Fearing for my equipment led me to disconnect the aerials and, in so doing, I suffered superficial burns to the fingers of my right hand.

It became agonisingly cold and we soon felt the depth of its penetration. The cloud seemed solid and without top as we struggled laboriously for height. We now heard ominous bumps as of something striking the aircraft and soon deduced that ice was being flung off the propellers. The captain asked me to shine the Aldis Lamp along the leading

edges of the wings and we could see the ice building up despite the action of the pulsating de-icer boots. The ice formed with great rapidity and soon we could see it building up thickly over the leading edges and we began to wallow very badly. We descended rapidly as low as we dared, but there was no improvement in our situation, which was now of extreme hazard.

The fear we all shared was aggravated by the effect of the arctic conditions and there was now ice inside the cabin – it was quite impossible to keep still. To me the navigator seemed to be performing the wildest gyrations, and I have no doubt that I appeared the same to him. The pilot was fighting with the aeroplane to keep it airborne and what the poor sod in the tail was doing only God knows. We were obviously not going to make it this trip and reluctantly decided to abort. I cannot remember for certain now, but I believe we dropped our bombs safe before staggering round to return to Jersey. We found that most crews had experienced the same as ourselves and only a few had, miraculously, avoided it and found the target; seemingly Turin was clear and with no blackout. We were airborne for 5 hours and 55 minutes.'

From a memoir by Squadron-Leader W. Jacobs, Bomber Command

Mediterranean and Far East there was no question that the theatre commanders should control the combined forces under their command. But in the European theatre a structure of command already existed. When Harris was asked to make his force available for the Normandy campaign he did all in his power to keep control of the Command in his own hands.

His efforts, and those of his American counterpart, the Commander of the 8th US Army Air Force, Carl Spaatz, to avoid handing over their forces to the new theatre commander, General Dwight Eisenhower, are well known. But their resistance to control by the air commander of the Allied Expeditionary Force, the RAF fighter chief, Air Marshal Trafford Leigh-Mallory, was not a result of simple rivalry or pique. Harris was convinced that the best service he could render the invasion campaign was to continue concentrated attacks on targets in Germany. He feared that his Command would be absorbed into a primitive tactical air battle in which concentration of effort would be squandered for little strategic gain. His intransigence almost provoked Eisenhower to resign in March 1944, but in the end a compromise was reached between Eisenhower's headquarters and British-based bomber forces. Harris agreed that for the invasion preparations and the first months of the campaign his bombers would come under the temporary command of Eisenhower himself, and

his deputy, the British airman Air Marshal Arthur Tedder. Leigh-Mallory was excluded.

The command crisis proved easier to solve than the deeper arguments about what the heavy bombers should be used for. Harris pressed from the start for the continued bombing of German industrial cities and targets linked to German air power, as laid down in the directive of June 3rd 1943 for operation POINTBLANK. The OVERLORD planners in January 1944 drew up a list of their priority targets: the German air force and its installations in western Europe; German coastal defences; and the transport net of north-western Europe through which German reinforcements would have to pass to meet the Allied invasion. The American bomber force agreed with Harris, and in March Spaatz drew up an alternative plan for the destruction of German oil supplies and the German oil industry. The conflict between the oil plan and the transportation plan was resolved, like the issue of command, at the end of March. American and British bomber forces were to concentrate for two or three months on transport targets and the German Air Force, but were free when resources or schedules permitted to continue attacks on targets in Germany itself. The OVERLORD air plan was issued as a directive on April 17th 1944; three days before, command over bomber forces in England passed to Eisenhower, and in practice to Tedder.

The OVERLORD Directive

'Directive by the Supreme Commander [Eisenhower] to Bomber Command for support of "Overlord", 17 April 1944

The overall mission of the strategical Air Forces remains the progressive destruction and dislocation of the German military, industrial and economic system, and the destruction of vital elements of lines of communication. In the execution of this overall mission the immediate objective is first the destruction of German air combat strength, by the successful prosecution of the Combined Bomber offensive. Our re-entry to the Continent constitutes the supreme operation for 1944; all possible support must, therefore, be afforded to the Allied Armies by our Air Forces to assist them in establishing themselves in the lodgement area.

The first pre-requisite of success in the maintenance of the combined Bomber offensive and of our re-entry on the Continent is an overall reduction of the enemy's air combat strength and particularly his air fighter strength. The primary role of our Air Forces in the European and

Mediterranean theatres is, therefore, to secure and maintain air superiority.

Our armies will also require maximum possible assistance on the ground preparatory to the actual assault. This can best be given by interfering with rail communication, particularly as affecting the enemy movements and concentrations in the "OVERLORD" area. A further Directive covering the employment of the strategical air forces during the assault period and succeeding land operations will be issued in due course.

The particular mission of the strategical air forces prior to the "OVERLORD" assault is:

(a) To deplete the German air force and particularly the German fighter forces, and to destroy and disorganise the facilities supporting them.
(b) To destroy and disrupt the enemy's rail communications, particularly those affecting the enemy's movement toward the "OVERLORD" lodgement area.

C. Webster & N. Frankland, *The Strategic Air Offensive against Germany* (HMSO, 4 vols, 1961); Vol iv, Appendix 8, pp 167-8

Harris recognised well before this that he was not going to win the argument, and it was to his credit that even before the decision to use the bombers for the transportation plan was finally taken on March 25th he had already begun to order railway attacks. The first was made on the night of March 6/7th against the rail centre at Trappes, and from then until the end of June Bomber Command made 81 attacks on rail centres and a further 21 attacks against smaller rail targets – bridges and tunnels. The greater degree of accuracy now possible in 1944, and higher standards of navigational training, meant that night attacks could be carried out on relatively small targets with much greater success than in 1940. By June the 37 rail centres assigned to Bomber Command were destroyed or heavily damaged. The subsequent collapse of rail traffic in the area slowed down the build-up of German forces and efforts at reinforcement. When bombers and fighter-bombers destroyed the bridges over the Seine during the week before the invasion, effective German reinforcement became impossible.

Bomber Command also contributed to the attacks on air force targets and the bombing of Germany's 'Atlantic Wall'. Some 14,000 tons of bombs were dropped on

these defences in the weeks leading up to invasion, and in the final attack on the beaches where Allied forces were to land, 5,000 tons of high explosives were deposited on the hapless defenders. Bomber Command was also called upon to attack other military targets, including the major military stores in northern France. The depot at Mailly Le Camp was attacked by 338 bombers on the night of May 3/4th, in bright moonlight to maximise the chances of accurate bombing. Night fighters and flak claimed 42 of the attacking force, but severe damage was done to the installation, and supplies to this and to four other major military depots.

Direct support for the ground campaign continued after the invasion, which took place on the morning of June 6th. Poor weather made it difficult for the 8th Air Force to bomb by day for the first two weeks, but Bomber Command was able to fly at night and continued its attacks on rail and military targets. When the weather improved Bomber Command began to fly by day as well, with strong fighter escort. The ports of Le Havre and Boulogne were attacked in mid-June and many of the small German naval vessels, gathered there to harass the Allied supply routes, were destroyed or disabled. The ground commander, Field Marshal Bernard Montgomery, asked the bombers to provide battlefield attacks at particular points in the campaign. While the result was terrifying for the troops who were bombed by hundreds of heavy aircraft, bombing of the battlefield had mixed results. The raid on Caen, designed to open the way for the GOODWOOD operation on July 18th, was too successful; the degree of destruction was so great that Allied ground forces found their own progress severely impeded, while German forces were able to withdraw from the city behind the shelter of the shattered streets in front of them.

Bomber Command did the same to the many strongpoints that remained in German hands as Allied armies swept past. The German garrisons at Le Havre, Brest, St Malo, Boulogne, Calais and Cap Gris Nez were subjected to pulverising attacks before their surrender. By September Allied armies had cleared most of France and on the 16th Eisenhower handed control of bomber forces back to the RAF. But Bomber Command continued to support the offensive into Germany when called upon to do so, and played a part in interrupting supplies and communications for the German counter-attack in the Ardennes in December 1944. When Allied armies invaded Germany, Bomber Command attacked German strongpoints and troop concentrations, almost obliterating the urban areas that housed them.

Halifax bombers on a raid against Calais on September 25th 1944. Allied air superiority over France was maintained after D-Day, enabling Bomber Command to fly more daylight missions.

Far left and left: Two photographs taken seconds apart during a daylight raid on Le Havre on September 6th 1944. Bombs are visible in the first frame, while explosions obscure the target in the second. Le Havre held out against Allied attacks until September 12th.

Cap Gris Nez, on the opposite side of the English Channel to Dover, was heavily attacked by Bomber Command in support of army operations in 1944. Here a Lancaster adds to the destruction on September 26th, four days before the garrisons of Calais and Boulogne surrendered.

OVERLORD was not the only diversion from the bombing of Germany. During 1943 British scientific intelligence identified German plans to build rockets and flying-bombs, the so-called V-weapons developed to counter the bombing offensive. On the night of August 17/18th, the rocket development centre at Peenemünde on the Baltic coast was attacked by a force of 596 Lancasters, Halifaxes and Stirlings. Once again the raid was carried out in bright moonlight to ensure visibility of the target. The defending fighters were drawn off by a diversionary raid on Berlin by nine Mosquitoes and returned only for the third, and last, wave of bombers. The main force attacked a camp of forced labourers until drawn back to the rocket complex itself by the Master Bomber organising the raid. Substantial damage was done, forcing the dispersal of the project and delaying the development and introduction of the weapons.

The effect was not, however, decisive. From December 1943 Bomber Command and the 8th Air Force were ordered to attack a network of launch sites for the V1 flying-bomb in Cherbourg and the Pas de Calais. Attacks continued through the period of OVERLORD preparation and beyond. The first flying-bombs were launched against London on June 16th, but the scale and intensity of the campaign were much reduced by the dislocation caused by bomb attack. The campaign, codenamed CROSSBOW, absorbed 60,000 tons of bombs between June and September 1944. Attacks had to be made in general from low altitude and with great accuracy, and direct hits were difficult to achieve. The mobile launch sites gave considerable flexibility to the V1 campaign. The rocket attacks, which began in September 1944, were harder to neutralise. The rockets were produced in deep underground factories, and launched from small and camouflaged sites in Germany until almost the end of the war.

Baling out

'It was a simple raid. It was east of Paris in daylight at the end of July [1944], and we were bombing this tunnel that stored V1 bombs 30 miles east of Paris. 617 Squadron were bombing the southern end and 9 Squadron were bombing the northern end to shut the tunnel. There were 300 planes with 12 single 1,000-pound delayed-action bombs to drop to prevent the Germans from salvaging the V1s. We had 12,000-pounders and we were at 12,000 feet to make sure we could see it. We went in in a gaggle. It was the first time I took my camera with me in the plane. It was supposed to be bad luck taking a camera! I took a few shots of the other planes. There was Flak ahead and the crew told me not to bother to take pictures of it because there were Mosquitoes covering the picture side. There were four and a half minutes left to stabilise the bomb sight. The bomb aimer said "Hold it. Hold it" and then bang! The outer engine fell off and something went through the plane. The stick went sloppy in my hand and I said, "Stand by to bale out".

My engineer handed me my chute. Took my helmet off and put my chute on. I shouted, "Bale out!", and the crew all dashed to the front to get their chutes and to get down the escape hatch at the front. If you have plenty of time you ask the rear gunners to come up, but in an emergency like this, with the plane beginning to spin down, they get out as soon as they can from the back. I could not get out of my seat, so I tried to open the side window but couldn't open it. I couldn't open the other window. I remember all the dinghies fell out. I turned the escape handle in the escape hatch, and as I turned it the whole nose of the plane must have come off, because the next thing I knew I was falling through the air and felt for my chute. There was quiet – no engine noise. I felt for my cord, pulled it. I thought it was not working when it suddenly jerked. I held on like grim death because I was not sure if I had put it on right. I could see trees coming up. I kept my legs together as all good men should do and slid into the trees. I thought I had broken my leg it was so numb. My hand was broken, hit when I came through the hatch, and my face was all burned.

I got down from the tree, took my chute off and poked it under a bush and then looked for my escape route. I could hear the bombs still going off because of the delayed action. I was quite near the target so I headed away. I had a dressing with me which you always carried and I sat and wrapped up my hand. I thought, "If I go further south I could speak French and make my way back".

The invasion forces were the other side of Paris. I stood up, and there were three big Germans with rifles and bayonets standing round me. They had seen the parachutes coming down into the trees. I saw the tail part of my plane in the trees and I pointed to it to see if I could go to it. By that time a German had come up who spoke better English than I did. He was wearing white jodhpurs. He thought I was American because it was a daylight raid. I went to my plane. The mid upper gunner was just inside, in the tailplane, dead. The rear turret was about 20 yards from the plane with the rear gunner in it dead with his chute. He had managed to get his chute on, but when he headed out he hit the ground. Twenty minutes later they came up with my wireless operator with his ankle all twisted. His chute must have opened in the plane and torn, because he hit the ground too fast and knocked himself out.

I took it that the rest of the crew were all safe. They had been in front of me and I had followed out after them. Our navigator was a French Canadian, so I thought he would be all right, and Chunky, my engineer, was a big strong chap. I thought, "Lucky devils, they are definitely away".

And it was not until we came back from prison that I found out they had all been killed. Whether they had been trapped in the nose, or their chutes had not opened, I don't know. They are buried in France.'

Bill Reid VC, Bomber Command pilot

The pilot William Reid seen visiting an anti-aircraft battery after his award of the Victoria Cross for pressing home an attack despite serious injuries. He was later shot down and captured, one of only two survivors from his crew.

The concentration of aircraft over a target area brought perils of its own: this B-24 Liberator of No 37 Squadron was struck by bombs released from another bomber overhead during an attack on Monfalcone on the border between Italy and Yugoslavia in March 1945. Incredibly, the stricken aircraft managed to return to its base at Tortorella despite the damage seen here.

Christmas Eve 1944

'There were certainly occasions when the weather was so bad you felt you should not be going out, but something had to be done. On one occasion towards the end of the war, at Christmas 1944 when the Ardennes push broke through [Battle of the Bulge], we had to bomb the supply lines and bridges and railways around Koblenz. We'd been grounded for about four days by fog. The whole country was fog-bound, but over there was brilliant weather. Eventually we took off in thick fog from Scampton. There was no way we were going to get back if an engine failed on take-off. We couldn't see the aerodrome, but the fog was only 100 feet thick. Once you got through it there were brilliant blue skies.

We flew to Koblenz and bombed those bridges and railways. But on the way back we were diverted to one of only two aerodromes in the country that were open, because there was a fog disperser in use there. We hitch-hiked into Margate or Ramsgate and went to a pub called the Cinque Port, and it was full of aircrew in flying gear. The publican realised something peculiar had happened and he asked me what it was about. I explained that we had been on a raid and had come back here because no other aerodrome was open, but it had no food there and no beds, so we were going to spend the night the best way we could.

It so happened that that day had been his daughter's wedding, and when the pub closed at about 10 o'clock, we stayed behind and had the remains of the wedding breakfast. We had duck and green peas. Then he found us beds for the night, and when I asked him how much we owed him in the morning, he said "Nothing at all". He had 5 shillings to send the bed linen to the laundry, but that was all he would take.

We went back to the aerodrome and rang up Scampton, which was still fog-bound. We were told to refuel the aircraft with enough fuel to get back to Lincolnshire. There we were on top of the wings refuelling our own aircraft when at 2 o'clock in the afternoon we got a message that two aerodromes were open. We landed at Binbrook and within 20 minutes of landing there was fog again. Fresh crews were sent in buses from Scampton to operate the next day from Binbrook. We were taken back in thick fog the 25 miles to Scampton. It was 24th December.'

John Gee, Bomber Command pilot

The Armstrong-Whitworth Albemarle was designed in 1938 and was regarded as a medium bomber capable of filling the gap before the heavy bombers appeared. The advent of the Mosquito in 1940 ended that interest and only about 40 were built, serving as glider tugs and for transport duties. This example flew with No 297 Squadron in 1944.

With Dimbleby aboard

'The army was bogged down about 10 or 15 miles short of the Rhine. February came and they were anxious to break out because V2s had been bombing the south of England. The armies were going to make their final push to get across the Rhine, and Bomber Command was asked to knock out a number of targets in front of the army. Cleve was one of them.

Cleve was a little town about 4 or 5 miles west of the Rhine, 10 miles from Nijmegen. There were 295 Lancasters and 10 Mosquitoes from 8 Group, and we had to bomb this target because it was thought to be a road and rail junction. The town had been virtually destroyed anyway, but it was a place where Panzer reinforcements might be brought up to resist the army push. Cleve was only just in front of our own front line troops, so we had to be jolly careful that we didn't bomb our own troops.

The weather forecast was good. There was no cloud about. Richard Dimbleby came up to Scampton that day, along with his engineer and his recording equipment. As I was the senior officer flying from 153 Squadron that night I was nominated to take him. I had two extra bodies on board which made us quite a lot overweight, so to reduce it we ditched some gallons of petrol. I was tickled pink to have him with me. He came up to the squadron and we sat with him and had a meal before we took off. He was a big chap, and of course when he sat alongside me the flight engineer, who would normally be there, had to stand behind and operate all his gauges and things. We were a bit pushed. You couldn't really get past in the fuselage with all the recording gear. He had an engineer to operate it. He had to squat down in the fuselage. I can't imagine anything worse than squatting in a Lancaster for 4 or 5 hours waiting to operate equipment for probably no more than 5 minutes.

It was only when we got near the target that he started to make his commentary. We were flying at 17,000 feet and couldn't see a thing. I thought, "What are we going to do? We can't drop our bombs on our own troops."

Suddenly we heard the Master Bomber calling us down below 4,500 feet. If you can imagine 295 Lancasters coming down from 17,000 to 4,500 feet through cloud. Why there was no collision I just don't know. Now they talk about a near miss if an aircraft goes within 10 miles of another. There were 295 near misses there all at one time.

There below us was Cleve, and the target was marked by the Pathfinder, and searchlights were reflected off the cloud – it was like daylight. And you could see the Lancasters coming out of the cloud like darts. Then we had to bomb the target from 4,500 feet. The bombs were exploding and the aircraft was being bounced all over the place. Richard Dimbleby made his commentary, which was broadcast the next day on BBC radio. We knocked Cleve out completely, so much so that when the army advanced the next day there were so many bomb craters and so many broken roads that it quickly came to a halt.'

John Gee, Bomber Command pilot

The Peenemünde raid

'When we were briefed for Peenemünde we were told this is top secret, can't tell you anything about it. It's the only briefing I ever went to where the briefing hut was surrounded by Service Police. You had to go to the door with your crew and show your identification with your pilot. We were told that if a word leaks out about the target you don't go tonight, and the source will be summarily executed. So we paid attention, we said this has got to be a biggy. We were also told if we didn't get it that night we would go back every night; tonight they won't expect you, but from then on they'll expect you but you will have to go back. Before we had been bombing at 16,000 feet with the Halifax, but Peenemünde was 4,000 feet.

It was the only low level I was ever on, and we were in the first wave. We were there before there were any markers. Our navigator had a movie camera and we were taking pictures that night for the RAF Film Unit. We kept flying back and forth over this target and the navigator kept saying, "I think the damn thing's working now, do another run." This was just terribly nerve-wracking. The fighters had all been decoyed to Berlin, which was fine for the first wave or two. But then the Germans caught on that it wasn't Berlin and the fighters refuelled. The ones that had the range headed for Peenemünde. They shot down a lot of aircraft from the Canadian Group in the last wave. When I was a prisoner of war I met a fellow in our hut who was the only one I met, until long after the war, to have been shot down over Peenemünde and survived. Very few got out in the dark. At 4,000 or 5,000 feet your chances of getting out are slim.

After we got back and the results came in there was a message from Air Marshal Harris saying, "Congratulations, boys, on a job well done". I don't think it was as successful as they said it was.'

Wilkie Wanless, Bomber Command rear gunner

A Pathfinder at Peenemünde

'A Minister was given the job of running the Peenemünde raid by Churchill, Duncan Sandys. We were told that it was such an important target that if we didn't get it that particular night, we'd go back until we did. For me it was one of the most memorable raids. In the Pathfinder force you had to be accurate. Your target indicators had to go down on time because the rest of Bomber Command, the main force, was waiting to see those target indicators at the time that they'd been told. Now in order to achieve your timing, you had to keep time in hand in case the winds were such that you couldn't get there at the time you expected. When you got near the target you had to get rid of that time, and one way of doing it was to do dog-legs. You would go 60 degrees to the left, say, for 2 minutes and then come back 120 degrees, and by doing that you'd have an equilateral triangle for every 2 minutes. For every 2-minute leg you lost 2 minutes along the main track. That wasn't the best way of losing, but most people did it.

But in our aircraft I had an arrangement with my pilot whereby I'd say a 1-minute turn or a 2-minute turn, and he would do a 360-degree turn and then go back on track. That would get rid of the time in one fell swoop. We did this in front of the thundering herd of Bomber Command behind us, but we reckoned it was worth it. We did that manoeuvre that night and it saved our lives. When we straightened up I decided to have a look at the war, pulled the navigator's curtain back, and immediately a German fighter came across our nose so close I could see the crosses under the wings and the wheels in place. The fighter had committed himself to a curve of pursuit against us in such a way that he'd expected us to be 4 miles further on and he couldn't reorganise his curves to get behind us.

After we'd bombed, the mid-upper gunner said, "There's a fighter coming in – it's got a Lanc, it's got another, it's got another." Three Lancasters were going down in flames. You didn't waste too much time thinking about it. So many things were going on – all sorts of lights in the sky, flashes on the ground.

I knew the first Master Bomber on that raid. When he got back to Wyton he was still bathed in perspiration. He'd had to fly above the target for the whole extent of the raid.'

Sam Hall,
Bomber Command Pathfinder navigator

Premonitions

'Everybody felt that every time they took off on a bomb operation there was a good chance that they weren't going to come back. They knew that some of them weren't coming back, but it was a question of who. Some people went down on the first, second, third, fourth, fifth operation, some did 20, 30, 40 – it was a matter of luck. There was skill in landing or combating the weather, and some aircraft crashed for lack of skill on the part of the pilot. But generally speaking you either survived or you didn't survive by luck.

The crews carried things like their girlfriends' stockings around their necks for luck. I had a piece of flak that had gone through the window of a Wellington on an operation fairly early in the war and lodged in my headrest. It missed my head by 3 inches. Next day the crew fished it out of the headrest and gave it to me. I carried this in my pocket for two and a half years, and one day it went missing. I thought, "I know what will happen, I'll go missing on the next operation." It was on the 13th, and it was my 13th operation of my second tour. You turn these things over in your mind.

There was a terrible case just after that when my crew went missing on a mining operation. It had been cancelled for perhaps four nights. On the day of the operation we went across the aerodrome. A sunny afternoon it was, and as we walked back from the aeroplane the pilot who was flying my crew said, "I feel a terrible premonition about this operation. If I had the guts I would take myself off the battle order, but if I did I would never be able to look the squadron in the face again."

I was terribly upset and told him I would fly. He wouldn't hear of it. These five aircraft went, three from my flight and two from another flight, on the mining operation. I waited for them coming back, and three came back but two were missing. One was my crew and I was absolutely distraught. I went back to my room and couldn't speak. It was only four weeks before the end of the war. A dreadful thing. When VE Day came only a month later and there was all the celebration, I sat there with my head in my hands. I didn't know where to put myself.'

John Gee, Bomber Command pilot

The mining campaign conducted by Bomber Command is one of its less well-known tasks, but mines dropped in German waters from the North Sea to the Baltic exacted a heavy toll of enemy shipping. The River Danube was mined too, disrupting the flow of oil from Rumania. Here, mines are loaded on to a Stirling Mk I of No 218 Squadron at Downham Market in Norfolk in 1943.

Bombing versus OVERLORD

'There could be no greater relief afforded Germany than the cessation of any ponderable reduction of the bombing of Germany proper. The entire country would go wild with a sense of relief and reborn hope, and get down to the prosecution of a purely land war with renewed determination and every hope of success. It is thus clear that the best and indeed the only efficient support which Bomber Command can give to OVERLORD is the intensification of attacks on suitable industrial centres in Germany as and when the opportunity offers. If we attempt to substitute for this process attacks on gun emplacements, beach defences, communications or dumps in occupied territory we shall commit the irremediable error of diverting our best weapons from the military function, for which it has been equipped and trained, to tasks which it cannot effectively carry out. Though this might give a specious appearance of "supporting" the Army, in reality it would be the gravest disservice we could do them. It would lead directly to disaster.'

From a Memorandum on the invasion of the Continent prepared by Harris, January 13th 1944 (PRO AIR 14/721)

A Lancaster Mk I of No 195 Squadron drops supplies to the Dutch population as part of 'Operation Manna', carried out to save the people from the very real threat of starvation. Some 16,000 civilians died during the winter of 1944-45 before the relief operation could be mounted.

Over six years of war, Bomber Command found itself called upon to fight many different battles. Bombing German industrial cities was one, but almost half of Bomber Command's efforts were devoted to supporting the naval and land war by attacking enemy shipping, military supplies, communications, airfields and a dozen other targets. Bomber Command crews and aircraft fought in different colours in the Middle East, Italy and the Far East. For the Allied invasion of Europe, despite the misgivings of its Commander-in-Chief, the Command played an indispensable part in neutralising the fighting power of the enemy and easing the path of Allied armies. For much of the war the distinction so commonly made between strategic and tactical bombing was blurred. Bomber Command played its part on every fighting front.

Chapter 3
Bombing Germany

The bombing of Germany began in earnest only in 1943. During 1942 some 35,000 tons were dropped on German targets; the same total was dropped in just one month in the spring of 1945. In 1943 the bomb tonnage dropped on German targets trebled, and in the last half of the year 85 per cent of Bomber Command's efforts was devoted to the German campaign. This was the strategy Bomber Command had planned to pursue from the 1930s, but only when there were heavy bombers in sufficient quantities, and great improvements in navigation and bombing tactics, was it possible to mount a campaign with serious strategic effects.

In the summer of 1940, when attacks on German targets at night were started, Bomber Command was directed to attack oil and communications as primary targets. The campaign began falteringly. Bomber Command was still a small force; it could attack at night only when the skies were clear; and on moonlit nights the bombers found a thick haze over industrial targets, that made identification difficult. Pilots were ordered to bring their bombs back if they could not get clear visual identification of the target. Bomber Command was asked to do so many other things that attacks when they were made were small and infrequent.

In October 1940 the Air Staff decided to concentrate on a single objective – oil. The belief was widespread that oil represented Germany's Achilles' heel, and that attacks on refineries and synthetic oil plants would somehow immobilise the tanks, aircraft and trucks on which Germany's new brand of mobile warfare depended. The Oil Plan was made the 'primary target' on October 30th 1940.

Oil had been the favourite target of the pre-war planners, and it was revived in 1940 because of the need to find some obvious vital target on which Bomber Command could concentrate its meagre forces. There were great expectations. In January 1941 the Command was asked to concentrate not on oil in general, but on the synthetic oil plants that had been built between 1938 and 1941 to

A Handley Page Halifax Mk II at Duxford airfield, Cambridgeshire, under evaluation by the Air Fighting Development Unit in April 1941. Despite the later interventions of Harris himself, defensive armament of the four-engined bombers was largely restricted to .303 machine guns, which were of limited value against German night fighters.

June 3rd/4th 1940: bombing the Ruhr

'First op in June was on the 3rd. Oil Storage Plant at Essen. Now we were to get a real taste of "Happy Valley". Our route

out took us over Rotterdam, which we had seen burning on 16th May. No smoke to hide us this time as the hatred came up thick and fast with searchlights for good measure: nose down and weave, loss of valuable height and a long climb back towards the target area, which we found quite easily, as we could see what was waiting for us some time before we got there. The night sky was lit by probing searchlights, flares, exploding heavy flak. Although horizontal visibility was good, the vertical was affected by industrial haze and I was called upon to add some of our flares to the illuminations: in flak conditions this could be a most unpleasant task.

In the darkened fuselage space, between the centre section access passage and the rear turret, was the flarechute. The flares were held in stowages on either side of the fuselage. About 4 feet long, the flares were not so much heavy as cumbersome in the confined space. The flarechute had a removable extension, not unlike a coal scuttle, at the top of which was a pulley holding a length of thin steel cable with a hook at the free end to take the loop of a cord attached to the striking mechanism. As the flare left the chute the cable ran off the pulley to its full length and pulled the cord out of its retaining pocket, thus activating the fuse as the cord left the main body of the flare. The height at which the flare ignited was determined by a calibrated fuse-setting ring, which had to be set whilst the flare was in the chute and before removal of the safety pin.

At the top of the chute was a handle that held the flare ready for release. It was easy enough when placing the flare, tail fins first, in the chute to let the lot go whilst holding the flare with one hand and trying to close the retaining handle with the other, all in the feeble light of a hand torch. Add to this the effect of evasive action or normal buffeting, the noise of exploding shells and the sickening stench of burnt cordite, and the reader will, perhaps, get some slight idea of what it was like to take action at the flarechute.

I was no sooner at the flarechute than we were held fast in a cone of searchlights that seemed to snap on to us instantaneously and we were immediately under fire. I could hear shrapnel peppering us as the nose went down and we started weaving. Eventually we came out and resumed our search for the target. We found nothing as a result of the first flare and I was asked for another, which I already had in the chute. The release technique was to pull the release with the right hand whilst giving the flare a good push with the left. I called out "Flare gone" and we started the turn.

"Where's that bloody flare?" came over the intercom, and, with the next one cradled in my arms, I looked down the chute and saw to my horror that it was jammed across the mouth of the chute; I had not imparted sufficient impetus and the slipstream catching the tail fins had forced them back far enough to cause the nose of the flare to jam across the chute exit, a good arm's length from the fuselage floor. This situation posed great danger in the event of ignition in the chute of a magnesium charge to the value of a million candle power, capable of causing serious structural damage and, most likely, fire. It had to be cleared and I asked for speed variations and erratic movement but to no avail.

Removing the chute extension and taking care not to further extend the cable attached to the fuse cord, I reached down into the chute with my left arm and found I could just touch the rounded cap covering the fuse setting mechanism. I could not move it even by using my torch as an extension to my arm. Somehow I had to get hold of it and pull it up the chute. My greatest worry was the possibility of ignition and it seemed wise, therefore, to try to unhook the fuse cord from the cable.

I removed my parachute harness and Mae West, slipped the Sidcot suit from my shoulders and took off my jacket. Now, with a bit of wriggling, I was able to get my shoulder further into the top of the chute and obtain a better grasp of the flare cap. I found the end of the cable, released the cord and knew that I was now fairly safe. Somehow, in sheer desperation, I found sufficient strength in my overworked left arm to pull the flare back up the chute a little way. I had thoughts of saving it but could not raise it more than a few inches, but enough to push it clear. All this happened in less time than it has taken to describe in writing, and the rest of the crew being otherwise occupied were quite oblivious to the lonely struggle going on in the mid-fuselage. Perhaps it was better that way; it was certainly a one-man job. How long I was at the flarechute I do not know, neither do I know how many more flares I released before I heard the bomb-aimer giving steering instructions to the target. This was the Command's heaviest attack so far...'

From a memoir by Squadron-Leader W. Jacobs, WOP/AG, Bomber Command

A Canadian-built Mosquito of No 139 Squadron, which was transferred to 8 (Pathfinder) Group. The Pathfinder force was established in August 1942 under the Australian Air Commodore Don Bennett, despite Harris's own reservation that the force would draw off the best pilots from other squadrons.

provide extensive oil substitutes. The Air Staff expected that sustained attack would produce an oil position of 'grave anxiety' by March, even of serious crisis. The expectations, however, proved entirely misplaced. The postwar British bombing survey found that none of the early attacks on oil – in contrast to the successful destruction of oil capacity in 1944 – 'achieved any significant measure of success'. Only the plant at Gelsenkirchen was hit out of all those attacked, and it was out of action for only three weeks. This could not be known in detail at the time, but there was accumulating evidence that the attacks were far beyond the levels of accuracy of which Bomber Command was currently capable. In May a lively debate was sparked off by Lord Trenchard, who had led the bombing campaign in the First World War. True to his belief that bombing would undermine enemy morale, he urged the Chiefs of Staff to begin round-the-clock bombing of German cities to 'make the civil population realise what war means'.

Trenchard did not argue for indiscriminate bombing, but suggested attacks on cities within which there were economic and military targets. But he did argue that the attack on precise economic targets, like oil, was a waste of effort. The Air Ministry agreed that concentration of effort was essential, but resisted the temptation to abandon precision bombing entirely. The Directorate of Bombing Operations, spurred on by the need to do something to help the Soviet forces, which now bore the brunt of German

armed power after the invasion of June 22nd, switched from oil to communications as the primary target. In a directive of July 9th 1941, Bomber Command was ordered to concentrate all its available forces on a ring of nine rail centres around the Ruhr industrial area to choke off supplies going into and out of the region. The canal and river system was also given priority. As with oil, it was assumed that the single target system was so vital and so fragile that it might have a decisive effect on Germany's capacity to continue the war.

A little under six weeks later the Butt report was published, confirming what had been widely suspected, even by the crews themselves, that Bomber Command's operations were remarkably inaccurate. The further afield the attack, the lower the level of accuracy. For the Ruhr, shrouded as it was in a permanent industrial miasma, only one in ten aircraft was found to have got within 5 miles of the target. Since this was the area in which first oil targets, then rail centres, were to be destroyed, the report showed that with current technology the force could only bomb areas, not individual targets.

In September 1941 the Air Ministry drew up a very different plan, based on a detailed assessment of the impact of German bombing on British cities during the Blitz. A list of 43 major German industrial cities was drawn up for heavy and repeated attacks by the Command. The campaign was calculated to require a front-line force of 4,000 heavy bombers, almost ten times the number available at the end of 1941. Attacks on this scale, regularly repeated, were expected to undermine the morale of the factory workforce and disrupt the operation of the war economy to such an extent that a successful army invasion of occupied Europe would be made possible.

The switch to area bombing was a recognition of operational reality. It is often seen as a radical departure, but the roots of the strategy can be found in earlier wartime directives. In July 1940 the Air Staff directed Bomber Command to attack cities in western Germany 'for their intrinsic industrial and psychological value' on nights when precise targets could not be identified or even located. The directive of July 9th 1941, which ordered the switch to transport targets, ordered the Command to attack urban industrial areas on the many nights in the month when precise targets could not be seen. The cities chosen as so-called 'secondary targets' were Hamburg, Bremen, Hanover, Frankfurt, Mannheim and Stuttgart.

The decision to switch to area bombing, made in the autumn of 1941, merely reversed the priorities laid down in July. Precise targets were not abandoned where they could be clearly identified or where they had a special significance. But the directive finally published in February 1942, Directive 22, (see page 80) ordered as a first priority the attack of 58 major German industrial cities and the morale of the industrial workforce that lived there.

This was a decision taken by the Air Ministry and the Air Staff in 1941. It was endorsed by the Prime Minister, and strongly supported by his scientic advisor Lord Cherwell, although it was never formally presented to the Defence Committee or the War Cabinet. It was not a policy developed by Bomber Command, but by Air Ministry planners. Moreover, it was not a policy devised by Air Marshal Harris, when he came from America to take over the Command in late February 1942, though his name has always been closely linked with it. Harris saw it as his job to carry out the directives he was given. He was a firm believer in concentration of force and accepted enthusiastically the idea of large-scale attacks on German cities in place of small, inaccurate and intermittent attacks, which had characterised the campaign until 1942. He was well aware that Bomber Command needed a commander willing to argue for a large share of Britain's industrial resources, able to defend the Command against the demands for bombers from other elements of Britain's war effort, and committed enough to restore the flagging morale of a Command whose efforts were subject to a growing chorus of criticism. Harris achieved most of this. What he did not do was invent the idea of the area bombing of Germany.

Harris's arrival coincided with the low point in the fortunes of Bomber Command during the war. In November Churchill had ordered the force to stop attacking Germany and to conserve resources for the spring. But by the spring the crisis in the Atlantic, the Mediterranean and the Far East sucked aircraft away from the Command, while the other services argued that the attacks on Germany had achieved too little to justify their expansion when the Army and Navy desperately needed additional air support and industrial resources.

Harris launched a series of attacks against Rostock and Lübeck, and a precision attack on the Renault works at Billancourt in Paris. Photographic evidence showed that these were all much more successful than the last attacks in 1941, though the numbers of bombers Harris could send were still little greater than a year before – 235 to Paris, 234 to Lübeck, 161 in the first attack on Rostock. What Harris wanted was a more spectacular demonstration of what his Command could achieve. In May 1942 he began to plan a raid using a thousand bombers in one night.

On May 18th 1942 Harris suggested the idea to Portal, and won the support not only of the Chief of the Air Staff but of Churchill too. The plan was to draw all the reserve aircraft from the Operational Training Units and the Conversion Units (where pilots were retrained to fly heavier four-engined aircraft), and to beg and borrow bomber aircraft currently on loan to other RAF Commands or to other services. In the end the Admiralty refused to release any bombers from duty with Coastal Command, and Training Command offered only four Wellingtons. The rest of the 1,047 bombers used in the raid were scraped together from Bomber Command's own resources, 365 of them from the Training Units. The bulk of the aircraft were the twin-engined Wellingtons; only 294 were the newer four-engined Halifaxes, Stirlings and Lancasters.

Harris introduced new tactics for the raid, which became the standard operational system for subsequent raids. Instead of a long-drawn-out attack, with bombers making their own way to the target, Harris sought to concentrate the force both in time and space. The 1,000 bombers were ordered to approach the chosen target, the Rhineland city of Cologne, in a narrow stream, and to bomb in waves covering no more than 90 minutes. The object was to try to swamp German defences. The defensive zone covering northern Germany was divided into small boxes of territory in each of which was a radar controller who identified intruders and directed a small number of night-fighters to intercept them. When aircraft came in twos or threes the system coped. Harris hoped that a large stream of aircraft would smother the night-fighter force and result in lower casualties.

The bomber stream was guided by highly-skilled pilots whose job it was to pinpoint the target. They were helped by a new navigational aid, TR. 1335, better known as '*Gee*'

Winning a VC

'We went to 10,000 feet over England, and then headed for the first track over the Dutch coast. I was at 20,000 feet and then the gunner asked me to come down a bit because he was feeling cold. His heating was not working, and I turned up the oxygen a bit. Suddenly, just after we had crossed the coast, there was a great bang from underneath. I thought it was flak because there had been no warnings, but the gunner had actually tried to fire. It was a Focke-Wulf 190. I dropped 2,000 feet because the windscreen had been shattered and I had been hit in the shoulder. It felt just like a hammer, not a spear. I did not feel as if I was going to drop off, so I thought there was no point in talking much about it.

I asked the navigator to set another course at about 19,000 feet. I kept looking at my watch. A quarter of an hour later we were attacked by a Messerschmitt, which knocked out the compasses, and the intercom and hydraulics on the port side. We dropped another 2,000 feet. It had hit the port elevator, so it meant holding the stick back in your belly to keep the plane flying straight. The engineer was wounded in the forearm. The bomb-aimer was still down at the front. He did not realise until the bombing run that anyone was hurt, because we could not talk to each other. This was probably a good thing, because there may have been panic.

I asked the engineer for another course because the compass was broken. He came back and indicated that the navigator had been knocked out. I had a feeling he would come to and take over again, but I looked round for the Pole Star and found it. That night we were heading for Cologne where we were dropping spoof flares to get their fighters away, and then turning and bombing Düsseldorf.

Our timing was very accurate. If you had to bomb at half past ten, you had to bomb at half past ten. We saw the flares going down, and I pointed ahead to the target. I held it steady and felt the bombs going off and headed back home. That was the difficult part, but I thought as long as I hit the English coast someone will find me a landing. The other thing on my mind at the time was to get back because we had wounded on board. There was no way we could bale out with all the wounded. On the way back we went up and down, up and down. Because we had no oxygen in the system, the engineer gave me the little bottles that we carried, like small fire extinguishers, that you can clip on to your mask. Eventually we ran out. I wanted to get down below oxygen height, which is 10,000 feet, but I didn't want to come down too soon in case there was a big flak area that would shoot us down.

When I saw the sea – it might have been the Zuider Zee – I came down to 7,000 feet. We were flying on and suddenly the four engines cut, and I thought, "Well, here it comes". The engineer remembered then that he had not switched the petrol tanks over. There are three petrol tanks on each wing and you normally try and keep them level in case you get hit, so that you don't lose all your petrol. He had left the main tanks the whole time as we had been so busy doing other things. He switched over to the other tanks and it started up. We flew on and saw a coast coming up. He kept telling me to get down, get down, because there was not much petrol left.

I saw this canopy of searchlights, so we headed for that. It was a fairly big aerodrome, so I just circled round and flashed my landing light on and off as a distress signal, because I could not talk to them. We had no hydraulics, so we needed to pull a bottle of compressed air to flood the system, so that I could put the wheels and flaps down. I had been hit in the head and it had frozen up, but it came alive again when we were lower and warmer and it began to bleed. I told them to stand by for crash landing. They stood behind me in case I passed out, and put out flares because there had been a touch of fog.

We came in and just touched down at the end of the runway, and as we did the undercarriage collapsed. It had been shot through. The plane was on her belly for about 50 yards, and it was only then that I realised that the navigator was dead, because he slipped forward from his cabin. It was an American aerodrome I had landed at, Shipton in Norfolk.

They scrambled on to the plane and opened up the dinghy escape and got us all out through the top. The wireless operator walked out even though he was wounded. They whipped us on to stretchers and into an ambulance and away. They had had a crash on the aerodrome 2 hours earlier that night with a Lancaster. The rear gunner was all but *saved but then burned as it caught on fire. We were sent to the air force hospital about three days later. The next day the wireless operator died. He must have been shot through the chest.*

The CO came down to see me in hospital. He asked me why I didn't turn back. I said that I thought it was safer to go on because we were still all flying in this big box of planes 10 miles wide and 10 miles deep, and it would have meant flying back through these and probably prang one. It was not a case of going on regardless. It was the safest thing to do.'

Bill Reid VC, Bomber Command pilot

(Ground electronics engineering), which supplied a radio beam that aircraft could follow to the target. First used against Cologne in an attack on March 13th, *Gee* made possible the tactic of 'streaming', and increased the weight of bombs that the Command could deliver on the designated target.

The attack was planned for May 27th, but was postponed because of poor weather. On May 30th, after four days of alert, the crews were ordered to embark, though weather conditions were far from ideal, with broken cloud and thunderstorms the best that the forecasters could offer. The first wave of aircraft operating *Gee* found the target easily, and the fires that resulted from the first attack guided the next waves to the target.

Out of the aircraft dispatched, 868 bombed the target, and did so with a degree of accuracy very much higher than the dismal results of a year before. A total of 41 aircraft – 3.9 per cent of the force – were lost, but only two of these resulted from a collision, despite the fact that there were four times the usual number of aircraft concentrated in a narrow stream. Photo reconnaissance over the following few days showed widespread destruction in the centre of the city. Almost 500 inhabitants were killed in the raid, and 12,000 buildings destroyed or damaged. Harris mounted two more '1,000 raids' in June on Essen and Bremen, but they were less successful. The plan to mount several such raids each month petered out for lack of aircraft.

Air Commodore Don Bennett (seated fifth from left) seen at a planning meeting for Pathfinder operations. The Pathfinder force began by visual marking of the targets with flares and incendiaries until the advent of effective radio navigational aids in 1943.

A Mosquito raid

'The weather closed down about 50 miles short of the target. We had to fly over mountains and then come down into the valley below and fly straight towards the target. We ran into cloud over the mountains, having had glorious sunny weather all the way. I was at the back of the second formation, and I, together with two others out of the 14, simply lost formation. We couldn't keep in touch with the aircraft next to us, but carried on on dead reckoning.

When I came down out of the cloud the visibility was still poor and I couldn't find the target at all. I set off to look for it, and the cloud base lifted to 1,000 feet. There was a large city spread out to my port side. I thought I would fly round the edge and look for some factory that looked worth bombing. I flew right round the edge of the city at 800 feet but it was all residential, a lot of prosperous-looking houses in the outskirts up in the hills. It turned out that this was Weimar, a university city that does not have an industrial complex. But right in the middle was a big railway station with an enormous goods train stationary in it. I dived down into the centre of the city and dropped my bombs from 200 feet straight into the railway station and then went down over the rooftops to fly away north-west of the city.

I had no sooner dropped my bombs than the most horrendous light flak barrage I had ever known opened up. When I got clear of the city and went up the river valley the flak was coming down from both sides of the hills. I was twisting and turning. When you are under light flak you have to throw the aircraft around because they are firing over open sights and trying to aim at you. We did get clear and I set off for home, alone of course. Having come through that and then realising, having looked at the map properly, that we were right down in south-east Germany, all alone, at 50 feet, I did feel a bit daunted, a bit desperate. But there was no alternative but to keep going.

We flew for a long time north, north-west until we were certain we were clear of Hannover, before turning to port and flying due west back to England. Once we started to fly across the open German plain I knew we'd got away with it. Once we got over the Dutch frontier it was getting dark and the Dutch farmers were amazing. When they heard low-level aircraft around – we would come up from 50 feet to about 300 feet – they would rush to the doors of their cottage or farmhouse and open and shut the door, flashing their lights inside to us as a sign. They risked death by doing that, just to give us encouragement. I've never forgotten it.'

Charles Patterson, Bomber Command pilot

Harris had nevertheless achieved what he wanted. The Cologne raid publicised the Command more effectively than anything it had yet done, and came at a time when bombing policy was under Government review. Ten days before the raid a report on the future of the bombing campaign was published under the signature of an independent assessor, Mr Justice Singleton. He had been asked by Churchill to resolve the dispute between his advisers over whether bombers should be used over Germany for tactical purposes. His report played down the idea that bombing could win the war on its own, but it did suggest that, with sufficient resources and a concentration of effort, bombing represented good value for money, and was the best Britain could do to ease the pressure of German forces deep in Russia. The Singleton report was far more encouraging than the Butt revelations. Taken together with the evidence of the Cologne raid, it was sufficient to win Bomber Command a reprieve. Harris was given the go-ahead to prepare the city campaign outlined in Directive 22.

No issue had featured more in the arguments about bombing than the problem of bombing accuracy. In 1941 the arguments had been about hitting single factories and railway yards, yet Butt had shown that aircraft were seldom capable of hitting even the right town. Harris knew that his force would only survive further efforts to divert the bombers elsewhere if he could demonstrate that his pilots could at least all hit the same area, and could do so with sufficient concentration of bombing effort to make the attacks worthwhile.

The problem was tackled in 1942 in two ways. Rapid progress in radio and radar technology provided Harris with the means to navigate fleets of bombers accurately in poor visibility and, eventually, to bomb through cloud. The first of the new equipment – *Gee* – was introduced in March 1942. The system worked on the same principle as the radio beams used by the German air force in 1940. Radio signals from a number of stations in Britain were sent in such a way that a navigator could calculate his position as the point where the signal beams intersected. The

Hitler's birthday present

'I was on the first night raid on Berlin done by Mosquitoes. Bomber Command decided to send 12 Mosquitoes to Berlin in the moonlight, because heavy bombers could not operate at that stage in full moonlight because of fighter interception. It was a raid to coincide with Hitler's birthday. The coincidence of the two was more than Bomber Command could resist, so to satisfy their whim we were sent off.

It was a wonderfully clear moonlit night, so clear that we map-read all the way to Berlin. When we got to blacked-out Berlin you could see this heavy dense black mass coming up in front of you with the moonlight glinting on the lakes at Potsdam. This was a high-level night raid. We looked upon it as a rather boring distraction from our normal operations and hardly took it 100 per cent seriously. But when I was running up on the target over Berlin in the centre of the city, suddenly I felt a loud, violent bump behind the aircraft. I recognised this from our medium-level Blenheim days as heavy flak bursting very close. The only reaction that went through my mind was "Bloody cheek! Hitting a Mosquito with flak at 18,000 feet in the middle of the night!"

I was irritated, but did not think anything of it until the next day when the Flight Sergeant invited me to look at my Mosquito. There at the rear end of the fuselage, just before the tailplane, there was a hole right through the fuselage where a piece of shrapnel had gone through from the burst of flak. It cut all the control wires except one and I'd flown home with one wire connecting me to the elevators. The aeroplane flew perfectly normally.'

Charles Patterson, Bomber Command pilot

The Singleton Report

'I think there is every reason to hope for good results from a sustained bombing policy. I do not think it ought to be regarded as of itself sufficient to win the war or to produce decisive results; the area is too vast for the effort we can put forth; on the other hand, if Germany does not achieve great success on land before the winter it may well turn out to have a decisive effect, and in the meantime, if carried out on the lines suggested, it must impede Germany and help Russia… If Russia can hold Germany on land I doubt whether Germany will stand twelve or eighteen months' continuous, intensified and increasing bombing, affecting, as it must, her war production, her power of resistance, her industries and her will to resist (by which I mean morale).

The important matter is to reach a greater degree of accuracy. If H2S comes up to expectations the load of bombs then carried will have a much greater effect than a like load carried today. Recent results are not encouraging except in ideal weather conditions, and there are few nights in the month on which such conditions can be expected, and few targets on which a night bombing attack can be really successful. At the same time, reports appear to show that the effect of our bombing is being more seriously felt in Germany than it was a little time ago.

To sum up, I do not think that great results can be hoped for within six months. I cannot help feeling that the six-months period ought to be looked upon as leading up to, and forming part of, a longer and more sustained effort than as one expected to produce results within a limited time. Much depends on what happens in Russia. The effects of a reverse for Germany, or a lack of success, would be greatly increased by an intensified bombing programme in the autumn and winter. And if this was coupled with knowledge in Germany that the bombing would be on an increasing scale until the end, and with the realisation of the fact that the German Air Force could not again achieve equality, I think it might well prove the turning-point – provided always that greater accuracy can be achieved.'

From Report by Mr Justice Singleton for the Defence Committee on the Bombing of Germany, May 20th 1942 (Webster & Frankland, Vol iv, Appendix 17, pp 237-8)

disadvantage of this first radar aid was its short range – confined to only 350 miles because of the curvature of the earth's surface. The signals could also be jammed by enemy counter-measures. This happened first in August 1942, though British scientific intelligence officers reacted quickly with anti-jamming devices of their own. *Gee* remained in use over the whole war period; by the summer of 1944 there were five chains of stations transmitting the *Gee* signal, and more were established in Europe once Allied armies were lodged there.

The Oboe *navigational aid was introduced into Bomber Command late in 1942. It operated on the basis of a fixed radio beam and two subsidiary tracking stations that indicated the point of the aircraft along the beam, and the point at which to drop the bombs. This is the interior of an* Oboe *control room.*

Harris knew that more sophisticated equipment was in the final stages of development. In December 1942 the first use was made of the 'Oboe' system, which allowed great accuracy in finding and hitting the target. Aircraft flew along a fixed radio beam and their position was tracked by two other ground stations that were able to locate precisely where on the main beam the aircraft was, and to relay exact information about when to release bombs. The early Oboe apparatus worked on a broad 11/2-metre wavelength, which was relatively easy to jam.

In the autumn of 1943 a short-wave centimetric radar was introduced, which saw service for the rest of the war. This second innovation was the H2S radar aid, which was also developed by the Royal Navy in the fight against the submarine. The system relied on a radar transmitter/receiver in the aircraft, which used radar pulses from surface objects to create a radar picture of the ground below. This allowed aircraft to fly well beyond the range of Gee and Oboe, and to bomb blind through cloud or fog. However, it was difficult to locate precise targets with H2S, and the apparatus proved temperamental. A new version using 3 cm wavebands was introduced in November 1943, which gave a much sharper image of the

ground features below. During 1944 H2S was installed on increasing numbers of bombers as long-range attacks were mounted into central and southern Germany.

Harris did not rely entirely on technology. The second prong of his attack on inaccuracy was to develop specialised crews who would lead the bomber streams and find and mark the target for the waves following behind. The origin of this tactical shift came with the introduction of the 'Shaker' system in the spring of 1942. Each operation would find aircraft divided into illuminators (a small group of aircraft whose job was to drop flares around the target area), target markers (another small group who would drop incendiaries into the illuminated area), and followers, who simply had to bomb the area lit up by flares and fires. The system worked intermittently: a mistake in placing the flares would distort the entire raid, and dummy flares lit on the ground diverted bombers from the true target. The introduction of the Gee navigational aid was therefore accompanied by a growing chorus of voices calling for the introduction of a specialised target-finding force to make the best use of it.

Harris and his Group commanders were not opposed to the idea of target-finding units, but they did not want such a

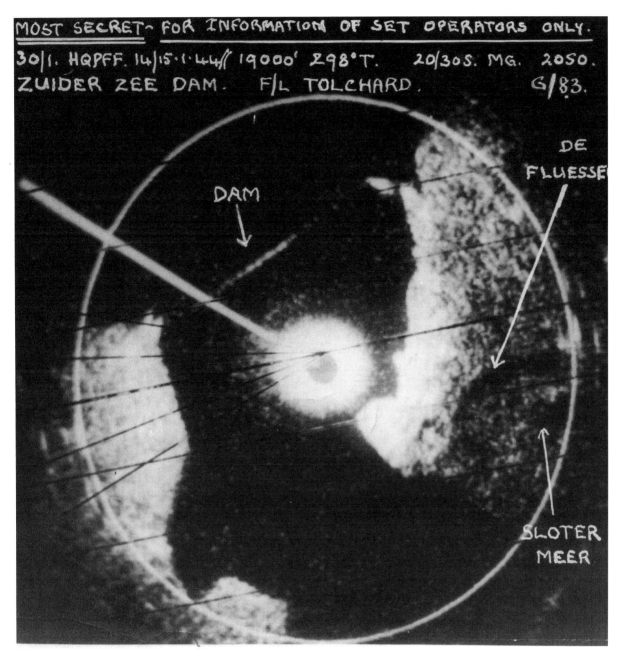

MOST SECRET~ FOR INFORMATION OF SET OPERATORS ONLY.
30/1. HQPFF. 14/15·1·44// 19000' 298°T. 20/30S. MG. 2050.
ZUIDER ZEE DAM. F/L TOLCHARD. G/83.

DAM

DE FLUESSE

SLOTER MEER

The screen of the H2S radar apparatus introduced into Bomber Command during 1943 to improve accuracy and enable aircraft to bomb 'blind'. The system provided a radar image of the ground and performed best against targets adjacent to bodies of water. This image shows the Zuider Zee dam.

force to be separated from the main body of bombers. They feared that the establishment of an elite corps within the Command would demoralise those left working in the groups, which would now be denied the best pilots and navigators. Harris favoured the idea of using the best squadrons within each Group to lead the attack and locate the target. In June he proposed a system of Raid Leaders for each Group, with their own distinct identity and insignia, but he was overruled by Portal and the Air Staff, who decided that the continued evidence of inaccurate bombing of cities in the Ruhr justified the creation of a special force of 'Target-Finders'. Harris reluctantly complied. On August

11th the force was activated under the leadership of the Australian airman D. C. Bennett, recently returned from Sweden after crashing during an attack on the *Tirpitz*. On August 18th, shortly after the Germans had succeeded in jamming the *Gee* apparatus, the new force undertook its first attack, against Flensburg. Harris could not stomach the Air Ministry title of 'Target-Finders' and christened the new Group 'Pathfinders'.

The change in tactics achieved an immediate improvement in the concentration of bombs dropped on the target area, but not on the accuracy of attacks. Not until the introduction of *Oboe* and H2S, and the development of

Defending the record

'Note by Air Marshall Harris for the Prime Minister on the Role and Work of Bomber Command, 28 July 1942

Those who advocate the breaking-up of Bomber Command for the purpose of adding strength to Coastal and Army Co-operation Commands and overseas requirements are like the amateur politician who imagines that the millennium will arrive through the simple process of dividing available cash equally between all. Ignorance of what is available for distribution is such that he does not realise that the outcome would be to give every individual £50 once at the cost of wrecking the entire industrial organisation and income of the country. Similarly, if the Medium and Heavy Bomber Operational Squadrons of Bomber Command were distributed between the many claimants for favour on the one hand, none of these claimants would receive anything more than a mere morsel towards the satisfaction of their alleged requirements. On the other hand, our only offensive weapon against Germany would be destroyed. One cannot win wars by defending oneself.

There is surprising ignorance about the effective strength of Bomber Command. On an average, it is able to produce about 30 operational medium and heavy night-bomber squadrons and six light bomber squadrons. The first-line strength of the operational squadrons of Bomber Command represent no more than 11 per cent of the total operational first-line strength of the Royal Air Force and Fleet Air Arm, and well over half of this 11 per cent is directed against Naval and Military targets.

Another common error is to suppose that the effort of the Command is devoted to the bombing of targets in Germany remote from and chosen without reference to the general military and naval situation. Nothing could be further from the truth. Approximately 50 per cent of the total operational effort of Bomber Command during the twelve months April 1941-March 1942 was directly employed against the enemy's sea power. During the last three months the proportion has been well over 50 per cent.

To the negative, but very worthwhile, credit of Bomber Command can be counted the strain upon the enemy of maintaining an enormous and ever-increasing mine-sweeping effort, and also the establishment and maintenance of the largest anti-aircraft and A.R.P. organisations in the world. Some three-quarters of a million personnel are employed on anti-aircraft duties in Germany. If one adds to that the A.R.P services, the damage and repair organisation and the manufacture of guns and their anti-aircraft ammunition, and also the mine-sweeping and mined ship repairing organisation, there is little doubt that the very existence of Bomber Command costs the enemy the whole-time services of at least three million able-bodied personnel... There is no doubt that, if the Bomber policy was to be abandoned, the release of this vast manpower for other essential work would be of the greatest value to Germany. The release of the twin-engined fighter bombers and the anti-aircraft guns for service on the eastern front and in the Mediterranean would have a powerful and perhaps even a decisive effect on those campaigns.

Finally, it is apparent that an extraordinary lack of sense of proportion affects outside appreciation of the meaning, extent and results of Bomber Command's operations. What shouts of victory would arise if a Commando wrecked the entire Renault factory in a night, with a loss of seven men. What credible assumptions of an early end to the war would follow upon the destruction of a third of Cologne in an hour and a half by some swift-moving mechanised force which, with but 200 casualties, withdrew and was prepared to repeat the operation 24 hours later! What acclaim would greet the virtual destruction of Rostock and the Heinkel main and subsidiary factories by a Naval bombardment! All this, and far more, has been achieved by Bomber Command; yet there are many who still avert their gaze, pass by on the other side, and question whether the 30 squadrons of night bombers make any worthwhile contribution to the war.'

Report from Harris to Churchill (Webster & Frankland, Vol iv, Appendix 18, pp 239-44)

special-purpose target-marker bombs, first used in January 1943, did the Pathfinders have the equipment to allow them to achieve a much higher level of precision in marking the centre, or aiming point, of the target. From early 1943 onwards Bomber Command experienced growing improvements in accuracy, and by 1944 heavy bombers could hit very precise targets, as they did in the supporting operations for the invasion of France, or the

later attacks on German transport targets.

The year 1942 was one of preparation and experimentation, a process of learning what the Command could do with its new technology and tactics, and the strategy of industrial area attacks. In 1943 the Command was at last in a position to carry out the kind of campaign against Germany envisaged in 1940, its size and lifting power being transformed by the arrival of the heavy bombers. In

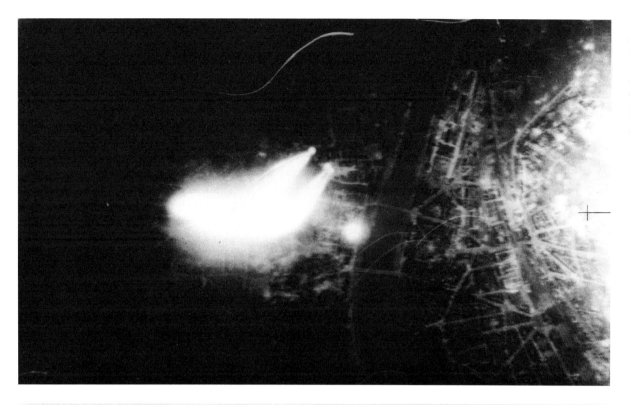

Target Indicators (TIs) burst and cascade over Frankfurt on the night of March 22nd/23rd 1944. TIs were laid first by the Pathfinder squadrons and served to guide the Main Force to the centre of the target. If the TIs were laid incorrectly, the whole raid could be diverted from its objective.

A Pathfinder's story

'I returned from leave once and was informed that we had lost the Commanding Officer and that a new Squadron Commander was in the Mess. My Flight Commander said he would introduce me. I went into the Mess and there were two Squadron Leaders there standing in their usual position with their backs to the fireplace. I was introduced to the new CO.

"I've heard of you," he said. "I believe you weave."

I said, "Yes, sir, I do weave."

He replied, "This will stop from henceforth. Pilots on my squadron will give their gunners a steady platform and will fly straight and level."

I said, "With due respect, sir, if you lay down this order you will lose most of your pilots."

He then accused pilots who did this of being yellow. I was upset about the accusation and wanted to vent my feelings by striking him, but my colleagues thought I was going to do something of the sort and I was whisked out of the Mess and told to go to bed. Before leaving I told the new commander that if he behaved like that he wouldn't last three trips, and he didn't. He was lost on his third or fourth trip.

There is a moral to the story. The aim as far as I was concerned, and for most of my companions in 83 Squadron, was to get to the target. We were Pathfinders; our policy was to mark the target and get back safely. We weren't there to battle with night-fighters.

Weaving was a method of flying that proved to be very successful. The aircraft flew in a kind of corkscrew motion, flying straight and level for a moment and then moving to the left and pushing the nose forward, diving 100 to 200 feet, and then moving it to the right and pulling the control column back. This was a gentle weave that could give the gunners a reasonably steady platform, so that they could see beneath the aeroplane where the fighter attacks came from. Our role was to get to the target and then fly straight and level for a long period while the bomb-aimer got the markers down on the target. What happened going to the target and returning was to stay alive by flying to the best of one's ability.'

**Maurice Chick,
Bomber Command Pathfinder pilot**

December 1942 there were 262 heavy bombers available on average over the month; by December 1943 the figure was 776, and a year later the average was 1,381. The bomblift of the force rose even faster: in December 1942 it was a mere 667 tons; a year later 2,930 tons; by the winter of 1944 an average of more than 6,300 tons. These figures did not approach the '4,000 bomber programme' on which Harris wanted to base his strategy, but during 1943 Bomber Command was joined by American forces in a joint assault on Germany's capacity to wage war.

The United States entered the war in December 1941 and almost immediately the decision was taken to establish strategic bombing forces in Britain to work alongside Bomber Command. The 8th US Army Air Force began to arrive in Britain in the summer of 1942 under the command of General Ira Eaker. The force flew its first combat mission on August 17th, a daylight raid against the railway marshalling yards at Rouen in northern France, heavily escorted by RAF Spitfires. The American air leaders believed that bombing could be carried out in daylight if the bomber force was heavily armed. The B-17 Flying Fortresses, some of which saw service in RAF colours, were the mainstay of the United States bomber forces. Bristling with guns, it was assumed that the aircraft could fight its way to the target and back, and bombing by day would ensure a high level of accuracy.

American planners had worked out the precise number of aircraft and bomb tonnages necessary to knock out Germany's key industries. When American attacks began on Germany in January 1943 they were directed at the submarine industry, rather than at whole cities. The two forces, British and American, complemented each other. In a joint directive issued on September 8th 1942, the RAF was given responsibility for night bombing and the 8th Air Force for bombing by day 'to achieve continuity in the bombing offensive'.

Over the last months of 1942 the two Allies collaborated to produce a coherent plan for the attack on Germany. The aim was to use bombing as a means of weakening the German war effort to the point where an Anglo-American invasion of Fortress Europe could be undertaken successfully. Portal told the War Cabinet that with a combined force of 4,000 to 6,000 bombers by 1944 the conditions for invasion could be met. Bombing on such a scale would, he argued, cripple the German air defences and divert German military resources to home defence, placing a 'heavy handicap' on German operations in all other theatres. By the time the Western Allies met in Casablanca in January 1943 to decide their strategy for winning the war, both British and American chiefs were committed to a heavy bombing assault on Germany.

A De Havilland Mosquito takes off into the sunset. This vital aircraft was, as Harris later wrote, 'the direct outcome of [the] controversy between supporters of the light and supporters of the heavy bomber'.

Planning German defeat, 1943

'(i)   The paper assumes that an Anglo-American Heavy Bomber Force would be based in the United Kingdom and built up to a first-line strength of 4,000 to 6,000 by 1944.

(ii)   Such a force could deliver a monthly scale of attack amounting to 50,000 tons of bombs by the end of 1943, and to a peak of 90,000 tons by December 1944.

(iii) Under this plan 1¼ million tons of bombs would be dropped on Germany between January 1943 and December 1944.

(iv)   Assuming that the results attained per ton of bombs equal those realised during the German attacks of 1940-41, the results would include -

   (a)   the destruction of 6 million German dwellings, with a proportionate destruction of industrial buildings, sources of power, means of transportation and public utilities;
   (b)   25 million Germans rendered homeless;
   (c)   an additional 60 million "incidents" of bomb damage to houses;
   (d)   civilian casualties estimated at about 900,000 killed and 1,000,000 seriously injured.

(v)   If the attacks were spread over the main urban areas the result would be to render homeless three-quarters of the inhabitants of all German towns with a population of over 50,000.

(vi)   Expressed in other terms, this scale of attack would enable every industrial town in Germany with a population exceeding 50,000 to receive, in proportion to its size, ten attacks of "Cologne" intensity.

(vii) If the attacks were concentrated on the 58 towns specified in Appendix I, each would receive, in proportion to its size, some 17 attacks of "Cologne" intensity.

(viii) A concentrated attack of this character would destroy at least one-third of the total German industry.

(ix)   A substantial proportion of the total industry of Germany is necessary to maintain a minimum standard of subsistence among the German people. As the German economic structure is now stretched to the limit this proportion cannot be further reduced. Consequently, the loss of one-third of German industry would involve either the sacrifice of almost the entire war potential of Germany in an effort to maintain the internal economy of the country, or else the collapse of the latter.

(x)   It is hoped that our bombing efficiency will prove to be substantially better than that achieved in the German attacks of 1940-41. In that case the process of attrition will be much accelerated.

(xi)   It is considered that the German defences will be incapable of stopping these attacks.

(xii) It is certain that the diversion of more and more of a waning aircraft production to the defence of Germany will heavily handicap all German operations by land, sea and air in other theatres.

(xiii) It is concluded that an Anglo-American bomber force of the size proposed could reduce the German economic and military strength to a point well below that at which an Anglo-American invasion of the Continent would become possible. This result might well be achieved before the combined force had built up to peak strength.

C.P.

From a Memorandum prepared for the British Chiefs of Staff by Sir Charles Portal, November 3rd 1942 (PRO AIR 14/739A)

For the first time in the war, Bomber Command was backed by a substantial economic commitment and a clear strategy. The so-called 'Casablanca Directive' for the 'progressive destruction and dislocation of the German military, industrial and economic system' was strongly supported by both Churchill and the American President, Franklin D. Roosevelt. The directive of January 21st 1943 picked out a number of primary targets: the German submarine industry; the German aircraft industry; communications; oil plants; and other essential war industries. The 8th Air Force was to bomb them by day, while Bomber Command was to hit the cities that housed them by night. Six months later, on June 10th, the directive was modified to take account of the increase in German air defences and their growing effectiveness. The German fighter force was given the status of 'intermediate target', and its destruction was made the primary goal. The campaign was given the unambiguous codename POINTBLANK.

Above: Ivor Broom and Tommy Broom in front of a Mosquito of No 571 Squadron in August 1944. Based at Oakington in Cambridgeshire, the squadron was part of 8 Group, the Pathfinders. The two men were not related, but became known as 'The Flying Brooms' with crossed broomsticks on the side of their aircraft. Ivor Broom was the air ace and survived the war to become an Air Marshal.

Above right: Air crew from a Lancaster pose for the camera by the rear gun turret. From left to right: Stan Thorne, Harold Swanton, Norman Daly (navigator).

Right: A crew member in a Whitley Mk V of No 51 Squadron, based at Dishforth in Yorkshire, prepares to push flares down the flare chute. In the early stages of the war the crew were expected to push bundles of leaflets down the same chute in the propaganda war against Germany.

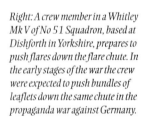

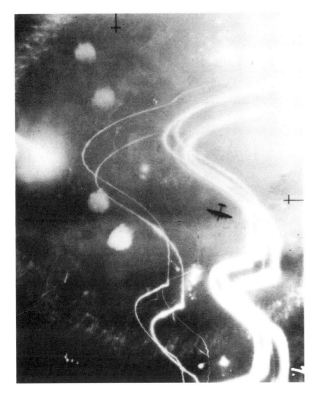

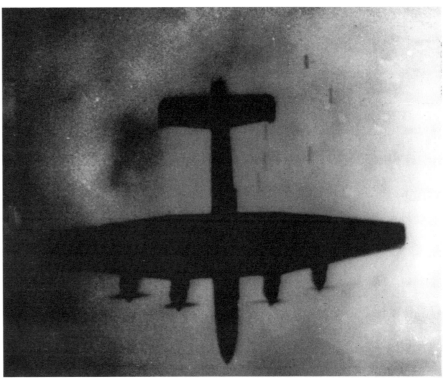

Above left and above: A Halifax bomber caught on camera at the moment of the photoflash explosion during a night raid on St Ghislain, near Mons in Belgium, May 1st/2nd 1944. The raid was part of the preparation for D-Day.

A relieved crew arrive safely back at base, ready for breakfast and de-briefing. 'You had to have luck,' recalled one veteran pilot, 'otherwise you didn't survive.'

The Casablanca Directive

'Combined Chiefs of Staff Directive for the Bomber Offensive from the United Kingdom, 21st January 1943

Your primary object will be the progressive destruction and dislocation of the German military, industrial and economic system, and the undermining of the morale of the German people to a point where their capacity for armed resistance is fatally weakened.

2. Within that general concept, your primary objectives, subject to the exigencies of weather and of tactical feasibility, will for the present be in the following order of priority:

(a)   German submarine construction yards
(b)   The German aircraft industry
(c)   Transportation
(d)   Oil plants
(e)   Other targets in enemy war industry…

5. You should take every opportunity to attack Germany by day, to destroy objectives that are not suitable for night attack, to sustain continuous pressure on German morale, to impose heavy losses on the German day fighter force and to contain German fighter strength away from the Russian and Mediterranean theatres of war.

6. Whenever Allied Armies re-enter the Continent, you will afford all possible support in the manner most effective.

From Webster & Frankland, Vol iv, Appendix 8, Directive xxviii, pp 153-4

Harris's first contribution to the Combined Bomber Offensive was the Battle of the Ruhr, launched in March 1943 and fought until July. Some 43 major attacks were made on a cluster of industrial cities, including Essen, which had proved all but immune in earlier attacks because of poor visibility in the area. The first attack of the Ruhr Battle was made on the night of March 5th against Essen. A force of 442 aircraft, including 303 four-engined bombers, was despatched in three waves. The attack was led by five Mosquitoes of the Pathfinder Force, which succeeded in marking the centre of the hazy target. The bombers followed in, dropping incendiary and high-explosive bombs. The attack lasted 40 minutes, 153 of the aircraft dropped bombs within 3 miles of the target, and extensive damage was inflicted on the Krupp works for the first time. The

attack set the tactical pattern for the rest of the Ruhr campaign. On occasion the Pathfinders failed to locate the target accurately enough and whole attacks were wasted. But the overall performance of the Command improved beyond recognition from the attacks of a year before.

In May Harris was persuaded to mount one of the most daring and technically complex raids of the war against a key target in the Ruhr – the raid on the dams. Harris opposed the scheme when it was first raised early in 1943; he doubted that the special-purpose bomb developed for the raid, the Barnes Wallis 'bouncing bomb', was capable of achieving what was claimed for it. He was unhappy about relinquishing valuable Lancaster aircraft for the project, having only won approval in January to mount a concentrated offensive on Germany for the first time.

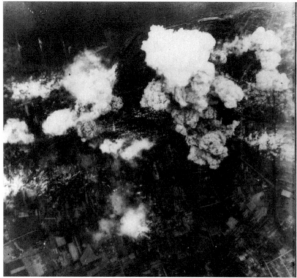 

These two photographs were taken 5 minutes apart during a raid on Emmerich on October 7th 1944. The target has become entirely obscured by the effects of high-explosive bombing. This made it difficult for the rest of the bomber stream to see what they were hitting, despite the great improvements in target marking.

Harris's objections were overruled. A unit already established in the Command to undertake specialist precision operations, 617 Squadron, led by Guy Gibson, was trained and equipped with the new bomb. The Combined Chiefs of Staff in Washington approved the operation. On May 17th 1943, 19 Lancasters set out in three waves to attack the Möhne, Eder and Sorpe dams in the Ruhr Valley. Flying at no more than 1,500 feet, seven of the 19 aircraft were shot

Fighting through

'What was daunting was the sheer size of the defended area. Essen itself was somewhere in the middle of the huge tent of light, but the searchlights and the flak were coming from an area far greater than that of a single town.

"I'm going to weave," called the pilot. "Watch out for fighters everyone and for our own aircraft."

His turns got steeper and more prolonged as we headed towards the astonishing display of light and smoke concealed in which, I had to believe, lay Essen and Krupps.

Now the action had begun in earnest and amid the constant winking of gunfire and the streams of tracer I saw the first red markers descending slowly, slowly. Almost at once they were followed by some greens, how close to the reds I found difficult to assess. Our instructions were to bomb the reds dropped by the Oboe Mosquitoes or otherwise the green "backers up", less certain to be accurate, dropped by Lancasters aiming at the reds in order to keep the marking going. Now there were more flashes on the ground and long strips of silver light betokened the first sticks of magnesium-based incendiaries.

It seemed an age before at last the navigator called, "George here, 3 minutes to ETA" (estimated time of arrival). Very soon came the bomb-aimer, saying, "OK, Paul, I've got a red and some greens straight ahead."

The bumps from the flak became more persistent and searchlights flashed across our wings, momentarily lighting up the cockpit.

"Hell," said the pilot, "they're getting too bloody close."

He turned quickly to starboard, then back again. "On course, all yours, Johnny," he called to the bomb-aimer. "Hurry up, for Christ's sake."

"OK, bomb doors open," from the bomb-aimer. Jerks and rumbles as the bomb doors opened with maddening deliberation. "Left a little, left, left, steady, steady, OK, bombs going."

I felt the aircraft lighten as each component of the load was released. I could see green target indicators to our left but the bomb-aimer's view directly below was obscured for me by the aircraft's nose.

With bomb doors shut again we turned steeply for home and it seemed that we would never get out of the defended area. We were rocked continuously by the blast from exploding shells. I looked back at where green target indicators were still falling, rather randomly now; some must have been many miles apart, and there were still streams of silver from incendiaries and flashes of guns firing and bombs exploding. Great areas were now covered with black smoke and the livid dark red of fires. I strained to see if I could see any ground detail but could make out nothing definite, only fire and smoke and the flashes of guns and the occasional larger flash of a 4,000-pound bomb exploding among the searchlights. It seemed incredible that so many aircraft could fly through that barrage of fire and light and survive.

We were still in the searchlight area but the pilot was weaving, turning, diving and climbing and using plenty of throttle so that the probing beams never rested on us for any length of time. There were still continual bursts of exploding shells above and around us and one of the gunners suddenly yelled "Fighter astern and to port", and both turrets fired long bursts of tracer while the pilot wrenched the aircraft into a steep diving turn to port in which I nearly lost my hold on his seat.

A few more minutes and the searchlights were behind us and we were out of the defended area; the weaving was less frenzied, and the fighter, which I had not seen and which must have been well astern in a blind spot for me, had apparently lost us. The shell bursts became more sporadic and ahead there was nothing but a blessed blackness.'

From P. Johnson, *Withered Garland: Reflections and Doubts of a Bomber* (London, 1995), pp 167-8

Below: One of the Lancaster BIII
(Special) aircraft of No 617
Squadron assigned to the
'Dambusters' raid of May 16th/
17th 1943. The 'Upkeep' weapon
installation, the famous 9,500-
pound 'bouncing bomb' designed by
Barnes Wallis, is clearly seen.

Below right: Wing Commander
Guy Penrose Gibson, with two
squadron leaders of No 106
Squadron, at Syerston in front of a
Lancaster Mk I. Gibson became a
legend after he led the 19 specially
converted Lancasters on the Dams
raid.

Breaching the dams

'When we were on our way in we were picked up by
searchlights. They were dazzling. The blue light was a
master light. Once the blue light was on you, the other ones
automatically picked you up. But we were fortunate. We
were able to shake it off. But we lost the two other aircraft we
were going in with. So we just carried on singly. As we got
down to the Möhne we started down the right-hand side, and
the light guns opened up on us. We picked up one hole. Then
we joined the other six aeroplanes circling the Möhne Dam
to create confusion and draw a little fire to give the one who
was doing the run a better chance.

We were the top end of the Möhne. The idea was that you
had to have 500 revolutions per minute and to be exactly 60
feet. Everything had to be right. You only had the one
weapon, and you couldn't waste it. That is what we had. We
ran down the Möhne water, when Guy Gibson crossed at
right angles and said, "This dam's gone!" Then he said,

"Number 6, number 6, B target." The B target for that night
was the Eder Dam. So we struck off for the Eder.

You could see the hole, and then a big gush of water. The
air was quite a sight as well. As a navigator I would not have
as good a view of it as the other crew members because I was
working from a white chart, and it takes a few minutes for
your eyes to get accustomed to the darkness.

Then we were on our way to the Eder. It was situated in a
hole. It was very, very difficult to get low enough, quick
enough and to have everything settled down – 240 miles per
hour at 60 feet. So we did this dummy run, but right ahead
of us was a hill. The pilot had to put on full power and go
screaming over that hill. It took exacting flying. The next
aircraft came along and hit the hill. We went round again
and made a decent drop. And then the next aircraft came
along and knocked it out. And that was it.'

Danny Walker,
Bomber Command navigator, 617 Squadron

down or had aborted before reaching the target. However,
five crews attacked and breached the Möhne Dam, and
three went on to attack and breach the Eder Dam. Attacks
on the Sorpe and Schwelme Dams were unsuccessful.
Three more Lancasters were shot down on the return journey.

The Dams Raid did not destroy the water supply for
Ruhr industry as had been hoped, and the defences were so
heavily reinforced to make repeated attacks too costly.
However, the raid gave the Command a new hero and much
publicity, though the loss rate was quite unsupportable. It
also demonstrated the great advances that had been made
in raising the operational skills of the force, and made
possible further precision attacks at night in 1944 against
tactical targets for OVERLORD. For the remainder of the
year Bomber Command stuck to the formula evolved in the
Battle of the Ruhr. Germany's major cities were subjected
to raids of increasing intensity and concentration. Harris

Two views of the Möhne Dam after the attack by No 617 Squadron. This and the Sorpe Dam controlled about two-thirds of the water storage capacity for the Ruhr industrial region. A third dam, the Eder, was also attacked that night and severely damaged. Both the Möhne and Eder dams were repaired within two months. The flooding caused by the raid killed 1,200 people, but did not severely impair industrial performance in the Ruhr. The attackers lost eight of the 18 bombers that reached Germany, a casualty figure among highly trained crews that persuaded Harris not to repeat the performance.

Coned

'We'd been briefed to attack an aircraft works at Hamburg. We bombed from about 9,000 feet, and were on our way back when some flak hit the rear turret. The rear gunner was trying to extinguish the fire, but couldn't put it out. The flames became obvious from the ground and we were caught in a cone of searchlights. About 20 lights homed in on us and it was like daylight. Though we got the turret fire out, a night-fighter had come in and lined itself up. He polished us off and some of the bullets he fired set off the flares inside the aircraft and set the aircraft on fire. I'd been hit several times, as had my navigator, and we were both lying on the floor of the aircraft.

We were lucky. The fire had put out the hydraulics on the rear turret and when the order was given to abandon the aircraft by the captain the rear gunner was not able to go out sideways as you would normally do, but crawled back inside the aircraft to get out of the hatch. He saw me lying on the aircraft floor and picked me up, sat me on the edge of the hatch, put my parachute on, put my hand on the rip-cord, said "For God's sake pull it!", and chucked me out.

I came to consciousness enough to pull the cord. We came down by parachute and I was taken to the nearest POW hospital, which was staffed entirely by French prisoners. No one could speak English, but there was a Professor of Surgery there from Strasbourg University, one of the few surgeons in Europe who was skilled enough to save my life.

The navigator was left inside the aircraft. He came to, looked around, saw that there was no one else there, got up to clip on his parachute, had a dizzy spell and dropped it through the escape hatch. He was in an aircraft that was on fire with no parachute. He walked up to the front, saw that there was no pilot there either, and got into the pilot's seat. He decided to end it quickly and dive straight into the ground, but then he had second thoughts and ended up bringing the aircraft down and landing it in a field in Germany about 1 o'clock in the morning, pitch black, with great skill. He ended up in the same hospital as I did a month later. He was badly wounded.'

Alex Kerr, Bomber Command pilot

Below: German soldiers beside the wreckage of a Stirling belonging to No 149 Squadron that crashed on May 18th 1942 near Abenra in German-occupied Denmark.

Below right: The Boulton Paul Type E gun turret, front and rear views, as fitted to the Handley Page Halifax and the Consolidated Liberator. The rear gunner had the most vulnerable post in a heavy bomber. The turrets were uncomfortable, difficult to escape from in an emergency, and often a German night-fighter's initial aiming point.

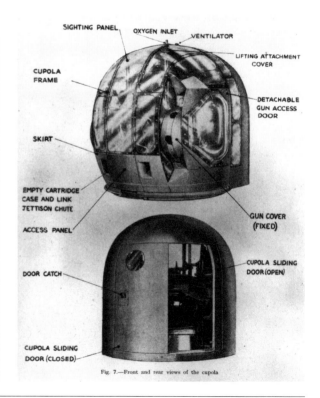

Fig. 7.—Front and rear views of the cupola

picked Germany's two largest cities, Hamburg and Berlin, as targets for further 'Battles' after the end of the Ruhr campaign in July.

The attack on Hamburg, carried out in a series of operations spread over the period from July 24th to July 30th by Bomber Command and the 8th Air Force, produced the most devastating results of the war. The sheer scale of the attack overwhelmed the rescue and fire services. Fires burning out of control created the first reported firestorm of the war. The intense heat destroyed three-quarters of the city and killed more than 40,000 people, one-tenth of all German deaths from bombing.

For the first time Bomber Command employed a new tactical device known as 'Window', which had been developed by 1942, but not used. It consisted of strips of paper covered with aluminium foil. The strips were 27 centimetres long and 2 centimetres wide, the exact size calculated to blind German radar by smothering the radar screens with false echoes. The effect was remarkable. The first use of Window rendered German radar quite useless, and made it impossible to organise the air defence of Hamburg. The German Air Force Chief of Staff, Hans Jeschonnek, was so horrified by the failure of his force that two weeks later he committed suicide.

Berlin proved to be a more difficult battleground. It was much further from British bases and was more heavily defended than any other area of the Reich. It was too large to identify the key bombing targets easily, and the H2S blind-bombing aid was itself blinded by the mass of ground information sent up from the German capital.

Above: A cloud of 'Window' anti-radar material descends during a raid on Gelsenkirchen on September 12th 1944. 'Window' consisted of strips of metallised paper that reflected radar emissions, clouding German screens with a mass of reflections and blinding their defences.

Left: The officers of No 106 Squadron, stationed at Syerston, in front of a Lancaster Mk I. Among them is Guy Gibson, who later led No 617 Squadron on the Dambusters raid. Each Lancaster carried a complement of seven or eight men.

Right: Handley Page Halifaxes of No 462 Squadron, Royal Australian Air Force, taxiing on the runway at Terria, Libya. Long-range attacks were launched from North Africa against targets in Italy and the Balkans.

Below: A Vickers Wellington Mk I of No 214 Squadron undergoing repairs in 1941. Few hangars could accommodate the larger aircraft introduced in the late 1930s, and a major construction programme was launched in 1940 to improve facilities for storage and repair.

Left: An Avro Lancaster runs up its engines before another mission. 'We knew every night some were not going to come back... We got used to it.'

Below: The chances of escaping from a stricken bomber over Europe were poor. Bomb-laden aircraft often exploded, or the 'g' forces trapped the crew inside as the bomber plunged to earth. However, some 10,000 aircrew survived to become prisoners of war.

An unlucky 13th

'There was a Flight Lieutenant whom I liked a lot. He'd done about 18 operations, but one day he got into the cockpit and he couldn't force himself to fly off. He was trembling, like a kind of shell-shock. He was reduced to the ranks and on his documents were written the words LMF – lack of moral fibre. He was a fantastic chap, and there were several like that. I think if I hadn't been shot down fairly early – it was I think my 13th operation – I might have gone that way myself eventually.

Thank God I used to be in my navigator's seat with curtains across the window. At times I could switch off the intercom and be miles away. When we were shot down I was off the intercom. The skipper was swaying the aircraft from one side to the other. I didn't take a great deal of notice because we often did that over Germany to avoid fighters. But suddenly there was this huge rat-a-tat and the whole plane shuddered and shattered. Soon it was on fire.

Fear is a strange experience. To begin with the plane was going down slowly, and we must have been at about 19,000 or 20,000 feet. We couldn't get the trapdoor open and I thought,

"God, I'm going to die". Now I was a coward and I sat down on the step and I went very calm. I gave the pilot his parachute; that was an agreement between us. I went very, very calm. It was a kind of peace. I was certain that one member was praying. Suddenly the door opened and I helped a very badly wounded man out. It was the bomb-aimer. He said he thought he would die before he hit the ground. The bomb-aimer's chute was all over the nose of the aircraft. Somehow in his haste he pulled the cord and the thing had opened.

Then I sprang, and counted 10 slowly like a good boy. I must have been going head-over-heels because every now and again the fire of the plane appeared only to disappear again. I counted 10 and then pulled the cord. My left boot shot off. I wanted to see clouds, but there were trees. I'd almost pulled the cord too late and I landed straight away in the corner of a field.

I hid the parachute under bushes as instructed. As soon as I realised I was safe I began to tremble again. All the fear came back. My first thought was to get to Holland. I knew that in September there was a triangle of stars, the base of which is roughly east/west, and I thought of going west. I'd only gone a few yards

A tunnel being dug at a prisoner-of-war camp. Captured airmen made many escape attempts, although only a few were successful. Evaders in France and the Low Countries were aided by resistance networks, which furnished papers and supplies. The most famous mass escape by airmen, from III Sagan on March 24th 1944, resulted in the execution of 50 recaptured prisoners as an example to the rest.

and there was what I thought was a huge German gun pointing to the sky. I went gingerly around it, but it wasn't a gun. It was a road barrier that was up.

I went on for four nights. I hid and slept in the day. I remember one 6 o'clock looking at my watch and thinking about this girl in York who would be waiting for me that day. We weren't supposed to be on this operation. A crew had gone sick. We were going on a week's leave the next day, but we were called in to take their place. I had this date with her, and I remember lying in this German wood looking at the watch. She would realise eventually what had happened when I didn't turn up.

It was sheer fear that kept me going. By my final afternoon my socks had worn out. I was so tired, even though I tried going to sleep in the day. I can remember being awakened by four boys, German boys, from a neighbouring village playing soldiers. One had got a dummy rifle on his shoulder, and he saw me lying behind a bush. He didn't come right across. He just stood there and looked and then went on to catch up his companions. He probably thought I was a forced worker. There were lots of them in Germany.

This final afternoon I was tired, demoralised – I'd got a growth of beard, I was dirty, hungry, and thirsty, lying in the early October sunshine. I'd gone to sleep and was wakened by three women sitting talking. I was in a copse overhanging a road. On the other side of the road was a river. I decided to remain in the copse. They were talking for 2 hours without realising that there was a British airman within a few yards of them.

I finally came out of my hiding place and arrived at three cottages. The door opened and a man came out. I said slowly, in bits of schoolboy German, "English airman". He was going to walk past me as I was giving myself up. I pulled back my brown innersuit and he saw the wings, and the penny dropped. He took me into the house. It was barely furnished and there was a baby in the corner in a wooden box. He left me with his wife and went off into the village to get the village policeman. He must have realised I was harmless even then. The policeman came and put handcuffs on me. He had a Hitler haircut and a Hitler moustache.'

Harold Nash, Bomber Command navigator

Conditions for captured airmen in German hands varied widely. Unsuccessful escapees risked transfer to a harsh prison regime in a concentration camp or even summary execution.

Silencing Goering

'On one occasion we had a bit of a shock. We used to work permanently on Mosquitoes, and every so often you were given a day off. You never knew when it would come. We would suddenly be told that tomorrow is a stand-down. We would plan to go out somewhere, make a late night of it, sleep in in the morning. It was surprising how often just as we were going out in the evening, someone would come rushing in and tell us it was all cancelled, we were on again, and we would be called at 6 in the morning.

That happened on one occasion. We got a call to say cancel your trip, go to bed, you'll be called at 5.30. Quite often I would be called in to the preparatory work on the raid, but on this one I wasn't. We got up the next morning and it was blowing a gale, the cloud base was about 3,000 feet, it was pouring with rain, horrible, dark and nasty. We got in the flight van to drive down to the briefing. My pilot, who was then the Flight Commander, said on the way down, "This one's a bit different. We start to climb after we've crossed the Elbe."

There was a stunned silence in the van. We thought, "Start to climb when we cross the Elbe? Where on earth are we going?"

We walked into the crew room and there was a tape on the map going from Marham to Berlin. Everybody without fail turned round and said, "Will we have enough fuel?" We hadn't been that far before, but that was it.

The Flight Commander was absolutely right. We flew low-level out to the south of Hamburg and we then climbed up to 25,000 feet. We had to bomb precisely on time, and the target was the radio station. The reason for the timing was that Goering was to make a speech. When we climbed there was unbroken cloud, and as we got closer I said, "We're not going to see anything – we're going to have to drop the bombs on the target area."

As I spoke there appeared a small hole in the cloud, and I could see the lakes of Berlin. It was the only hole in the cloud over the entire horizon. Quite incredible. We bombed, and there was no gunfire until after the bombs hit the ground. The guns started firing, but miles away from us by then. We came back and later on heard a tape of the broadcast. They announced that the Reich Marshal would make his speech, but he never said a word; there was a bang in the background, and the radio then played martial music. He never did make his speech.'

Ted Sismore, Bomber Command navigator

Missing a lynching

'We were briefed for Kassel. We were doing the diversion; we flew past Kassel and then turned and came back. After the turn coming back we got hit by a fighter. Nobody saw him. He came up underneath us with his upward firing cannons. He hit the starboard wing and he must have hit the fuselage too because he killed the mid-upper gunner. We were a ball of fire. Everyone got out except the mid-upper gunner and the pilot. Why the pilot didn't get out I have no idea. I spoke to the pilot from the rear turret. I said, "This is the rear gunner – I'm going out, everyone else has gone."

I pulled my chute in, buckled it on and flipped out backwards. I was always very apprehensive about getting run into by another aircraft in the stream, so I did a delayed drop, landed in a potato patch, undid my chute, buried it under some potato tops, took off my sheepskin trousers. I'd taken my helmet off in the aircraft, otherwise you would break your neck if you baled out with it on. It was about 9 o'clock at night, October 3rd 1943. I walked out to what I thought had been a river, but it was an Autobahn. I walked out on to the highway and trundled along until I became absolutely exhausted when the nervous reaction set in. I crawled into some brush and went to sleep.

I thought I'd get to Switzerland. We had escape kits, and I had a beautiful silk map so I knew where I was. I was a mess, I'd fallen in a few ditches. The second night I hid, and the third day I was in a ditch by a farmer's field. He came to look at his hay crop and saw me there. I pretended I was French with my schoolboy language. He just shrugged and walked away.

Within a short time three men arrived and arrested me, marched me into the town hall. The Gestapo called in and one man interpreted, an old man who had been in England in the First World War. They phoned Berlin. Now, my name is William Alexander Wilkie Wanless, and when they phoned Berlin they said Vilhelm Alexander Vilkie Vanless. I kept saying, "No, no, no – William Alexander Wilkie Wanless."

They locked me up in the city jail, and during the night a couple of Luftwaffe guys arrived in a black Maria and took me to the air base. They assigned me an armed guard and he took me by train to Frankfurt and the interrogation centre. I was amazed to look up in Frankfurt station and see all the glass. I thought we would have broken it all by then.

An elderly German went by and saw "Canada" on my shoulder. He looked terribly disturbed and started screaming. It was a mob scene in seconds, and my escort had to get his Luger out. He grabbed me by the arm and said "Run", and we just ran down the platform as the train was coming in. You couldn't hold it against anybody. The RAF had been there a night or two before; the Americans had been there a day or two before. You could feel for them.'

Wilkie Wanless, Bomber Command rear gunner

RAF prisoners in German hands. In the camps escape committees were formed, identity papers forged and civilian clothes made. Guards could be bribed or blackmailed to help. Prisoners displayed remarkable ingenuity in their efforts to flout the system.

Above: Airmen were posted to three main camps after passing through the screening camp, Dulag Luft at Oberusel outside Frankfurt-am-Main. The camps were III Sagan, Heydekrug and Dobrilugk-Kirchbain, a converted youth hostel. Some were sent to other camps or to the special prisons for recaptured escapers at Colditz and Posen.

Right: The interior of a tunnel dug by prisoners-of-war. At the camp in Dobrilugk-Kirchbain two former miners excavated a tunnel 227 feet long. However, all 52 escapers were caught and the camp closed down.

Baptism of fire

'I can remember my first operation quite clearly, because when we went to the squadron they said, "Oh, you're all right. At first they give you a couple of easy ones to do."

When we went to the briefing room we'd no idea what the target was. But as a Flight Engineer I knew it was a long trip because I knew what the fuel load was. I also knew what the bomb load was, and I had worked out that we were going quite a distance. But when they revealed on the map the actual route to the target, it was Berlin, the "Big City".

It was rather frightening at first, and then I thought, "Well, you start at the deep end; it can only get shallower."

We went out across the North Sea going northwards. We crossed over northern Denmark and approached Berlin from the north. We were followed by an enemy aircraft for quite a while. The rear gunner was the first to spot the aircraft. At one point he closed in on us, and we thought "The attack's coming!". The rear gunner opened up followed quickly by the mid-upper turret, and the aircraft suddenly swerved over and dived and went down somewhere below us.

It was my first operation, and I had no idea what a target looked like. We could see in the distance the coloured markers that had been laid down by the Pathfinder Force. The enemy had laid above an avenue of huge lights, some gigantic form of flare. It felt as if you were flying down a fully-lit avenue and you expected to be attacked at any moment. My skipper had a pact with the bomb-aimer that when we got to the target he would fly as far as he could straight and level across the target so that the bomb aimer had every chance of releasing the bombs at the right time. The skipper always said, "But I won't go round again."

You did nearly everything in as near as you could to total darkness. The navigator had to have lights on his navigation charts and he was enclosed by curtains, and the wireless operator the same. The gunners sat in total darkness just searching the sky. The bomb-aimer would be down below in his compartment. The skipper and I would be left in the cockpit. He would look out to the port side, and I would look out to starboard. We had an agreement amongst us that while we flew we wouldn't talk to each other, so it was a lonely flight. We didn't exchange any normal conversation. If somebody had something to say, it had to be important. The skipper and I arranged a mutual sign language where he would point to things in the cockpit and I would manipulate the various gadgets as he required them. That worked well unless I got it wrong. He was a big fellow, and I would just feel his hand on the back of my head. You knew you hadn't done the right thing, and then he would point again.'

Norman Berryman,
Bomber Command flight engineer

A De Havilland Mosquito takes off, with a formation of Boeing B-17 'Flying Fortresses' seen overhead. By 1944 eight Bomber Command squadrons were equipped with Mosquito bombers.

A Pathfinder operations room with operations board after the raids of April 4th/5th 1944 against Berlin and Magdeburg and the Leuna synthetic oil plant, details of which are written up on the blackboard to the right.

In three exploratory attacks in late August and early September 1943 the accuracy and concentration was well below the standards set in the summer, while the loss rates of more than 7 per cent were among the worst of the war. Flak damage was also heavy, and a further 7 per cent of the force sustained heavy damage. The German defences, temporarily swamped at Hamburg, had regained the initiative. The concentration of defences along the Kammhuber Line, with its intricate system of radar and night-fighter boxes, was replaced by a more flexible system in which a ground controller operated a much larger force, directing them to the bomber stream as a whole with a constant commentary. Night-fighter tactics and radar development matched the changing tactics of the bomber force. In late 1943 the German night-fighter force brought

Bomber Command's offensive to a point of crisis.

Nonetheless Harris persisted with the Battle for Berlin, which he regarded as a particularly important target. The long winter nights were exploited from November onwards, but loss rates remained unacceptably high. In January raids on Berlin cost more than 6 per cent of the attacking force, but raids on other cities exceeded even this. The last attack on Berlin on the night of March 24th was even worse. Strong winds blew the markers to the south of the city and scattered the bomber stream. Little serious damage was done by the 811 aircraft despatched, but almost 9 per cent of the force was lost. This was the last major attack mounted by Bomber Command on the capital, although small forces of Mosquitoes continued harassing attacks.

In the hands of the Gestapo

'We came down north-east of Paris, and got in with the French underground. A Frenchman turned us in for the reward. The German army took me and put me in their local jail. I was in a private cell, where I was interrogated by the Gestapo every day. Finally they took me to what was called a private house in which there was a bed set in concrete with handcuffs. I was interrogated there for about 8 hours. What they really wanted to know was who the people were who had helped me in the underground. They did not want military information, for they knew about as much as we did. They wanted to know who had done everything for me. They did everything in the world. They fired guns at you and around you. They would slap you around. They took all your clothes and had you handcuffed naked to the bed. There isn't much you can do. I waited out. They just kept working and working to try to get the people's names. I made up my mind that I wasn't going to tell them. Name, rank and serial number were all we were supposed to give. One guy laughed. He knew I was American and he showed me his coat with "Made in Florida".

"America, the land of milk and honey," he said. "When the war's over, I'm going back."

That was the only time I answered and said what I wanted to say: "Well, don't let me ever catch you there."

But I never did see him again.'

**Wilfrid John 'Mike' Lewis,
Bomber Command pilot**

Collision over Berlin

'There was always tension going into Berlin. I always tried to get in early. I tried to get in with the Pathfinders when I could, because I fancied that I was as good as any Pathfinder. When you went in all hell let loose. They had extraordinary devices that exploded with a tremendous bang and lit up the whole sky to frighten you. The Pathfinders were remarkably good. You saw the flares and incendiaries go down. Then 600 bombers were all around you. The risk of collision was very great. Looking down you gradually saw the city explode with bombs dropping and with incendiaries. Looking back you saw Berlin burning.

This was the turning point at which extreme caution had to be exercised. If everyone did not turn at the same time the risk of collision was very great. On one particular night two Lancasters collided in front of us and one of them exploded and went straight down. The other did two upward rolls with all four engines burning and exploded right in front of us, a hundred yards away.

The pilot shouted to the gunners to turn away so that their night vision would not be impaired. One gunner asked why, and when he was told his knees shook. Quite an extraordinary scene.'

Lord Mackie, Bomber Command observer

When, a week later, another long-distance attack, this time on Nuremberg, met with fierce night-fighter defence, the loss rate rose to 11 per cent, and Harris came close to admitting the defeat of the night offensive. The diversion to the OVERLORD air campaign to some extent disguised the crisis. When Bomber Command returned later in the year to large-scale attacks on Germany the balance again swung in favour of the attacking force.

During the OVERLORD period the bomber force, now very much larger than a year before, and equipped with improved H2S, made occasional attacks on industrial cities in Germany, but the overwhelming bulk of its activities were confined to tactical targets. The first major raid carried out after D-Day came against Kiel on the night of July 23rd. The loss rate was only 0.6 per cent, and the accuracy and concentration of bombing was considerably improved. Raids on the more distant Stuttgart produced loss rates of 4.6 and 2.2 per cent. In mid-August the main phase of support for the Allied invasion was over, and although Bomber Command continued to divide its operations between tactical and strategic targets, the regular bombing of German cities began again.

In the interval between March and August a great deal had changed. The high losses of the autumn of 1943 had affected the US 8th Air Force as well as Bomber Command, and the answer was found in the 'strategic fighter', a long-range fighter aircraft capable of flying with the bombers far into Germany. In late 1943 experiments with a number of aircraft fitted with additional drop fuel tanks demonstrated remarkable gains in range with little loss of performance. The American aircraft industry began a crash programme. The P-51 Mustang, with a Rolls-Royce Merlin engine, began to pour in hundreds from American factories. The Spitfire was also modified, though with less success. The American P-47 Thunderbolt and P-38 Lightning extended their range significantly over the winter of 1943-4, but the Mustang proved to be the true strategic fighter, flying as far as Berlin and having the overall performance to fight the German air force in its own airspace.

In the spring of 1944 the American air force began a two-pronged assault on German air power. The bombers were directed to destroy the German aeronautical industry, while the fighters were detailed to destroy the German fighter force wherever it appeared. In the first month the Luftwaffe experienced exceptional loss rates, running at 25 per cent. The aircraft industry, in the midst of a large expansion programme, was forced to disperse away from the main factories. A cycle of attrition set in, from which the German air force never recovered.

The defeat of the German air force was the key to a successful bomber offensive, as had been recognised in mid-1943. But there were other tactical innovations to explain the growing power of the night-bombing force. In November 1943 a special force was set up, designated 100 Group, to organise and operate radio countermeasures against the enemy. Armed with jamming apparatus known as 'Mandrel', the group flew on major operations to prevent the night-fighters from getting a fix on the size or direction of the bomber force. Other aircraft, mainly the fast high-flying Mosquitoes, engaged in sophisticated deception operations, luring the German fighters to the wrong destination.

The main bombing force was now divided into two or three separate streams, flying by unpredictable routes to different targets. Each stream was ordered to maintain almost complete radio silence, to prevent the night-fighters from listening in and finding the direction and height of the attacking force. Divided and confused, the shrinking German night-fighter force was no longer able to feast off the bomber mass as it had done in 1943. When long-range British night-fighters began to infiltrate into Germany with the bomber streams, German losses rose sharply. By that point Bomber Command was flying again by day, heavily escorted by long-range fighters.

Bomber Command also had much greater hitting power. The accuracy of attacks was greatly improved, and the weight of bombs carried increased sharply. Almost half of the bombs dropped on German cities fell between August 1944 and May 1945, and the high-explosive carried had much greater destructive power thanks to the introduction of aluminised explosive. It was found that the blast effect of the new explosive was anything up to ten times greater than conventional products, and in late 1943 it was gradually introduced into Bomber Command armament. The combination of better bombs with heavier and more accurate attacks contributed to the very high levels of destruction achieved in the last months of the war. So, too, did the emasculation of German air power for the rest of the war, and the return to daylight bombing in September 1944, which the weakness of the Luftwaffe made possible. The operational and tactical maturity of the force had taken a long time to achieve, but by late 1944 its the striking power was formidable and terrifying.

The return to the regular bombing of Germany revived all the old arguments about targets. The technical improvement of the force was seen as an opportunity to move back to the strategy of precision bombing abandoned in 1941. A good proportion of Bomber Command's activities was already devoted to tactical targets, such as bridges, viaducts or railway lines, which had to be attacked with pin-point accuracy. The first directive to the Command following the decision to remove it from Eisenhower's direct control in September 1944 stipulated attacks against primarily tactical targets. When this was revised by the Combined Chiefs of Staff on September 25th top priority was once again given to oil, with transport and the German tank industry second. Harris remained unconvinced that what he called 'panacea targets' could yield results as quickly as his persistent attack on the industrial cities of the Reich.

In October, with Allied forces bogged down in the west, the Combined Chiefs ordered what amounted to a compromise. Two operations were ordered, HURRICANE I and HURRICANE II. The first was a concentrated attack on the Ruhr area to try to unhinge the German war effort in the region directly facing Allied troops. The second was a reiteration of the assault on oil and transport.

Harris did not reject more precise targets out of hand, although he made his views clear to Portal and the Air Ministry. Bomber Command was now large enough (and resistance so much lighter) that it proved possible to spread attacks over a whole range of targets, as well as giving direct support to ground forces, undertaking reconnaissance and signals operations, and supporting the activities of the British Special Operations Executive. Harris felt as keenly as ever that area attacks were likely to be more decisive, but he was no mutineer. In December 1944 the Command devoted 30 per cent of its effort to city attacks, 20 per cent to attacks on communications

and 8 per cent to oil, hitting many more oil targets than the 8th Air Force. In January, when Harris's disagreement over the oil strategy was expressed in a series of angry and vehement letters to Portal, the Command actually devoted 20 per cent of its effort to oil, dropping 10,000 tons against the 5,500 tons of the two American bomber forces, 8th and 15th.

Harris could point with some justification to the uncertainty that prevailed at the highest levels over what use to make of the bomber force. On January 27th 1945

cities were again given a higher priority. The new operation, codenamed THUNDERCLAP, was intended to support a general Soviet offensive in the east after months in which the eastern front had slowed almost to a halt. It was also deliberately intended to create demoralisation and disorder in the cities of central and eastern Germany in order to hamper the movement of troops and supplies, already confused by the flood of refugees from the Soviet advance.

The inspiration for this new wave of city attacks was

John Gee (second from right) poses with his crew in front of a Lancaster bomber 'Vicious Virgin'. 'From being a young man, you aged ten years overnight,' Gee later recalled.

A Lancaster takes part in a daylight attack on Germany late in the war. Using drop tanks, American fighters were able to escort their bombers right across Germany. From mid-1944 the Luftwaffe suffered heavier losses over Germany than on any other front and eventually lost control of its own airspace.

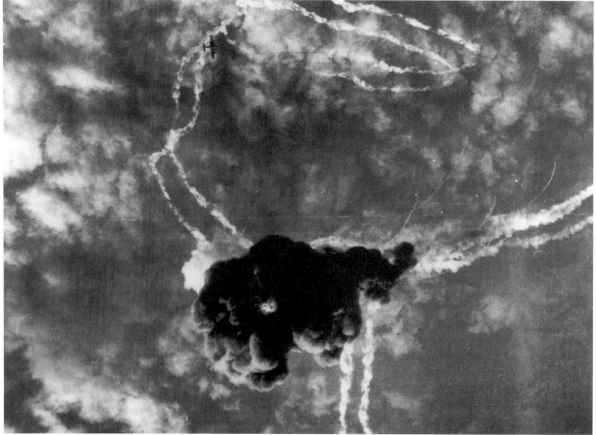

German heavy anti-aircraft guns could reach targets at up to 45,000 feet. Here a heavy bomber explodes in mid-air during a daylight attack on Germany in February 1945. The background is criss-crossed with Sky Markers guiding bombers to the target.

Directing the Hurricane

'Operations "Hurricane I" and "Hurricane II"

I am directed to inform you that it has been decided in agreement with the Deputy Supreme Allied Commander and the Commanding General US Strategic Air Forces Europe to undertake special operations for the following purposes:

(i)   In order to concentrate bombing effort on the vital areas of the Ruhr. Outside the question of the great concentration of enemy economic and military resources in the Ruhr, the Supreme Commander has stated that our best opportunity of defeating the enemy in the West lies in striking at the Ruhr and the Saar.

(ii) In order to demonstrate to the enemy in Germany generally the overwhelming superiority of the Allied Forces in this theatre. This is to be done as soon as weather and other circumstances permit.

The common object of these demonstrations is to bring home to the enemy a realisation of this overwhelming superiority and the futility of continued resistance.

"Hurricane I"
This plan provides for the concentration of effort in time and space against objectives in the Ruhr. The intention is to apply within the shortest practical period the maximum effort of the Royal Air Force Bomber Command and the VIIIth United States Bomber Command against objectives in the densely populated Ruhr… The initial stage of this operation is aimed at the maximum disorganisation of the Ruhr and the denial to the enemy of essential facilities and particularly its communications. Apart from the direct destruction caused, it is anticipated that administrative chaos will follow…

"Hurricane II"
This plan provides for the maximum concentration of Allied air attacks against precise targets in Germany on the first occasion when visual bombing conditions obtain over that country generally.

The maximum effort of RAF Bomber Commands, and the VIIIth and XVth Air Forces will be directed, on the first day on which the weather permits, against the major oil targets throughout Axis Europe. The RAF Bomber Command is to contribute to this plan by making a maximum effort against the Ruhr-Rhineland synthetic oil plants.

From Webster & Frankland, Vol iv, Appendix 8, Directive 42, pp 174-6

---

not Harris. The idea developed in the Air Ministry, and was also suggested by the Joint Intelligence Sub-Committee of the Combined Chiefs of Staff. Churchill was keen to have something to tell Stalin and hurried the idea along. The result was a joint strategy, pursued by both the American and British bomber forces. The first attacks of the THUNDERCLAP campaign were made by the American 8th Air Force, not Bomber Command. When Bomber Command carried out its part of the campaign Harris was directed to Dresden. It was attacked with a large force, against light opposition. Another firestorm was created, like the one at Hamburg. The attack had ghastly consequences for the thousands of refugees packed into the town, but it was not intended as a mere act of terror or retribution. The Dresden attack was part of a series of operations designed to dislocate Germany's final efforts at resistance and to speed the Soviet advance. A month later Churchill himself asked the Chiefs of Staff to review bombing policy in the light of Dresden. He deprecated the use of air power 'simply for the sake of increasing the terror', forgetting in the process that he

had asked his Air Minister in January when the RAF was going to start 'basting the Germans'.

From mid-February the Allied front was on the move in both the east and the west. Both the British and American bomber forces were shifted to tactical targets in support of the ground offensive, including a ring of bridges around the Ruhr that were attacked by the precision bombers of 617 Squadron using the 22,000-pound 'Grand Slam' bomb developed for the purpose. On April 25th Bomber Command attacked Hitler's retreat at Berchtesgaden to prevent fanatical Nazis from using the area as a centre for a final do-or-die stand.

The last attack on Germany by Bomber Command was made on the night of May 2nd when 126 Mosquitoes attacked Kiel, where it was feared German shipping was mustering to carry German troops to Norway to continue the fight from there. As the offensive petered out Bomber Command crews found themselves ferrying thousands of Allied prisoners-of-war back from Germany, and dropping relief supplies to the starving population of the Netherlands. The unlucky ones found themselves preparing for transfer to the war in the Far East.

The German research facility at Peenemünde on the Baltic coast where the V1 'Flying Bomb' and V2 rockets were being developed. This aerial reconnaissance photograph shows part of the installation before the concentrated attack mounted on August 17th/18th 1943.

Peenemünde after 560 bombers attacked, causing extensive damage and forcing the dispersal of the German rocket development programme. A total of 44 aircraft were lost on the raid, but the threat was not ended. The first V2 rocket fell on Chiswick in London on September 8th 1944.

The target map for the last major Bomber Command attack on Germany, which took place in daylight on April 25th 1945. The target was Hitler's mountain retreat at Berchtesgaden in southern Bavaria where, it was feared, he might make a final stand. The 359 Lancasters and 16 Mosquitoes demolished many of the Nazi leaders' buildings, but Hitler himself was in his Berlin bunker where he committed suicide five days later.

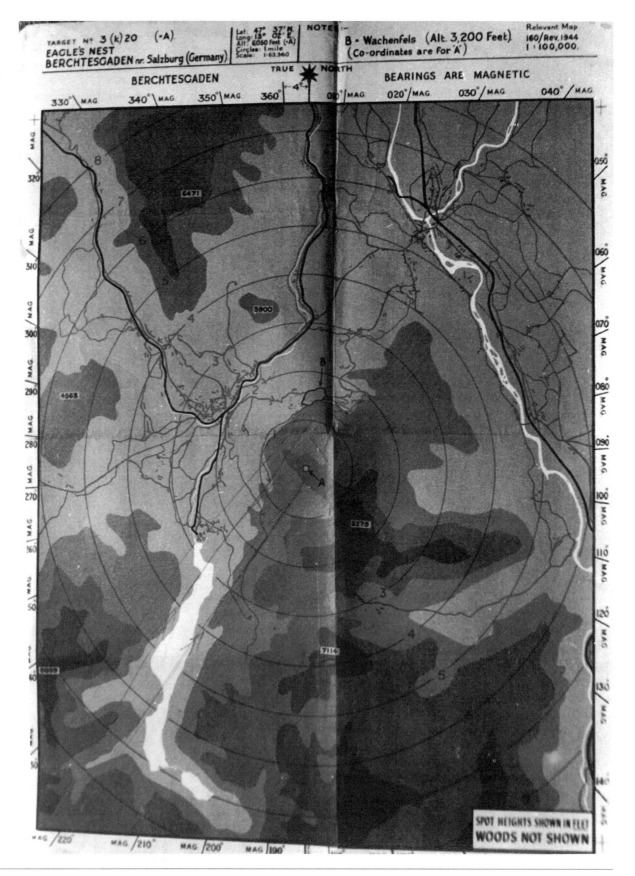

Chapter 4

The Home Front

Unlike most British and American servicemen in the Second World War, the crews of Bomber Command spent most of their time in England. Some were trained overseas, some were posted to other theatres of war, but those who stayed in the Command did their fighting from British bases. Air crew were part of the Home Front. The vast network of airfields, stores and maintenance units brought thousands of Britons into day-to-day contact with the war effort, which they saw at much closer quarters than they had in the Great War. The thundering noise of hundreds of heavy bombers making their way across the English countryside to join the bomber stream became an almost daily occurrence by 1944. The sight of stricken bombers, torn by Flak and fighter fire, limping back to base, must have been familiar to the inhabitants of much of southern and eastern England. Bomber Command fought a war that people could actually see.

The very visibility of Bomber Command was part of its appeal when, in the early years of war, it proved also to be the only means of bringing the war directly to the German people. The bombing raids were widely reported in the press and in popular magazines at a time when there was little else for the British public to cheer about. The presence of the bomber crews among the people for whom they were fighting produced a special bond between them, and helped to sustain the popular view of the air forces as both more glamorous and more effective than the other services. Figures like the 617 Squadron leader, Guy Gibson, achieved a level of popular acclaim equalled by few if any from the Army and Navy.

For the RAF this was all to the good, for Bomber Command was throughout the war a volunteer service, and there was no serious shortage of volunteers. Bombing was a dangerous and arduous occupation, but flying was regarded by many of those who joined as uniquely exhilarating and challenging. Above all, it avoided army life, with its image of square-bashing and pointless drill, and the memories of senseless slaughter in the trenches. During the war Bomber Command attracted 125,000

A Bomber Command pre-raid briefing in front of the film cameras. Once the target was selected at Harris's morning situation meeting at Bomber Command headquarters, details were sent to the Groups and then to individual squadrons. Navigators were usually given an earlier briefing to allow them to work on the route.

volunteers to fly as aircrew. They came from all over the world, but most came from Britain and the settler Dominions – Canada, Australia, New Zealand, South Africa – or from British colonies. There were volunteers from defeated states – French or Poles – and there were volunteers from neutrals – from Ireland or from the United States before December 1941. The Dominion volunteers at first entered British squadrons, but were soon formed into units of their own to give them a distinct sense of unity and identity. Bomber Command was a multi-national force, drawing on the skilled manpower of a whole empire.

The crews were the tip of the organisational iceberg. They were serviced by hundreds of thousands of ground crew, administrators, medical staff, and technicians. The training scheme was based on hundreds of overseas facilities, and an extensive operational training system in Britain. The whole Command was held together by a communications net that was centred on the Headquarters in Buckinghamshire. It was here that the Bomber Command Commander-in-Chief ran operations. The other aspects of the bombing effort were organised from the Air Ministry and authorised by the Air Staff, with the exception of air strategy, which could only be sanctioned

by the Chiefs of Staff, or from 1942 onwards by the Anglo-American Combined Chiefs of Staff.

Harris's responsibility was to organise the Command and its operations within the framework of the directives and instructions issued from the Air Ministry and agreed by the Air Staff. These were issued at intervals during the course of the war by the Deputy (later Assistant) Chief of Air Staff responsible for operations. Harris had the freedom to decide which targets should be hit on a particular night, and by which Bomber Groups, but he operated within the broad context of the directives he was given even when he disagreed with them, as he sometimes did. For much of the war the Chiefs of the separate RAF Commands met regularly with the Chief of Staff to air their views, a practice that became more difficult to operate once Bomber Command had been subordinated to Eisenhower's Headquarters in 1944.

Harris was the longest serving head of Bomber Command, and its most forthright and energetic defender. He gave to the Command a sense of its own worth and identity that his predecessors had failed to do. He worked tirelessly and continuously. The bombing campaign gave him little respite. He once remarked with characteristic acerbity: 'The Army fights half-a-dozen battles a year. The

Harris studying maps at the 'bunker' headquarters in High Wycombe, Buckinghamshire. The day's operations were planned early in the morning once meteorological reports were available. After Harris had given his decision, he interfered little with the conduct of each operation.

Navy fights half-a-dozen a war. But poor Bomber Command! Every night that the weather gives us a breather … the critics accuse us of doing nothing yet again!'

There were few nights on which Bomber Command crews did not do something, even in poor weather. Not every night saw a major attack, but they occurred regularly enough for Harris to face an almost constant stream of activity. Despite periods of failing health, he stuck to the job with an extraordinary will, and did not take a single day of leave during the entire time he commanded the bomber force. He worked a long day, filled with paperwork and meetings through which he chain-smoked. Each morning at 9 o'clock he held his situation conference in which plans for the day were discussed and finalised after consultation with the Command's meteorological and intelligence

Harris at work

'As one of the controllers at Bomber Command Headquarters we took our turn in the ops room. The morning briefing was fairly standard. The senior Air Staff officers would gather in the underground ops room and around 9 o'clock the Commander-in-Chief would come in, look at the state board which showed the aircraft and crew availability for that night, and then sit down at a table to receive a briefing from the Command Met Officer. The target or targets for the night were discussed depending on the weather forecast that was given. The C-in-C always spoke very quietly and I never heard him raise his voice. After he left we got down to the detailed side of planning the night's operations, allocating targets to the various groups. This was telephoned to them on a secret line, and the groups would then allocate these targets to the squadrons.

As operations controllers we took it in turn to man the operations room at night, and we had several telephones on our desk, one of which was directly linked to the Commander-in-Chief's residence. From time to time he would ring up to enquire how the operations were going. We just prayed that it wouldn't happen when we were there. I remember one controller saying that the experience was equal to one sortie over the Ruhr. We held him in such great awe. I don't remember him ever saying thank you. If he asked you a question, you gave him the information and he terminated the conversation.

The Commander-in-Chief was a very direct, down-to-earth person who exuded authority and commanded great respect and loyalty. He very seldom visited stations. He didn't have very much time to do so, but in some mysterious way his personality and influence pervaded the whole Command. What he had was leadership.'

Wilf Burnett, Bomber Command pilot

In the bunker

'My job at High Wycombe was on the navigation staff, where I mainly looked after operational requirements. But like the other members of the navigation staff I had to take my turn in the Operations Room. We would wait there for the Commander-in-Chief to come in. In the large room there was a central desk with information relating to the squadrons, the aircraft, the manning. There would be the latest intelligence photographs of the most recent raids, and there would also be up on a board the current bombing directive from the Directorate of Bombing Operations in the Air Ministry. It would be known roughly from what family of targets the particular selection would be made.

Harris would come in with his staff and liaison officers from the Navy and the United States Air Force, and there would be a short discussion and you would see files being handed over people's heads. There would be perhaps 10 or 12 people around the desk. Small fry like me would prop up the wall some distance away. You couldn't hear what they were saying very easily. After about 10 minutes, never very long, there would be a short pause and then just one word would be ground out – Cologne, or Düsseldorf, etc – and the Commander-in-Chief had selected the target for the night.

He got up immediately. There would be no small talk. He would go to the door and Saundby would hand him his cap, and then all hell would let loose because the detailed planning had to start. What was the armament? What was the route? What was the fuel? How many aircraft?'

Sam Hall, Bomber Command navigator

officers. He then pronounced the objective for the night, and the size of the force it required. His deputy undertook the detailed operational planning, while the Bomber Groups were notified by secure teleprinter of their targets. The Groups then passed on the operational requirements to the squadron commanders, who finally briefed the crews not long before their departure.

Harris made little attempt to meet the crews he sent off every night. His schedule left very little time for cross-country tours, and the Command was widely dispersed. He met airmen as they passed through his Headquarters, or through the meetings in London. He occasionally invited them back to his house in High Wycombe, close to his Headquarters. He was known by reputation, which preceded him wherever he went. Hard-working, diligent, unyielding in the exercise of his authority, a man who suffered fools not at all, Harris commanded by example. His long and arduous tenure of office was emulated and endured by very few among the commanders of the Western war effort.

The structure of command was taut. Harris's decisions, taken in the middle hours of the morning, were relayed out to the bomber Groups, which could then discuss the operations directly with Harris's headquarters. Before Harris returned for his briefing meeting on the following

morning most of the crews would be back at their bases, eating the regulation post-operation breakfast. The Command was spread out by 1944 over 128 airfields, a handful of them in Scotland, and the rest scattered down the whole of eastern England, from 5 Group in North Yorkshire to the Operational Training Units of 92 Group dotted to the north of Bomber Command Headquarters in Buckinghamshire. In January of that same year the Command had 1,465 operational aircraft, and a further 1,860 divided between the Training Units.

At the start of the war all 27 Bomber Command airfields were grass covered. All but two of the 128 airfields in 1944 had hard runways, although runways of sufficient length to cope with large numbers of heavy bombers were only authorised in October 1941, and few were completed before 1943. An integrated and extensive system of airfield lighting was gradually introduced on all Bomber Command airfields, but the provision of hangars to house the large numbers of heavy aircraft in 1942 and 1943 lagged well behind schedule, forcing mechanics to work long hours on aircraft in the open air.

Each operational airfield was a unit complete in itself, a fact acknowledged by Harris when they were all upgraded to the status of Air Station in 1942. The main airfields had small feeder fields where aircraft could be stored and

A large network of stations, with outlying storage depots and sub-stations, was set up across Eastern and South Eastern England. This is the bomber station headquarters at RAF Tuddenham in Suffolk, which operated Short Stirling Mk IIIs.

Above: A group photograph of No 214 Squadron at Downham Market in Norfolk gives a dramatic impression of the size of the four-engined bombers, in this case a Short Stirling Mk I.

Left: The lead navigator explains the route and operational plan to other navigators at a briefing for an attack on the Zeiss optical works in the eastern German city of Jena.

Romance was one of the great casualties of the bombing campaign: thousands of young crewmen who died left behind wives and girlfriends. Arnold Derrington, seen here with his future wife, was one of the lucky ones.

repaired. They also contained all the necessary facilities for organising and running local operations and for servicing the aircraft. Levels of amenity for the personnel varied widely from station to station. Medical and catering services were standard, but facilities for recreation and relaxation were introduced piecemeal. Leave was regularly granted, though it could be rescinded in periods of fine weather, when Bomber Command operated all it could. The curious situation in which airmen found themselves, at war in the midst of regular civilian life all around them, gave them opportunities to make close contacts with local communities and to share their social life. Bomber crews gravitated between these extremes of arduous and dangerous combat and the relative tranquillity of the areas in which they lived.

All Bomber Command crews began their career in training, which was long and thorough; the last part, in the Operational Training Units, was run by the Command itself. Their preliminary training was undertaken by Training Command, later known as Flying Training Command. Much of this was done overseas, thanks to an agreement reached on December 17th 1939 with the British Dominion governments to establish the Empire Air Training Scheme. Courses for aircrew began in April 1940. At its peak the scheme had 333 flying training schools, 153 in Britain and the remainder in Canada, Australia, South Africa, Southern Rhodesia, India, New Zealand and a handful of other territories. Some was done at bases in the southern United States, where 14,000 British Empire aircrew were trained during the war.

Of the more than 300,000 aircrew trained, more than 220,000 were trained overseas. There were evident advantages in the scheme, but some disadvantages. When aircrew were sent to England to complete their training they found an entirely different flying environment from the clear skies and open landscapes with which they were familiar. Flying in England was more hazardous and uncomfortable; flying four-engined heavy bombers with a full bombload against a heavily defended area of Germany was about as different as it could be from flying light trainer aircraft over the African savannah. It was the job of the Operational Training Units to prepare the crews for combat.

The men who arrived at the OTUs had all been trained for a particular role – as pilot, navigator, air gunner, wireless operator and bomb aimer. The nature and length of that training changed over the war with the shift from light to heavy bombers. The transition from light Anson

A Canadian training

'There was a great response in western Canada to the British Empire Air Training Scheme. All the flying schools in Canada became training centres under the supervision of the air force. There was a big manning pool opened in Edmonton where I lived. We stayed there a few weeks, but they didn't have any stores or uniforms. We finally got kitted out and we had to go to different stations on what they called Tarmac Duty, or guard duty. I went to a service flying school in southern Alberta, where I was driving a tractor. Then they opened an Initial Training School at Saskatoon and we went over there on one of the coldest days of the winter. I had not been issued with a greatcoat, and we had to march 2 or 3 miles up the road to the training station.

Most of the navigation instructors were ex-schoolteachers, recruited from schools. Some of us who didn't have as great an education as others had to learn logarithms and so forth. We were billeted in this old school and there were blackboards up all over the place. At night those who understood navigation and logarithms – and I didn't know a logarithm from a hole – taught us our classes. One was a mathematical genius, and he used to stand up and pound the blackboard because we were all so dumb.

"Don't you guys get it?" he would say, and he would bang the board until chalk came out of the cracks.

That is where we were selected as pilot, or navigator or wireless operator.

Wilkie Wanless, Bomber Command rear gunner

Starting up

We first of all had our medical, which lasted three days. This was when you first signed on, when you were called for your medical. I took mine at Uxbridge. It was pretty thorough for the time. Afterwards we stayed at Uxbridge and were eventually called six months afterwards to an aircrew receiving centre on different parts of the coast. The one I went to was at Babbacombe in Devon, where we received our uniform, had our inoculations and learned the elements of rudimentary drill. We were there for something like a fortnight, then immediately moved to an initial training wing. These were also dotted around the pre-war seaside resorts.

The one I went to was at Newquay in Cornwall, No 8 ITW. By then a large number of the hotels had been requisitioned to house the recruits and permanent staff and instructors. It was well organised. The only trouble was that being a young lad just breaking out of my late teens, I was continuously hungry. With the emphasis on PE, which was done on the beach with well-known professional sportsmen, footballers or runners, I had a perpetual hunger. We never got enough food.

The subjects were the kind of thing you'd expect to find: basic navigation, signals, about gases, aircraft recognition. We all had to pass a proficiency test before we left, and the whole course lasted about eight weeks. We were then posted from there after a fortnight's embarkation leave. We were all earmarked to go to Canada. We were shunted up north to Wilmslow, just outside Manchester, where there was a huge pre-war hutted camp. We eventually set sail from just outside Glasgow. I went over to Canada on an ex-P&O cruise liner. There were about 3,600 of us on board. The ship had received all its previous supplies down in South Africa, so it was full of luxuries that we had not seen for ages, like big chocolate bars, with whole nuts and raisins, and so on. Initially you couldn't get around the deck of the ship, there was such a long queue. But two days out the sea was so rough you could go up to the dry canteen, as it was called, and you could buy what you wanted any time. All the bad sailors were strung along the ship's frame.

We got to the fringes of Canadian territorial waters and because of the speed of the ship we didn't go in convoy. We had two destroyers to escort us, but one broke down and had to go into Reykjavik in Iceland. The other escorted us as far as the Newfoundland fog banks, where the Royal Canadian Navy took over. U-boats were in operation in that part of the world, and you can imagine the 3,600 aircrew, all absolutely spot-on with their Aldiss lamp signalling, when a destroyer came just abeam of us and flashed with his bright signalling lamp that a periscope had been seen 5 miles to starboard. The ship heeled over at 90 degrees and the next thing we saw were the depth charges. It all passed off all right. The fog bank came down and within a day and a half we were into Halifax, Nova Scotia.'

Harry Le Marchant, Bomber Command observer

or Oxford trainers to multi-engined bombers was carried out by the Conversion Units set up for that very purpose. Not even these units could replicate the conditions of combat, and for most crews combat was the toughest but the most useful part of their apprenticeship. With the coming of the heavy bomber there also came a complete overhaul of the crew structure. In the early part of the war all bombers carried two pilots and crew members who performed multiple roles – the navigator was also the bomb-aimer, the wireless operator was also an air gunner. In 1942 the second pilot was dropped from the crew, allowing many more crews to be formed, and a more thorough training of the reduced number of pilots now required; the pilot was given a flight engineer as a replacement. The navigator was confined to the task of navigator, and was joined by a specialist air bomber and a wireless operator. The air gunners were no longer required to learn wireless operation. The effect of these changes was to increase the competence of the crew and to rationalise its functions.

Operational training was standardised at approximately 80 hours flying time. In 1942 crews began training on twin-engined aircraft and were then sent to Heavy Conversion Units for further flying. When Lancasters were brought in they were regarded as too valuable an asset to be used in training, and small Lancaster Finishing Schools were set up to give crewmen familiarity with a very different aircraft. When Lancasters became more widely available in 1944 they were placed in the Conversion Units and the finishing schools closed down.

Above and right: Simulator training for would-be aircrew. At his desk the trainer has a map on which he monitors the flight of the trainee. The trainer has controls that can alter wind direction and strength, affecting the simulated movement of the aircraft. Models of friendly and enemy aircraft hang from the ceiling.

Far right: De Havilland Mosquitoes assembled for review. The much-feted hero of the Dams Raid, Guy Gibson, was to meet his death in a Mosquito over Holland in 1944 after insisting on a return to active duty.

Left: The Avro Anson served as a transport and training aircraft in Bomber Command as well as an early patrol aircraft for Coastal Command.

Below: Lancasters of No 50 Squadron at Skellingthorpe. They were part of 5 Group, whose policy of carrying the maximum possible bomb load has been advanced as an explanation for their higher losses in 1943-44.

A simple memorial to a bomber crew who died over Europe during the bombing campaign. By 1942 crews had a 44 per cent chance of surviving one tour of operations (30 missions), but less than a 20 per cent chance of surviving two.

An avoidable accident

'In the year when I was going on to Mosquitoes, we were still flying Blenheims non-operationally. It was April 1st at 11 in the morning, and I was on a navigational trip with my navigator. There happened to be a rather stupid Beaufighter pilot who saw me and pretended that I was an enemy. He made a mock attack on me, which I knew nothing about until I realised my aeroplane was falling out of the skies. What had happened was that he had hit the tail fin, and the rudder and the elevators and ailerons had come off. I proceeded to go into a steep dive, but unfortunately my navigator couldn't get out. All I could do was stand up in the cockpit and somehow managed to get the canopy away from me. I couldn't get out of the pilot's seat, so I pulled the parachute. Now a parachute

has a small parachute which opens first, and it got out of the cockpit and then dragged the big parachute and finally me. As I went out I hit the rest of the tailplane, was concussed, broke an arm and a leg and finished up in a tiny little river, 12 feet across. I must have got out at 600 feet.

I shouted for help and two Land Army girls came along and hauled me ashore. All I remember was wanting to have a cigarette, and when I got them out they were completely wet. It gave me nearly a year in hospital. My navigator was killed. In the Blenheim the navigator had to get out through the floor, and he must have had the same difficulty I was having. I think the pilot of the other plane that hit me was court-martialled.'

Peter Swan, Bomber Command pilot

Women radio operators working at a Bomber Command station. This was a demanding and sometimes demoralising task. 'Mine had been the last voice they heard – would ever hear,' wrote the operator Pip Beck about the fatal crash of a returning bomber. 'I felt shaken and sick.'

Women took over many jobs on the bomber bases, including loading bombs into aircraft, driving the crews in station buses to and from their aircraft and, as seen here, performing engineering work on the aircraft themselves. A handful of women pilots were also employed ferrying four-engined bombers from factories to airfields.

All aircrew completed their training with long cross-country flights at night, which produced hazards of their own if the bombers were not clearly identified as friendly. The final training exercises tried to simulate the conditions of an attack with searchlights and an illuminated target, but even that can have borne little resemblance to the real conditions of combat to which new crews were cautiously introduced when they arrived at the squadrons.

Operational Training took a heavy toll of the apprentice crews. Problems of adjusting to different weather and terrain, the difficulties of flying at night, the complexity of heavier aircraft, all contributed to a succession of accidents. Over the course of the war 5,327 were killed in training (some 10 per cent of all Bomber Command deaths) and a further 3,113 injured. Flying always carried a large element of risk, and the high casualty rate in training brought home to new aircrew the fragile nature of their occupation.

After a period of up to 18 months the volunteer airmen finally reached the squadrons. Novice crews were given easier assignments wherever possible, but they also found themselves sent out on urgent operations with little flying experience at the station. Crews came together by chance rather than design. Assembled together in a hangar, the aircrew chose each other with little or no knowledge about the skills or character of the team they joined. As the war went on, the high casualty rate meant that crews seldom

stayed together for long. Those who survived from crashed crews were slotted in with others that had also suffered losses. In air warfare unit cohesion was difficult to maintain.

Once Bomber Command crews joined operational units they were faced with one of the most hostile and dangerous combat environments of the war. Unlike the men of the other services, or indeed of the other Air Commands, the men of Bomber Command were asked night after night 'to go over the top'. The dangers they faced came from every quarter. Accidents were routine with the large numbers of bombers on the runways and in the bomber streams. Once in the air the crew faced the hazards of high flying. Cold was the chief enemy, and frostbite one of the main causes of non-combat casualties. Efforts were made to improve temperature levels with electrically heated suits, but they were cumbersome to wear and prone to technical hitches. At high levels the loss of pressure could produce the 'bends' – acute muscular distress – and shortages of oxygen. Damage to the oxygen supply in combat could be fatal as pilots and crew blacked out or suffered severe dizziness. Flying large aircraft in the early 1940s was an exceptional endurance test. Flights could last for up to ten or a dozen hours, with no rest and little refreshment.

Over the battlefield itself the crew faced their severest test. From the moment the bombers approached the enemy coast they were exposed to a barrage of anti-aircraft fire. By

Armstrong Whitworth Whitleys are loaded with bombs. Whitleys performed the first of the futile leaflet-dropping missions over Germany in September 1939 and were the first RAF aircraft to bomb Italy in June 1940. After withdrawal from Bomber Command the type was used by Coastal Command and some were converted to drop paratroops.

1944 over 55,000 heavy and light anti-aircraft guns defended Germany. Around heavily defended targets in the Ruhr, or over Berlin, the barrage was intense. From the ground, searchlights sought out an identifiable aircraft so that it could be caught in a cone of light and shot down by anti-aircraft fire or fighters. Flare shells illuminated the sky to help fighters fix on to their prey. Night-fighters tracked the bombers using sophisticated radar equipment, attacking them where they were most vulnerable and the fighter least visible. Over the target area the bomber crews risked collision with the stream of bombers around them in the dark, or even the danger of being hit by the bombs from another aircraft. On the return trip night-fighters and anti-aircraft fire accompanied the aircraft back to the coast of Europe. For many aircraft, severely damaged over Germany, the flight back to base was a constant battle against fire or technical failure, and the grim prospect of a crash landing.

Casualties were high, but the surprising thing is how many crews and planes returned to the air stations from each mission, albeit drained and exhausted, their adrenalin spent. They were greeted with breakfast and de-briefing – usually, but not always, in that order. Each crew reported on their raid, the hazards they experienced, their own estimate of accuracy and bomb damage. They would then stand down and return to the routine of station life. They would not normally be asked to fly again that evening. After a particularly harrowing or dangerous raid, crew were given a brief period of furlough, but a day, or days, later they would be in the air again.

Early on in the war the Command settled on a figure of 200 hours of combat as the standard first tour of operations, after which aircrew would expect a period of six months with an Operational Training Unit, before returning for a second tour. In practice the crews came to see 200 hours as equivalent to 30 missions, and expected to be released from operations after that.

Airmen asleep in the mess at a Bomber Command station. Airmen found themselves constantly forced to adjust to periods of inactivity and relaxation after brief but intense operations in the air, exposed to exceptional dangers.

Preparing for a daylight operation

'You were called quite early in the morning. You went through the usual routine. We would go to a briefing first. The navigators would start off with a pre-briefing so that they could draw up their charts. When all was done the main briefing was held in the station cinema. The station commander and the wing commander would come in and go through their routine. The curtains would be drawn back and the route would be on the map behind them. It was the first time most people in the hall had seen it. The further it went, the worse people liked it. We didn't much like going to Nuremberg, or other places that were a long way.

Then there would be a briefing by the Intelligence officers, and a briefing on the raid itself – how many aircraft would be taking part, who would be coming from where, the heights and the timings. Last there would be the Met briefing, in which we were told what to expect over the target, and what to expect when we got home. Finally the station commander or the wing commander would get up and say a few words along the lines that we had not done too well last time, or the aiming point photographs had not been very satisfactory.

We would go and get changed. Then the crew buses would come round, and we would all pile in. The bus took you out to your aeroplane where the pilot and engineer checked all the bits and pieces. I laid out all my navigation materials. Everyone smoked in those days. There would be a last cigarette and then the time came to clamber into the aeroplane. We all started up at a certain time, and you could see all the aircraft gathering from all around the airfield. It was a very impressive sight.'

Sir John Curtiss, Bomber Command navigator

Soviet officers visiting a Bomber Command base. The Soviet regime was keen on the bombing offensive, but would allow very little direct help to western air forces. Reciprocal visits to Soviet bases by British airmen were vetoed.

Superstitions

'Rituals, and superstitions. I prayed a lot, I prayed always before I went on operations. We had our talisman. We took all the WAAF parachute packers out for a pie and a pint, and a little WAAF very kindly and very sweetly got out her purse and gave me a Victorian bun penny, one of the very old coins with Victoria when she was young, with the bun of hair at the back. It had a hole in it. She said, "Here, take this as a lucky charm for the future", which I did, and I always flew with it. My uncle gave me a silver cigarette case, and I never failed to fly without that too. I always kept mine in my breast pocket, over my heart. This was very much a superstition.

I and many of my friends had girlfriends' stockings too. When you flew you had a white pullover, but you were not allowed to wear a collar and tie because the collars in those days were detachable, and if you went in the water the clothing might shrink and suffocate you. So everybody had gay coloured scarves, be they old school scarves, or girlfriends' stockings, which you wore round your neck. There were lots of teddy bears, even teddy bears in flying kit, and things made by wives or girlfriends.'

Harry Le Marchant, Bomber Command observer

A Lancaster Mk I of No 467 Squadron, Royal Australian Air Force, from Waddington, Lincolnshire, seen on a friendship visit to a base of the US 8th Air Force in early 1945. Relations between the two forces were generally cordial, although a strong sense of rivalry persisted beyond the end of the war.

After a raid

'Most people lit a cigarette. You waited for the crew bus to come and take you to the interrogation and debriefing session. The CO of the station and everyone else was there asking you questions, making out the report on the effectiveness or otherwise of the raid. What were the defences like, and similar questions. Your main feeling was to get that part of it over and get back, have a meal and get to bed. Having got to bed, you couldn't sleep because you could still hear the engines and you were really wound up. I never slept after an operation, by which time it was daylight anyway. You couldn't sleep in the daytime, you were just so highly strung. You tried to calm down, but you had to let off steam to calm down. Possibly the next day you would not be flying. You would have a number of beers and get yourself into the state where you could go to sleep. That was how you got over it. You were just glad to have got back and survived.'

John Gee, Bomber Command pilot

Left: Each station had its own pigeon farm and carrier pigeons were carried aboard the bombers, to be released in an emergency with details of the bomber's position. Some aircrew shot down over the North Sea owed their lives to this apparently primitive communications system, which could alert rescue aircraft to their position.

Below: Two officers on horseback exercise across the airfield at Dishforth in Yorkshire, passing an Armstrong Whitworth Whitley Mk V.

For Pathfinder pilots, whose job was in many ways the most arduous in the whole campaign, the tour length was 45 missions. The chances of surviving a whole tour were poor. By 1942 the Command calculated that aircrew on heavy bombers had a 44 per cent chance of making it through the first tour, but less than 20 per cent chance of surviving a second. During 1943 these odds fell even further as Bomber Command began its systematic attack of German cities. Only 17 per cent might expect to complete one tour, and 2.5 per cent a second.

Loss rates such as these would have eliminated the whole force several times. In fact, of the 125,000 who served in the Command, over the war some 55,000 died in combat or in accidents, a loss of 36 per cent of all flying crew. There were periods in the war when loss rates were exceptionally high – the battles in 1940, the attacks on German cities in the winter of 1943/4 – and other periods when they were much lower. By 1944, when the Luftwaffe

was pushed back to the point of defeat, the chances of survival were much improved.

Terrible though the levels of casualty were, they were not unique to Bomber Command. At the time that it was calculated that 44 per cent of heavy bomber crews would survive one tour, the Air Ministry noted that day-fighter pilots had a 43 per cent chance of survival and night-fighter pilots only 39 per cent. Over the war considerable efforts were made to find ways of improving survival rates. Better training and more efficient crews contributed to survival, and the coming of the long-range fighter also helped. Navigational aids not only helped crews to find the right target, but also reduced losses in operational training or on the long haul back from a combat mission. Nevertheless the very nature of the bombing war, with its relatively small numbers engaged in an almost continuous attrition war against the German war effort, made high loss rates inevitable.

This Mosquito of No 109 Squadron at Marham, Norfolk, is in the process of conversion for Pathfinder duties. This included the addition of the most recent navigation equipment, H2S.

Above: Unloading boxes of incendiary bombs at a Bomber Command station. An increasing proportion of incendiaries was carried as the campaign continued: in combination with conventional explosive, the incendiaries caused tremendous damage.

Left: The RAF began the Second World War with few bombs larger than 250 pounds, but 500-pound and 1,000-pound bombs became standard, with 4,000-pound 'blockbusters' also widely used. Specially converted Lancasters could carry the special-purpose 12,000-pound 'Tallboy' or the 22,000-pound 'Grand Slam' bombs.

Right: Bombing up a Lancaster of No 463 Squadron at Waddington, Lincolnshire. Winter weather added to the difficulties of keeping heavy bombers flying night after night. Maintenance was harder and accidents more common.

Below: Lancasters on the snow. At least Bomber Command had the advantage of better weather forecasting than the German defenders. By 1943 most German weather ships in the Atlantic had been intercepted and German air bases had less warning of an incoming weather front.

A Hampden Mk I of No 50 Squadron is bombed up at Waddington. The weather conditions made little difference to Bomber Command operations; its aircraft flew on 71 per cent of all nights during the war and 59 per cent of all days.

The Armstrong Whitworth Whitley Mk V could carry 7,000-pounds of bombs, 4,000 in the bomb bay and 1,500 in bomb cavities in the wings. This example belonged to No 51 Squadron in October 1941.

Above: Maintenance Command was established in March 1938 as a separate organisation. The work was carried out by 40, 41, 42 and 43 Groups. Between 1942 and 1945, 13,778 bombers were damaged on operations and all aircraft required re-servicing at intervals. Nearest to the camera here is a Lancaster from No 44 Squadron.

Right: A Lancaster seen at the point of take-off. 'I was shit-scared every operation,' admitted one veteran, 'but I don't think it ever showed. It didn't interfere with my performance…'

The vital contribution of the Handley Page Halifax has been overshadowed by its more famous contemporary the Lancaster. There was some prejudice against the type, stemming partly from the disappointing performance of the early versions like this Halifax Mk II of No 78 Squadron. The later radial-engined versions were a dramatic improvement.

The crews of No 199 Squadron at Lakenheath in Suffolk assembled for a pre-operation briefing. Airmen changed crews a number of times, unless they were particularly fortunate. 'The crew formed the focal point,' recalled a veteran navigator, 'the nucleus, the sense of belonging.'

Crews from No 218 Squadron at Mildenhall in Suffolk are briefed for a raid. Many men became superstitious to cope with the strain, performing particular rituals before entering the aircraft, or carrying a talisman on operations.

A Piper Cub Coupé communications aircraft seen under the wing of a Halifax Mk II bomber, which is being serviced by ground crew.

Left: Final days – a Lancaster of No 149 Squadron at Juvincourt in France, May 1945. The Lancaster continued in service after the Second World War, particularly in the Middle East. A civil airliner version was developed and Lancasters helped to carry out a thorough aerial mapping of northern and eastern Africa.

Below: Fuel is pumped into the wing tanks of a Vickers Wellington and bombs lie on trolleys ready to be hoisted in. The Wellington served not only with Bomber Command but with the Fleet Air Arm and Coastal Command against the submarines and German minefields.

Above: A bomber crew arrive at the moment of departure. They were commonly driven out by WAAFs. 'You never asked where they were going,' recalled one former driver, 'because a secret could get out if there were any spies around.'

Right: 'It was not unknown for a crew to go missing,' wrote a WAAF after the war. 'They just disappeared and we never heard their fate ... lost in endless blackness.' Here a group of airmen wait for the return of the crews from an operation.

Left: Navigator Ted Sismore lights up next to his aircraft. 'You always got to the aeroplane 10 to 15 minutes too soon… Most of us lit a cigarette. It was a way of filling those few moments.'

Below: One of the Lancaster Mk BIII (Special) aircraft converted for the Dams Raid in May 1943. The hand-picked crews for the raid trained from March with blue-tinted windows and yellow goggles to simulate conditions of bright moonlight.

Right: Radio control operators at a Bomber Command station. Pip Beck, a veteran WAAF from whose collection this photograph is taken, found herself having to listen for the return of the man who had asked to marry her: 'When he was flying and I was on duty, I would listen on the R/T, willing them back.'

Below: A sergeant air-crew enjoying a post-operation breakfast. One veteran recalled how it felt to return to base after a raid: 'Most people lit a cigarette... Your main feeling was to have a meal and get to bed...'

A North American B-25 Mitchell in RAF colours flies over camouflaged barrack blocks. Designed in 1938 and in production by February 1941, the B-25 became the standard medium bomber of the US air forces and also served with the RAF and Russian Army.

The effect of losses on the crews became part of the daily strain of the bombing war. On every operation one or two, or more, aircraft would fail to return to each station. Airmen coped in different ways. A great many carried good luck charms or a talisman of some kind. Chapels were available on the stations. Many airmen developed a gallows humour to cope with the constant fear of death. The bombers were decorated with their own symbol or motif. Bombs were routinely scrawled upon before loading into the bomb bays. There was no way of disguising the risks the aircrew ran every night. Heavy drinking was allowed between operations, and young airmen, freed temporarily from the tensions of combat, were notoriously high-spirited, even violent. The periods between operations were especially tense as airmen wound down from the strain of the flight only in the knowledge that they would have to repeat it all again within days. The greatest strain came in the hours just before operations, as the air crews were briefed for the target and waited, tense with expectation, for the order to embark. When operations were cancelled for any reason commanders observed a sharp fall in station morale. Once the crews knew that they were to fly, they hoped to start as soon as possible. Once in the air the drama of the flight took over.

The great strains placed on the crews of Bomber Command took their toll. Morale was always a major concern, and the Command leaders were well aware of the exceptional demands they made of their men. There were inevitably psychological casualties as well as physical. Even the most courageous flyer could find the constant strain hard to endure, and the longer a flyer survived the greater the strain became. Over the period from 1942 to 1945 the RAF classified 8,402 men as suffering from some form of neurosis, of whom only about one-third came from Bomber Command. Lesser cases were dealt with at the stations, where an extended period of leave or a temporary posting to ground duties reduced the condition.

In addition to personnel from the Commonwealth, airmen from several Allied nations joined Bomber Command. These Polish crew are fitting a Vickers 'K' gun to the turret of a Whitley bomber. A total of 749 Polish aircrew were killed or posted missing presumed killed while flying with Bomber Command during the war.

Left: The undercarriage of this Consolidated B-24 Liberator collapsed on landing. Over 3,200 of Bomber Command's aircraft were damaged in accidents between 1942 and the end of the war.

Below left: The epitome of a British airman. Flying Officer L. A. Cox poses in full operational dress plus pipe. The crew of bomber aircraft possessed a popular glamour denied to most of the other services, but the reality of bomber operations was anything but glamorous.

Below: Ground crew examine the damage to an Avro Manchester Mk IA of No 61 Squadron after a raid on the German battleships Scharnhorst and Gneisnau in Brest. The intensity of British air attacks drove the Germans to withdraw these heavy units back to their home waters.

Right: This Lancaster Mk III of No 619 Squadron was forced down at Rinkaby in Sweden on January 14th 1945. Some pilots deliberately flew over neutral territory, but most Bomber Command aircraft that landed in Sweden or Switzerland did so because of damage. Of the 13 bombers that landed in Switzerland, 12 were badly hit and half of the 64 that landed in Sweden were damaged or destroyed.

Below: This veteran Wellington Mk IC on its way for repair was damaged while flying with No 75 Squadron. It survived to enjoy a further career with an Operational Training Unit.

No writing home

'When the flight crews arrived in the Mess you got an idea from their general behaviour and attitude how long they would last. We would bet among ourselves – "Oh, he'll make it" or "He won't make it". Sitting in a corner writing home was not the sort of thing the average chap did. There were too many things to do to worry about your mother. The young marrieds were the ones who suffered most. We just enjoyed ourselves in our free time. We loved flying. There were sadder times, if a crew didn't return. One night we lost three aeroplanes, 21 people. There was the ritual of moving their kit from the room. Not 24 hours later, or even less, a truck would come through the gates with the new crews to replace those lost. They would come into the Mess where those who had been on the Squadron for a month or two were considered old hands.

I don't think we worried about it at the time. We had a job to do. Our role was flying aeroplanes to do whatever we could for the war effort. Of course, one never got to know people for any length of time. On the Squadron we knew that it was short-lived, that we would move on if we survived to the end of our tour. When people arrived you would look at them and you either took to them or you didn't like them. We sorted out our friends, and were not concerned with the others. The loners, the ones who sat writing letters home, these were the ones that didn't seem to last. The ones who enjoyed life, who seemed a bit juvenile at times, survived.

My best friend on the Squadron survived with me. There were others that I knew very well who were killed. That was Mess life, Squadron life. It was an odd feeling. I could look back and think I was very hard, people were hard, but they weren't really. It was a matter of accepting it. This is what happened in war.'

Maurice Chick, Bomber Command Pathfinder pilot

Three airmen pose in the snow at their base. Relaxation time was short but cherished. 'Eating, flying and sleeping were the main things in squadron life,' remembered one veteran. 'There seemed to be very little time for any sort of social life.'

Life on the station

'We had our normal stand-down days, when we knew that operations were not on and we had a free evening. In those days there was not a lot to do. We were in stations that were normally miles from anywhere. There was invariably a local pub somewhere nearby. Apart from those who wanted to play bridge or poker, we would all wander down to the pub. Beer was rationed, but the landlord would look kindly on us as he knew where we had come from. We would have our usual two or three pints. On occasion we had Mess parties and high jinks were had by all. We had one game where one of us stood with their back to the wall while the others crouched down in a long line. You would run as fast as you could and leap on to the backs of these people. We had two teams and would probably get six or eight large men on the backs of 10 or 12 people before the whole thing collapsed. Enough beer was taken beforehand to make it enjoyable for everybody. I remember another occasion on which the Mess tables and chairs were piled into a pyramid in the centre of the anteroom. One person, with blackened feet from the soot from the fireplace, would climb to the top and put his footmarks on the ceiling, along the wall and disappearing into the chimney.

On returning from a flight the younger ones would get down to some serious drinking. They would sit at the bar and discuss the night before. Occasionally we had an expert at the piano and we would stand around and sing the songs of the day until the late afternoon, probably three, four or five hours. Then we would go to bed. There was one of us who used to take his dog on operational flights with him, against all the rules and regulations. Just once he didn't take it and he went missing. The dog was in a terrible state. It had gone out on to the airfield and just would not come back. He knew his master was gone.'

Maurice Chick, Bomber Command pilot

'On your night off you didn't waste time thinking about operations, you just wondered who was going to buy the next round.'

A Bomber Command crew relaxes on a beach on the East Anglian coast. Friendships could be hard to sustain: 'I often wondered how the civilians looked at us,' said one survivor. 'We used to make sure we enjoyed ourselves… What was the use of a roll of banknotes in your pocket. You spent and you drank.'

Between peace and war

'I don't think anyone in history has been required to fight such a war as the Bomber Command crewman. He was fighting, but he didn't see the effect of his blows, he seldom felt the effects of his enemy's blows, or if he did it was sudden death. Then in the morning you all break up with the coming of dawn, go back to your airfields and say, "Well, that's it for another night".

You would report to your air crew station, go to bed, get up about 11 o'clock and report into flights about 2 o'clock. If you were lucky enough you had that evening off. We used to do about two on, two off, or two on, one off. If you were on again it was just a repeat of the previous night's routine, but if you were off then you got your little banger out, or your friend's banger, and went down to Cambridge and reinserted yourself into civilian life. It was a strange atmosphere. I often wonder how the civilians looked upon us because we used to make sure that we enjoyed ourselves. It wasn't worth saving money. What was the use of a roll of banknotes in your back pocket if you were going off again tomorrow night? You spent and drank.

There were one or two saints among us, but not many. To the civilians standing alongside us at the bar we must have looked a very strange bunch. Many of them said they envied us the camaraderie we had. We also used to meet American 8th Air Force crew in the local bars in Cambridge. We had a little harmless enmity between us. They would, of course, have the best-looking girls because they had the most money, but we had the best-looking aircraft. We made sure on the next day on the night-flying test that we went over towards the American fields until you could find a Fortress in the air somewhere. You would stalk it, make sure you had about 5,000 feet above him and then you would dive past him making sure that you feathered an engine on his side so that he would be chugging along in his Fortress and see a Lancaster go sailing past with one engine feathered on his side. That was great fun.'

Rod Rodley, Bomber Command pilot

An American invasion

'The next Americans arrived in Flying Fortresses! Forty-nine of them. They were diverted to Barford on their way back from a daylight op because their base at Podington in Northants was closed in bad weather. It was an incredible sight as one after another the B17s came in. I thought they were never going to stop. Eventually, they were dispersed all around the airfield... I was making tea, so started giving cups of tea to the Americans as they came up feeling that they must need it. But soon I ran out of tea and could do no more. The Met girls from downstairs produced another supply but that was rapidly exhausted. There were Americans crowding out Control, in the Met Office, sitting wearily on the stairs, and sitting outside, men in leather jackets and flying boots, hung about with flying gear.

There were nearly 500 men... I asked the pilot if we could go and look at their aircraft. Several of them said they'd be happy to "show us around", and we went to look at, and in, it. It was named after a popular song of the 1930s – "I'll get by".

We were given handfuls of candies and gum – each of the crew gave us the remainder of their candy rations, and pockets and hands were filled. Another of the crew – the tall navigator – took out a Met Report card, and got the rest of the crew to autograph it. He wrote, "A swell bunch of people, you English – thanks for everything".

Next day trucks with their own ground crew arrived, and they swarmed around the B17s, getting them ready for departure. Later, their aircrews were driven out to their aircraft and soon, one by one, they lined to take off. This was another enthralling spectacle as the first big aircraft became airborne, then the next – and the next – and the next – all 49. When they had all departed, the ground crews left and the station, from heaving and buzzing with activity and noise, was strangely quiet. Everything was rather flat after our American invasion.'

Pip Beck, Bomber Command WAAF
(from *A WAAF in Bomber Command*, Goodall Publications, London, 1989, pp 159-60)

Boeing B-17 'Flying Fortresses' head for Germany. Like Bomber Command, the US 8th Air Force suffered terrible losses in its early daylight raids until long-range fighters could accompany them. Camouflage was of little value to four-engined bombers in mass formations, and polishing the airframe added a few precious miles per hour.

A Royal Visit

'When I was in 114 Squadron on Blenheims in the summer of '41 at West Raynham the King and Queen paid a visit to the station in the middle of an intense operational period. Our Station Commander, Lord Bandon, was a friend of the King and he had been at Sandringham, which was nearby, staying the night and duck shooting.

At 8 o'clock in the morning on the way to London the King and Queen paid a visit. I was a Flight Commander at the time (I went from Pilot Officer to Squadron Leader in six weeks due to the casualties) and each Flight Commander had to take first the King and then the Queen and present their flight to them, all lined up in the crew room, one flight down one side, one flight down the other. We had all been very strictly briefed that the only thing we said when the King or Queen offered us their hand was "How do you do, Sir" or "How do you do, Ma'am" and nothing else. If they asked you a question, you answered it.

I brought the Queen up the line, presenting each one by name, and she took each one by the hand and looked up at these young chaps – none of us was more than 22 – looked up at each one as much as to say "I think you're wonderful". Then to my horror one young Yorkshire Sergeant Air Gunner, a tall rawbone youth, was so overcome that he seized the Queen's hand with both of his and said, "I am so pleased to meet Your Majesty".

I nearly passed out. I thought I'd had it now, but all she did was put her other hand on top of his and say, "No more pleased than I am to meet you, Sergeant, I assure you."

That absolutely made his day, he was on cloud nine. A week later he was dead.'

Charles Patterson, Bomber Command pilot

Princess Elizabeth, the future Queen Elizabeth II, visiting a Bomber Command squadron. Young airmen were ordered to say nothing more than 'How do you do, Ma'am' when Queen Elizabeth, now the Queen Mother, came to visit.

Nose art on two Stirling Mk IIIs of No 199 Squadron at Lakenheath in Suffolk. Most aircraft were decorated with their own unique motif and a record of their operations.

Maurice Chick (standing centre, with moustache) with flying crew and ground crew of his Lancaster bomber 'The Saint'. Chick survived the whole war.

A much smaller proportion were classified under the unfortunate term Lack of Moral Fibre (LMF). This broad category included the very small minority whose morale did crack completely under the strain, and who were removed from the force, as well as those whose courage was never in doubt but who, like the shell-shock victims of the First World War, were psychologically incapable of continuing in combat. It was an evident injustice that they carried with them the stigma of LMF classification, but the Air Ministry failed to provide a broader range of categories for psychological disablement, or sufficient psychiatric care to ensure that men who had suffered extraordinary levels of trauma could be nursed back to psychological health, and to the Command. It is remarkable how small a number did give in to the strain. Over the war an estimated 200 cases a year were classified as LMF, or slightly less than 0.4 per cent of all bomber crews.

The aircrew of Bomber Command found and gave a remarkable courage in everything they did. They were, of course, volunteers. The operational crews were the elite of the force, and during training those who were clearly not up to the severe demands they would face were weeded out and confined to ground duties. The great army of technicians, armourers, officials, nurses and caterers, though some carried a higher rank than the fliers, fought a very different war, bound by the routines of station life. However, this was an existence not without its own dangers. Airfields were subjected to air attack early in the war. The handling of large quantities of armament, day in, day out, produced a string of fatal accidents. Crashes at base were frequent. The station personnel were also able to see more clearly than the crews the effects of a persistently high casualty rate. They played an important part in maintaining the morale of the airmen who passed through the squadrons, and were occasionally rewarded with telegrams from Harris who regularly acknowledged the part they played.

Nonetheless, medals and awards went largely to the fighting force. Over the war the RAF awarded 20,000 Distinguished Flying Crosses, for officers, and 6,600 Distinguished Flying Medals for non-commissioned aircrew. Any crewman who completed a 30-mission tour was likely to qualify for an award. Exceptional acts of bravery were recognised by the Distinguished Service Order or by the Victoria Cross. The highest award for bravery went to 23 Bomber Command airmen, but most were awarded posthumously. Those who survived, like the pilot William Reid who, though severely wounded, carried on to bomb his target, became national heroes.

The sergeants' mess at Lakenheath, seen in April 1944.

'The Rhodesians were so unmistakably not English,' wrote a WAAF who worked with them. 'Their independence and disregard for the finer points of discipline were a by-word on the camp.' Here, No 44 (Rhodesia) Squadron celebrate Christmas at RAF Waddington in Lincolnshire.

An official march-past to honour William Reid, winner of the Victoria Cross for his bravery in continuing to fly his aircraft on to attack the target despite severe wounds.

A WAAF's day

'We were asked to drive anything and everything. We had a licence to drive vehicles up to 3 tons. We did crew coaches, taking the crews out to the aircraft. I was an ambulance driver for some of the time. Sometimes we would be asked to drive a staff car with a high-ranking officer, sometimes the ration wagon, when you drove round to all the different Messes. We did a lot of crew coaches, which we all liked because we would chat to the fellas.

We would get up about 7, unless we had been on night duty. Over to the Mess for breakfast and then to your Motor Transport section. If you had a vehicle allotted to you, you would then have an inspection. We also had to do 500- and 1,000-mile inspections. I don't know how I got through that. I used to get one of the chaps to help me.

We used to get leave, but we were always glad to get back. I used to get bored after a while. We had ten days leave four times a year, and I always wanted to go back after five days seeing the family and being home. We were really like a lot of kids. We were all very young. Most of us were teenagers.

There was a dark side of it. When you picked up crews and took them out you never discussed where they were going. They were very good at hiding their feelings, and we all tried to take our cue from them. We didn't want to admit that this was life and death. I think they would not have shown anything, but it must have been there, the fear. I always found that if you picked them up after they had been over they were very quiet. They were very tired but so quiet. I look back now and I feel so, I can cry now about things more than I did then.'

Eileen Richards, Bomber Command WAAF

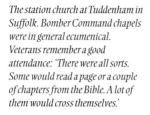

The station church at Tuddenham in Suffolk. Bomber Command chapels were in general ecumenical. Veterans remember a good attendance: 'There were all sorts. Some would read a page or a couple of chapters from the Bible. A lot of them would cross themselves.'

You had to have luck

'We were all volunteers. Nobody was forced to fly. Their own ego and self-esteem kept them flying. If they did turn and run they were treated as lacking in moral fibre and dealt with in various ways. I'm sure that during a tour of operations everybody at some time or other had that fear and would willingly have given up, but they didn't. They went on. At the height of the bomber operations a great many would not survive the first 30 operations. They knew that every night some were not going to come back. Sometimes it would be two or three aircraft from a squadron, maybe sometimes five, maybe only one, sometimes none. We knew the chances that some were not going to come back.

The WAAF officers and the WAAFs who had done the parachutes and bombed up the aircraft would come down to the runways and wave us off. It was all very emotional, but it was part of life. You just had to do it. We knew that if we did not, we would be letting ourselves and the squadron down. I was just lucky. You had to have luck. There was a certain amount of skill, but you had to have luck. Otherwise you didn't survive.'

John Gee, Bomber Command pilot

Members of No 342 (Lorraine) Squadron of the Free French air force attend mass in the station chapel in Hampshire. The French pilots flew the American Douglas A-20 Havoc light bomber, designated the 'Boston' by the RAF. The type had originally been ordered for the French air force before the war.

Life on base

'Whenever possible I got out of parades, which I detested. I suppose Pay Parade was the only one I did not make strenuous efforts to avoid. Shift workers had a definite advantage when it came to either being on duty or sleeping after night duty. In the morning, knowing that an inspection would take place around 11.00 hrs, we would put a notice on our door that said "Please do not disturb – sleeping after night duty", which gave us considerable satisfaction. Of course, we had to be in bed; sometimes the door would open gently and we knew someone was checking that we really were sleeping.

Periodically FFI inspections were carried out – "Free From Infection" – at WAAF Sick Quarters. This was a basic medical inspection of skin and hair to make sure we were clean and free of lice. We hated it, but appreciated it as a necessary precaution…

We felt Gas Drill too to be a necessary evil. Gas masks and steel helmets were carried at all times… Gas Drill was held in a small hut behind No 1 hangar, and the procedure was for a number of us to be shut inside after a capsule of tear gas had been broken. We wore our respirators, and if anyone felt stinging eyes or was aware of the choking smell, they were unlucky. They had a leaky mask. After a few minutes of this we filed out, removed gas masks, and entered again, one at a time. This ensured that there'd be no doubts in our minds if we were ever unfortunate enough to encounter the gas in reality. After my first experience of the Gas Hut and the mild but unpleasant effects of a whiff of tear gas, I decided the best method of coping with the drill was to take a deep breath before entering, hold it, and once inside close my eyes and rush around and out as quickly as possible. This way the effects were minimal.'

Pip Beck, Bomber Command WAAF
(from *A WAAF in Bomber Command*, Goodall
Publications, London, 1989, pp 46-7)

On the runway

'I was posted to my first station in Suffolk straight from my driving course in Morecambe. I'd never seen an aerodrome before. The sergeant from the Motor Transport said, "Right, you can go on night duty because we need a night duty driver". In those days they had a cardboard disc over the headlights, so that the light went down rather than up. There was complete darkness because of the blackout. The aerodrome was quite foreign to me. I'd never seen planes on the ground before. While it was still light I had to take the flight mechanics from their Mess up to the flight, which was quite a way out on the aerodrome. It was dark when I took them back and I asked how I was to find my way back. They told me to go between the lights of the perimeter track until I reached the control tower. I set off, and I thought the lights were rather brighter than when I came. I drove along between them, in a 15 hundredweight truck. It seemed very wide, and the lights very bright. Then suddenly I heard a roar, and I realised that a Stirling aircraft was about to take off and I was driving straight up the runway towards it. I pulled the vehicle over on to the grass verge and drove along over bumps until I came to a stop. My heart was thumping. The aircraft took off and I got back to flying control. The officer was waiting for me and absolutely tore me off a strip. He told me I was on a charge. I told him I didn't know what I was doing.

"You must know you don't go up the runway," he replied.

I told him I didn't even know what a runway was. He asked me how long I had been here, and I told him I had only arrived this morning. He asked who had put me on duty, and the sergeant was torn off a strip. I wasn't on a charge, but for me and the crew it could have been fatal.'

Eileen Richards, Bomber Command WAAF

Above left: Three WAAFs from the meteorological office at RAF Waddington pose by a bomber.

Above: Back from the raid on the Zeiss works at Jena, the crew of the RAF film unit's Mosquito. Left to right: Flt Sgt Leigh Howard, Charles Patterson (pilot) and Wing Cdr R. W. Reynolds DSO, DFC who was wounded by flak during the operation.

A Polish Wellington is bombed up for another raid. Note the slogans chalked to the bomb casings: another occasional feature on bomber stations throughout the campaign.

This portrait of a bomber crew was taken in York during 1944 and supplied by a survivor, F. Moss, seated in the centre of the first row.

When the war in Europe ended, Bomber Command was already winding down its organisation. The number of trainees began to decline during 1944, and the Training Units of the Command closed 27 of their 69 airfields before the end of the war. When in May 1945 the war in Europe was won, the greater part of Bomber Command was demobilised. A number of squadrons were earmarked for transfer to the Far East where the war with Japan was also

drawing to a close, but the so-called Tiger Force was still in Europe when the Japanese surrendered in mid-August. Harris spent the remainder of the year winding up the affairs of the wartime command and writing his Commander-in-Chief's despatch on bomber operations, which was delivered to the Air Ministry in December 1945. In the New Year's Honours List he was promoted together with the head of Fighter Command to the title of

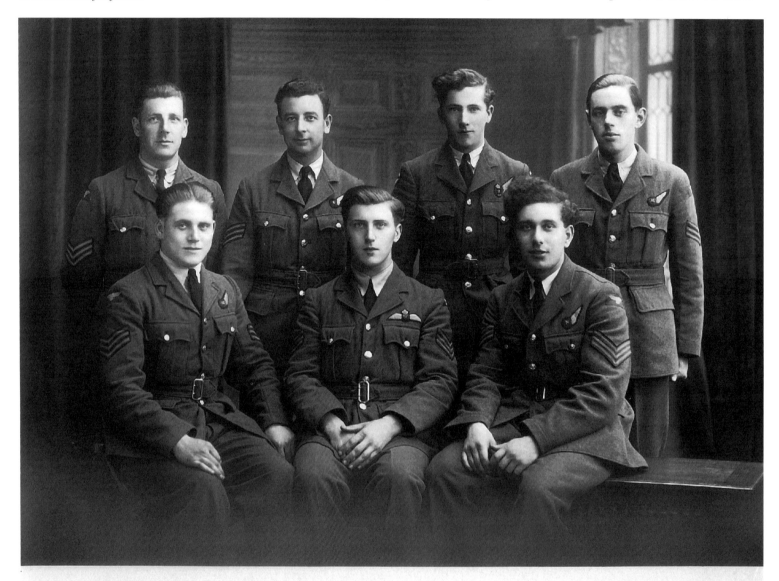

Herbert Speed.   York

F. Fearnley   H.W.Tasker   1944.   L.Webster.   L. Fowler.

S. Hodgson   F.Moss.   R.E. Davenport.

Not so great escape

'After nine months in hospital I was sent to a regular prison camp near Berlin. There were about 200 prisoners in the camp and I was number 182. When I got there some of the boys had started on a tunnel. We worked on it for several months and we got out exactly a year to the day I was shot down, May 10th 1942. Fifty of us got out – 49 were recaptured and one was shot.

We were sent then to Stalag Luft 3, which was the Great Escape camp. The tunnel we had made was 153 feet long, the longest constructed at that time. We had a couple of Canadians who were used to mining and they helped shore up the tunnel with bed boards and that sort of thing. We were all recaptured. I was with a couple of others and was recaptured after ten days. We'd spent most of the time at night jumping trains. We were heading south to Yugoslavia and where one of the three of us had been dropped as a paratrooper and had a radio buried. We pinched what we could from vegetable gardens to live on.

One night we just couldn't get off the train. By the time it slowed down enough for us to jump off it was getting light and we couldn't make our way into really thick cover. German pilot training in the area had been suspended and they had their training aircraft out looking for us. The three of us were lying in a hole in the middle of a field. We heard German farmers ploughing all around us. An aircraft went across and he must have spotted us, because about an hour later a German appeared with a shotgun and just walked to the edge of the hole and told us to get out. There had been quite a bit of feeling generated against Britons in Germany as a result of the raids and we had agreed that if we were picked up, I would just talk French all the time and tell them we were escaped French prisoners. They accepted this, for there happened to be a French prison camp quite close and one or two prisoners had broken out of there. They took us to the French camp and when we were in the hands of the authorities rather than civilians, we revealed our identity and they sent us back to the Luftwaffe camp.'

Alex Kerr, Bomber Command pilot

'An infinity of hope'

'In prisoner-of-war camp you met people of all kinds – lecturers, ordinary working chaps who got into the RAF, dynamic people. There was one who became well-known on the stage afterwards, one who became a Cabinet Minister in the Labour Government. We used to have debates in a big hall. They were marvellous debaters. We put on plays. We got costumes from the Red Cross and put on Girls, Girls, Girls, with chaps dressed up.

My father sent me my Sunday best suit, and on Sundays I would walk round the compound in it. You always walked interminably round this compound; you saw the same wire when you went to bed, when you woke up in the morning. Everything on the other side of the wire seemed to be heaven. It was freedom – you could eat what you wanted, you could go with whom you wanted, you could meet the girl you wanted. There was an infinity of hope. Inside you were limited not only physically, but gradually mentally as well, because you couldn't maintain your dream.

There were so many already there when my batch of prisoners arrived in the middle of Lithuania. Those fellows who had been shot down early in the war hadn't seen a woman for months and months and months. One day a German officer walked by the wire in the other compound with a blonde. The prisoners ran out of the huts from all corners just to watch this blonde go by. I'd only been in the prison camp for about four weeks, and it seemed to me the most unexpected, inexplicable phenomenon, that we were to live like monks.'

Harold Nash, Bomber Command navigator

Marshal of the Royal Air Force. In 1946 he left the air force and emigrated to South Africa. In the 1953 New Year's Honours Churchill made him a baronet.

When the war ended almost 10,000 Bomber Command airmen who had become prisoners-of-war returned to their native countries. Those liberated by Western armies were returned by air to England, where they were de-briefed then sent on, if they were Commonwealth airmen, to the Dominions. Those liberated by the Red Army could, if they were permitted, find their way to American or British lines. The rest were sent on a long journey to the Black Sea port of Odessa, whence they were transported by sea back to Britain. A few airmen who had landed or parachuted into neutral territory in Sweden or Switzerland were returned home from internment.

Bomber Command shrank back to its peacetime strength. The network of airfields and workshops did not disappear entirely, but the wartime communities created around the dozens of air bases soon evaporated. The dead of Bomber Command were buried in thousands of graves spread across the churchyards of eastern England and the air battlefield across northern Europe, and a permanent monument to their sacrifice was raised at Runnymede.

The crews of Bomber Command fought a unique war. They were in contact with the enemy throughout, more often than not in the skies above his home territory. The front line they attacked was heavily defended and continuous, and they attacked it repeatedly. Over the whole war period, Bomber Command was in action on 71 per cent of all nights and 59 per cent of all days. Airmen fought in small units, in which each had a critical individual part to play. For long stretches they were isolated from other crews, fighting their own way across Europe and back. They suffered a high level of casualty and battle fatigue, but they returned from each mission into the incongruously safer world of the home front, where they hovered uncertainly, disarmingly, between peace and war, life and death.

Chapter 5

The balance sheet

The balance sheet on bombing was already being drawn up before the campaign was over. Bombing had always had its critics, even within the RAF. The capture of German-occupied Europe, then the invasion of Germany herself, provided a unique opportunity to assess what bombing had or had not done. In 1944 the American Government set up the United States Strategic Bombing Survey for this purpose, with instructions to examine not only what the American bomber forces had done, but also to look at the damage done by Bomber Command to Germany's economic performance and the morale of her population. The RAF set up a much more modest group to begin Bomber Command's own survey, but this was then superseded by the establishment of the British Bombing Survey Unit staffed by civilian experts as well. The final report of this Unit was drawn up by a young intelligence officer, Hugh Trevor-Roper, who shortly afterwards published his best-selling *Last Days of Hitler*, and went on to become a senior Oxford historian.

The surveys were not kind to Bomber Command. Implicit in the American reports was the criticism that night-time area bombing had done very little at all to dent German war production. Indeed, the evidence accumulated in the first weeks of the American team's activities showed that the greatest achievements of the German economy coincided with the peak of Allied bombing. This discovery led one member of the American Survey, the young economist, John Kenneth Galbraith, to broadcast his own view that bombing had been nothing short of a strategic blunder, costing more to the Allies to mount the campaign than it cost Germany in lost production. If anything, Galbraith suggested, bombing actually stimulated German production and made firmer the resolve of Germany's bombed population.

Galbraith's was by no means the only voice raised in protest. As it became clear that bombing had apparently achieved little before the summer of 1944, and nothing after that to actually decide the outcome of war, the terrible cost in lives and destruction in Germany's cities was seen as an unnecessary evil, the product of a flawed strategy. The survey of German morale conducted by psychologists attached to the American Survey team showed that at no time did morale crack in the sense expected by the advocates of morale-bombing. Materially and morally the

case for bombing evaporated after the war. Even the Bombing Survey Unit's conclusions were lukewarm, and the main report, largely authored by the scientist Solly Zuckerman, was critical, even hostile to the Command. Its conclusions were not widely publicised.

Only Harris stuck to his convictions, sending his official Despatch on Operations in December 1945 to the Air Ministry. In a surprisingly terse survey of the campaign, Harris concluded that under the circumstances his force had done everything that could have been expected. Left to itself bombing could, he argued, have ended the German war as it ended the war with Japan in August 1945.

Who was right? Galbraith or Harris? This is not the place to speculate about whether this target or that target would have ended the war sooner, or made the Command more effective. The place of Bomber Command in the war effort of the British Empire can be assessed only on the record, and critics of bombing have hardly ever looked at the whole of it. From Galbraith onwards the view has taken root that the only thing that Bomber Command did, or was ordered to do, was to attack German cities with indifferent accuracy. The Bombing Surveys devoted most of their effort to measuring the direct physical damage to German war production through city-bombing. This has produced since the war a narrow economic interpretation of the bombing offensive that distorts both the purposes and nature of Britain's bombing effort to an extraordinary degree.

To understand the contribution made by Bomber Command it is necessary to go back to basic strategy. It was the task of the Command to provide the bombing component of the RAF. Part of that bombing effort was intended to be directed at the enemy's military and economic structures on the home front if Germany attacked civilian targets indiscriminately. From May 1940 onwards this aim was present in almost all Air Ministry directives to the Command. But a very large part of the bombing effort was devoted to all the other many functions for which bomber aircraft were required. Less than half the bomb tonnage dropped went on the campaign against Germany's industrial cities, and in the later stages of the war many of these attacks were 'tactical', carried out in support of the advancing western and Soviet armies. The rest of the effort went to supporting Allied armies in other

The distinguished American economist John Kenneth Galbraith was a member of the team sent to survey bomb damage in Germany in 1945. His view (see below) that bombing was largely a waste of effort and time laid the foundation for widespread criticism of the campaign over the past 50 years.

theatres of war, where bombers had an important part to play in assisting the land campaign. The war at sea absorbed a great deal of the bomber force for the first three years of war, while during the greater part of 1944 the home-based bomber forces were under the direction of the Allied Supreme Command, to be used in support of the invasion of western Europe. Bombers were used extensively for reconnaissance, for propaganda flights, in support of secret service operations, even for flying relief and aid operations. Bomber Command was a Jack-of-all-trades, so much so that its Commanders-in-Chief had to spend much energy trying to prevent the complete dissipation of their force among all the competing demands for bomber operations.

Bombing must also be understood in the wider context of British, and later Allied, grand strategy. Air power was embraced in Britain, and in the United States, as a way of reducing the horrendous combat losses of the Great War. The memories of the Somme battles of 1916 played their part, as Lord Cherwell once remarked to Roosevelt's Army Chief of Staff, General Marshall. High though the proportion of losses was in Bomber Command, the 55,000 dead over six years of war was a tiny figure compared with the millions who died on the Eastern Front, or in the war in China, or even with the 200,000 casualties

The US Strategic Bombing Survey

'However bitter the disagreements between the USAAF and the RAF on which industrial targets to hit, there was total agreement that much damage was being done to the German war economy. This we in the [United States Bombing] Survey also assumed.

Our first indication that something was wrong came in London before the fighting stopped. It was a superb statistical find, the Statistische Schnellbericht zur Kriegsproduktion or the German statistical overview of war production. The factories producing the guns, tanks, self-propelled guns and assault guns were not a primary target. But they drew on labor, coal, steel, ferro-alloys, machine tools, transportation and all the lesser resources and fabrics of industrial life. A general disruption of the German economy could not be meaningful if it did not affect the production of these items. In 1940, the first full year of the war, the average monthly production of Panzer vehicles was 136; in 1941 it was 316; in 1942, 516. In

1943, after the bombing began in earnest, average monthly production was 1005, and in 1944, it was 1538. Peak monthly production was not reached until December 1944…We were beginning to see that we were encountering one of the greatest, perhaps the greatest, miscalculations of the war…

German war production had, indeed, expanded under the bombing…strategic bombing had not won the war. At most, it had eased somewhat the task of the ground troops who did. The aircraft, manpower and bombs used in the campaign had cost the American economy far more in output that they cost Germany. …The purposes of both history and future policy would have been served by a more dramatic finding of failure, for this would have better prepared us for the costly ineffectiveness of the bombers in Korea and Vietnam, and we might have been spared the reproach of civilized opinion.'

From K.J. Galbraith, *A Life in Our Times: Memoirs*, 1981

The judgement of Harris

'To sum up, it can be said that Bomber Command successfully achieved the tasks allotted to it, notwithstanding the limitations imposed by inadequacy of means. The progressive solution of the numerous outstanding problems eventually brought the force to a state of effectiveness which, had it been available a year or more earlier, would undoubtedly have ended the German war as abruptly as the Japanese war was ended, by concentrated and overwhelming bombing, without the need for an invasion by land forces...when it began to be able to hit hard, it dealt mighty blows at German war production, devastating German industrial cities, and by doing so hampered and reduced the production of every war necessity.

But in addition to all these direct achievements, Bomber Command made a further very great contribution to the Allied victory. To counter the combined bomber offensive the enemy was obliged to employ a most considerable part of his army, navy and air force, and his potential manpower for war production, in a purely defensive role...The fighting power of the Wehrmacht was, according to their Armaments Minister, "considerably weakened" by the diversion...

Another war, if it comes, will be vastly different from the one that has just drawn to a close. While, therefore, it is true to say that the heavy bomber did more than any other single weapon to win this war, it will not hold the same place in the next. The principles will, however, hold true: the quickest way of winning the war will still be to devastate the enemy's industry and thus destroy his war potential. But the means by which that end is achieved will certainly be different from those which were used, with such far reaching effect, to destroy the most powerful enemy we have faced for centuries.'

From Sir Arthur Harris, *Despatch of War Operations*, February 23rd 1942 to May 8th 1945 (October 1945)

suffered by Allied forces in only three months in the invasion of France. For Britain, with its small population and the lack of a large standing army, a small force of specialised volunteers was arguably a more effective way of mobilising British manpower than the development of a large and inexperienced ground army.

Second, the bomber offered Britain an important political and psychological weapon in the early stages of the war. Churchill made it clear that bombing was entered into not just for its probable effects on Germany, whose scale and effectiveness he soon came to doubt, but for its effects on British and world opinion. Bombing was the only way that Britain could signal to potential allies, or those already conquered, that she intended to stay in the war. It had an important effect on American opinion, and on Roosevelt in particular, at a time when there were serious doubts abroad over British resolve to continue the fight against Nazism. Bombing also helped to maintain domestic morale at a low ebb in the war. It was widely and conspicuously reported, and its propaganda value was appreciated by the Home Office and the Ministry of Information, which both played a part in developing the public image of bombing. If this image was often widely at variance with the capabilities of the force, the effect was to give the British public the sense that their country was still actively fighting an enemy whose geographical immunity might otherwise have reduced Britain's role to that of a distant spectator.

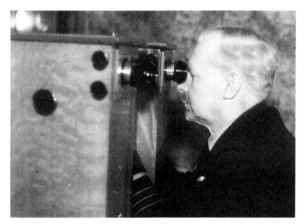

Air Chief Marshal Arthur Harris examining reconnaissance photographs of bomb damage through a viewfinder. Harris ended the policy of drift and uncertainty when he took over in 1942 and restored bombing as a central plank of Allied strategy. He became a forthright defender of Bomber Command as politicians began to distance themselves from bombing plans that they had originally endorsed.

The use of bombing as evidence of Britain's commitment to the war was even more important after the invasion of the Soviet Union in 1941. Stalin's constant complaints about western inactivity were parried by Churchill's insistence that bombing did constitute a 'Second Front' in its own right (a claim that will be examined more closely below). At the least it was a way to demonstrate to both the Soviet and American allies that Britain remained committed to an offensive war. The directives to Bomber Command in the middle years of the war laid special emphasis on the contribution bombing was to make to the Western strategy of gaining re-entry to Continental Europe.

Above: A Lancaster of No 44 Squadron takes off from Dunholme Lodge for an attack on Friederichshafen in June 1943. The Lancaster was the mainstay of the British bombing offensive; its range and lifting power were essential to the strategy set by Harris in 1942, and without them the bombing offensive would have been far less effective.

Right: A total of 1,690 bomber versions of the De Havilland Mosquito were built. Unarmed, it relied on speed and high-altitude performance to escape interception. While four-engined bombers had suffered heavy losses attacking Berlin in 1943, Mosquitoes kept up the attack on the German capital throughout 1944-45.

Left: A total of 7,373 Lancasters were built during the war, more than either the Stirling or the Halifax. They carried a heavier bomb load than either of the US bombers in Europe, the B-17 and B-24.

Below: A Boeing B-17 'Flying Fortress' seen in RAF colours in March 1944. Some 12,677 were built for the US Army Air Force. The USA manufactured an incredible total of 97,810 bomber aircraft during the Second World War.

Detail of the camera fitted in the nose of a Mosquito Mk IV. The high speed of the Mosquito made it a useful photo reconnaissance aircraft.

Mosquitoes were capable of carrying a single 4,000-pound 'cookie', and even the fighter-bomber version could carry 1,500 pounds of ordnance. Mosquitoes carried out a number of daylight raids over Germany in 1942-43, the last one being against the Zeiss optical works in Jena in May 1943.

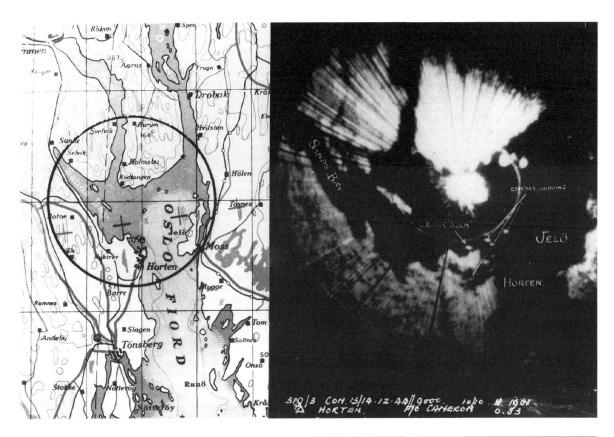

Left and far left: A map and an H2S image of Oslo Fjord taken during an anti-shipping strike. The H2S equipment was introduced into the Command in 1943 but took some time to perfect.

A Halifax going down with its wing fuel tanks ablaze on March 24th 1945. By 1945 loss rates were down to 0.9 per cent, but the hazards of anti-aircraft fire and fighter attack had not disappeared entirely. During the first four months of 1945 some 597 aircraft were lost.

For crews trained on light bombers or twin-engined medium bombers, the transition to the new generation of four-engined aircraft required a period of intensive retraining. These aircrew are training on a Lancaster at a heavy bomber conversion unit. Such units were run down in 1944 and operational training was carried out by front-line squadrons.

The Short Stirling's undercarriage was a known weakness and the cause of a number of landing accidents. This is the aftermath of one such incident at Wyton on June 2nd 1942.

Thus bombing was both strategic and tactical in purpose, pursuing an independent campaign to pave the way for a combined-arms invasion of Hitler's Europe. During the run-up to invasion in June 1944, and for the critical following three months, Bomber Command was at the disposal of the ground commanders and its activities were coupled with the course of the ground assault. Any historical assessment of bombing has to recognise that the Command played a direct part in the military outcome of the war.

Nothing was more central to the achievements of the Combined Bombing Offensive than the defeat of German air power. The German air force was central to the success of German arms in the first three years of war, as an essential element of modern warfare. When the modified Casablanca directive ordered the bombers to concentrate on undermining the German air force as an 'intermediate objective', the circumstances were created for the defeat of German air power, and the result in the spring and summer of 1944 was catastrophic for the German war effort. Direct attacks on German aircraft production, airfields, aircraft in transit, together with the use of long-range fighters to contest German air space, crippled the Luftwaffe. German air power evaporated at the fighting fronts, weakening the military effort everywhere. Albert Speer, Hitler's armaments minister, later reflected in his prison diaries

that this was 'the greatest lost battle on the German side'.

This amounts to an impressive list of strategic objectives beside the direct and indirect effects of the bombing campaign on Germany's economy and morale. It is now time to return to the central issue raised by the critics: what *did* Bomber Command do to the economy and morale of the enemy? The answer to this question goes well beyond the assessments made by the Bombing Surveys of the loss of actual weapons output. The effects of the bombing offensive were both direct and indirect. The latter were in many ways more damaging to Germany's war effort, and they were not unintended. British air leaders recognised that bombing would produce all kinds of secondary effects in Germany in the effort to defend against it, in the general disruption to social and administrative life, and the damage it would do to general levels of social efficiency.

The direct damage was also nonetheless significant. Bomber Command played its part in the campaigns against oil and transport in 1944 and 1945, when German domestic oil production fell from 673,000 tons in January 1944 to 265,000 tons by September, and aviation fuel was reduced temporarily to 5 per cent of requirements. Bomber Command also contributed to the attacks on the aircraft and tank industries, which by January 1945 had produced, according to one contemporary German estimate, a shortfall during 1944 of 35 per cent of

The German port of Hamburg was subjected to a shattering assault from July 24th-29th 1943 when Bomber Command attacked by night and the US 8th Air Force by day. More than 40,000 people were killed and 70 per cent of the city destroyed.

armoured vehicles and 31 per cent of aircraft, excluding further heavy losses sustained from the effort to distribute aircraft and tanks under almost continuous air attack.

Some of this direct damage was achieved, however, by the American air forces, which were directed at very specific industrial targets. The so-called area bombing campaign contributed, according to another German estimate, about 20 per cent of the direct production loss. Detailed surveys of bombed cities showed that the loss to infrastructure and utilities from city bombing also played a part in undermining economic performance. In Berlin, where 45 per cent of all industrial and commercial buildings were destroyed – not all of it by bombing – the supply of gas to the city was slowly eroded by bombing. Stocks in gasometers were reduced from 2.25 million cubic metres early in 1943 to 480,000 by March 1944. Random destruction of electricity supply had a similar effect: in 1943 Berlin received 2,297 million kwh, but in 1944 only 1,946 million. The bombing also soaked up very large labour resources. In Berlin an average of 4,000 workers were employed every day in 1942 on repairing bomb damage; in 1943 the figure was 10,000; in 1944 it was 9,000, or the equivalent of 2.7 million working days. Over the whole country in 1944 an estimated 800,000 workers were engaged in essential repair work to communications and factories, with a further 250,000 to 400,000 working to supply the equipment and resources for repair.

City-bombing also forced German industry to adopt a policy of dispersal or de-centralisation. The authorities began this programme in 1942, well before the onset of American bombing. Although dispersal allowed production to continue when the bombing became severe in 1944, it had a number of debilitating effects. It proved highly disruptive to firms that had become highly centralised as a result of efforts to rationalise German war production. Dispersal meant longer hauls between the different premises making an aeroplane and a tank, and area bombing interrupted this delicate net of distribution and supply. Dispersal also meant greater reliance on skilled labour in smaller, less rationalised workshops. Where skilled labour was lacking, new labour was drafted in that was less well-equipped to cope with complex engineering, and the quality of German weapons also declined.

The cathedral at Cologne rises out of the ruins of the city that was the target of the first 1,000-bomber raid in April 1942. Bomber Command attacked it repeatedly thereafter, and by 1945 70 per cent of the residential area was destroyed and the population had shrunk from 770,000 to a mere 20,000.

Left: The ruins of Dortmund in 1945. Like Cologne, the city was in the Ruhr, Germany's industrial heartland, and a prime target for Bomber Command throughout the war. Some 65 per cent of Dortmund's residential area was destroyed.

Below left and below: Aircrew from a shot-down Wellington are buried with full military honours by the Germans. These photographs were given to one of the survivors, rear gunner Harry Jones by the Germans during his captivity. Towards the end of the war popular hostility to the bomber crews or 'terror fliers' was more marked.

The price of freedom

'I never spent much time wondering what was going on down below. I eased my conscience by feeling that the Germans must do what we'd been doing, which was to evacuate non-participants. I never pictured what a bomb could do to a human frame. I'd done my duty, which was to take a load of high explosive to an aiming point laid down by those in authority above me, whom I trusted. If I'd been an imaginative character I might have wondered exactly what happened when those bombs hit, but I merely hoped that I was hitting a factory, or machine tools or something of that ilk. The only way I could have got a picture of the effect of bomb attack on people was to go to the East End of London. I had no great desire to do that.

I was not troubled in my conscience because we were fighting a very ruthless enemy. We all knew this. Our families were home behind us and we were rather like a crusader with his sword in front of them. My thoughts at the time were that I have a family, and a bigger family – the public – and I was going to do my damnedest to stop the Germans coming across. If you go into war you've got to win it, and if you are too weak you suffer the trials and tribulations of being a slave race. Some of our intelligentsia are writing in the peace and warmth of their homes about how wicked the bombing campaign was. They don't realise that they wouldn't have had that freedom to do so if we had not had 55,000 aircrew who lost their lives for their sake.'

Rod Rodley, Bomber Command pilot

German soldiers guard the wreckage of Harry Jones' Wellington bomber. Bomber Command lost a total of 8,325 aircraft during the war.

One of those things that had to be done

'If we had a precision target to hit, that gave us greater satisfaction than just aiming at a point in a big city like Berlin or Cologne. There was no way you could single out a particular factory in Cologne and make sure of hitting it. You had to aim at the aiming point and hope that some of the bombs hit the target. I don't think anyone gave any real thought to the fact that if it was an area raid civilians were going to get killed. It was just our contribution to the war and it had to be done, just another flight. Nobody came up to me to say, "You know, these poor civilians down there are being killed". It just never occurred to us. We'd seen it happen over here. It was not in any way "Here's one for you' or "Have this one back", it was just a way of getting on with the war. It was one of those things that had to be done.

I'm sure the crews of Bomber Command would like to be remembered as having fought a very arduous war, a very difficult war, and having made a significant contribution to it. We are certainly not making any excuses for it, but we would like to be remembered in a different way to the way we are portrayed now by historians as a lot of murderers. We thought that what we did had to be done, we were ordered to do it, and we did it to the best of our ability.'

John Gee, Bomber Command pilot

The point of the spear

'We accepted the fact that as a necessary part of the prosecution of the war there were civilian deaths. It occurred in Britain, it occurred in Germany. One got used to the fact that civilians were suffering, and they were suffering all over the eastern front and the Jews in eastern Germany. Everyone accepted that this was total war. We were doing the job we were asked to do, and we thought it was essential under the circumstances we were in.

While I was in training France was conquered, and there was the Continent under the heel of Hitler. While I was training we had the Battle of Britain and the Blitz. Without America in the war the only way we could hit at the Germans was through Bomber Command. The whole attitude of Bomber Command was that we were the point of the spear, and we had a job to do. It was highly dangerous. We had to accept that in modern war civilians were killed. In our eyes we were in a desperate situation, and we knew it. The trials of the German nation did not worry us an awful lot.'

Lord Mackie, Bomber Command observer

Coffins of the Wellington crew at their funeral in Germany. Bomber Command's casualties were high as a proportion of the force, but a fraction of the losses suffered by British forces on the Western Front during the First World War.

Right: Bomber Command left a trail of wreckage across Germany, much of which was collected and recycled into German aircraft production. Scrap aluminium became an important source of metal during 1943 and 1944.

Below: Accidents were frequent in training or on the long haul back from a raid on Germany. Inexperience, exhaustion, bad weather or just bad luck all played their part. Here a Stirling Mk III of No 196 Squadron lies entangled with a Halifax Mk V of No 298 Squadron at Tarrant Rushton in February 1944.

In some cases large resources were tied up in building new factories in bomb-safe areas in a situation where building labour and materials were in desperately short supply. None of this proved critical, but it provided a constant attrition of managerial energy, and denied German industry the opportunity to plan and operate a rational, centralised industrial structure, in which optimum output would have peaked at levels very much higher than those achieved in the teeth of bombing in 1944 and 1945.

The impact on German morale was equally debilitating. Bombing did not, of course, produce the popular overthrow of the Hitler regime, which was an unrealistic expectation at best. Workers continued to work and soldiers to fight, even beyond the limit of endurance. But the effect on those regularly subjected to bombing in the major industrial centres was nonetheless intensely demoralising. The destruction of the urban environment and urban amenities did not make workers want to fight and work harder, but induced panic, nervous exhaustion, apathy and listlessness. These were hardly the ingredients for revolution, but neither did they produce an active and enthusiastic labour force. The head of the Labour Section in the Speer Armaments Ministry described the effects of city bombing as follows:

> '…accommodation in mass and emergency quarters, difficulties of going to and from work, loss of personnel and personal property on account of bombing, disturbed rest at night on account of air-raids, difficulties of supply, change of place of work when the firms were evacuated, working in factories without a roof, or underground…'

Germans interviewed after the war were almost unanimous in their view that bombing was the hardest thing for civilians to bear. The effect fed through into levels of absenteeism. In 1944 the average level of absenteeism was 23.5 days, or almost four full working weeks. At the Ford works in Cologne one-quarter of the workforce was absent on any one day of the year. The efficiency of industrial labour was reduced by the terrible strains imposed by bombing. In the cities directly under the flight path of the bomber stream, hours were spent in cellars and cramped shelters, often by day and by night. In Mainz between January and November 1944 a state of air-raid alarm existed for a total of 540 hours, or almost ten weeks of work. The populations evacuated the cities. The population of Berlin declined from 4 million in January 1943 to 2.7 million in May 1944. Almost 9 million Germans were evacuated from German cities, reducing the number of potential women workers, and placing

enormous strains on the reception areas to supply food and shelter. The production of civilian goods actually went up in Germany in 1943 and 1944 to supply bombed-out families with basic provisions.

The urban populations that stayed behind were subjected to a uniquely dangerous and unnerving experience. The levels of productivity achieved in 1944 in German industry were without doubt lower than they would have been if Germans had been free to work, like American workers, in an environment free of hazards and the constant threat of death. In many cases production was kept going by an army of unfortunate forced workers and camp inmates, whose atrocious conditions produced a productivity rate two-thirds or less of the German worker, and whose commitment to the German cause was presumably nil. Bombing produced in German society and in German industry insupportable strains, which by the winter of 1944/5 brought the German domestic war effort to crisis point.

Bombing had other profound effects. It distorted German strategy and forced the massive diversion of resources – men and weapons – to fight the bomber threat. The establishment of an extensive air defence system of searchlights, radar, anti-aircraft guns and fighter defence shifted valuable resources away from the main battlefronts. In January 1943, 59 per cent of the German fighter force was already tied up in the west facing the bomber threat, and one-quarter was on the eastern front. By January 1944 the proportion was 68 per cent and 17 per cent respectively. The air war also absorbed a large share of German artillery output, one-third by 1944. There were by that year 14,489 heavy guns and 41,937 light guns pointing skywards. Anti-aircraft guns took one-fifth of all ammunition, while air defences took half the production of the electro-technical industry, and one-third of optical equipment, leaving German forces in the field short of air protection, guns, and radio and radar. The manpower of the air defence system was formidable: 439,000 by 1942, and 889,000 at its peak in 1944. Though air defence was not organised into divisions and army corps, and its manpower and equipment was scattered across German territory, it would hardly be an exaggeration to argue that German air defences constituted a real 'Second Front' during 1943 and 1944.

The air defences had a further unforeseen effect on German military performance. German armies during 1943 found themselves slowly starved of air support at just the point that their enemies' production of aircraft began to rise steeply, and the balance between defensive and offensive aviation shifted decisively in favour of the former. By 1944 bombers constituted only one-fifth of German aircraft output and they were frittered away against much larger enemy fighter forces on the eastern and western fronts. German commanders were almost unanimous after the war in picking out air power as the decisive difference between the two sides. Without the bombing, both British and American, German forces at the fighting fronts would have had much greater protection in the air, and might well have been able to maintain some of the initiative that was irreversibly lost by the summer of 1944.

Bombing also caused unpredictable diversions of effort. Two were especially damaging to Germany's military prospects: the decision to push German production underground, and Hitler's insistence that Germany should produce weapons of revenge (V-weapons) to counter aerial terror with aerial terror. The underground programme developed from the autumn of 1943 when it became evident that German industry was going to be subjected to an ever heavier and more accurate bombardment. It was a vast plan. Hitler ordered the construction or conversion of over 93 million square feet of floorspace. During 1944 work began on 71 million, but only 13 million were completed. The effort took half Germany's building

Targets

'If we could have seen what we were doing, if we could have seen little babies and women burning to death, screaming in agony, we wouldn't have been able to do it. It's sheer distance that allows you to do these things. You don't see the people you're blowing to smithereens, you don't hear the shrieks and screams. All you hear is the propaganda. I remember Lord Vansittart saying that the only good German was a dead German. You are taught to hate. I wasn't a good soldier. I don't think I hated enough. But I do ask the question, "What's the difference between me and an IRA terrorist who plants a bomb in a station and has no idea who it is going to kill?" We're terrorists.

They never mentioned people in targets. They just said targets. We had to aim at the flares and drop our bombs. There was never any mention of people. We might have thought we were dropping them on factories or military centres. All I thought of was not the people below but for God's sake let's get home. When a person is facing death, your primary object, right from your very guts, is the survival instinct – look after yourself. Survival was our thing.'

Harold Nash, Bomber Command navigator

The eternal dilemma

'There was always at the briefing some military reason given for our attack. It was either a steel-producing town or there was a lot of small industry making precision instruments. But the policy was the destruction of towns. You destroy a town, you hinder the war effort in many ways, and that in itself was the justification. The big mistake was to think that by breaking German morale it would end the war. The morale of the German population was utterly and completely broken, but this had no effect on the hierarchy, the people who were actually directing the war. In the Third Reich the popular voice could not have any influence.

Something we do have to remember is that from D-Day in June 1944 to the end of the war, the losses among Allied troops were less than for any one major battle of the First World War. When the Americans and British landed in France they were facing a continent that was completely softened up by the Allied bombing. Had that bombing not taken place, leaving aside the morality of it, God knows if we would have survived as an invading force. There are people who say if that had been done, or if this had been done, but you do what seems to be right at the time, and bombing Germany as we did seemed to be right at the time. In fact there was very little alternative.

I personally have no regrets in having participated. I do think about these things. It was terrible, but everything you do in war is terrible. If you stick a bayonet into someone it's terrible; if you shoot someone it's terrible; if you put people in concentration camps, it's terrible. But what is the alternative? Should we not have used the force in the best way that seemed possible? Or run the risk of concentration camps in our country? It's the eternal dilemma of peace and war.'

Peter Hinchliffe, Bomber Command

workers, half a million men, and quantities of construction materials and machinery. Much of the completed underground plant was never occupied or utilised. The scheme was an economic fantasy; the reality was the diversion of valuable resources to a project of little strategic worth.

Much the same could be said of the V-weapons programme. During 1943 Hitler became obsessed with the desire to get back at Britain for the night-bombing of German cities. Efforts to renew the 'Blitz' failed. Instead Hitler ordered into production two new weapons that he hoped would deter Britain from further bombing, or might even prevent invasion from the west. The first was the Fieseler 'flying bomb', known as the V-1; the second was the first true missile, the A4 rocket, known as the V-2. These programmes distorted efforts to produce more conventional weapons; it was later calculated that the materials in the V2 programme could have provided 24,000 additional fighter aircraft.

Neither weapon proved decisive. In the end, and partly due to the bombing, only 9,500 V-1s and 5,000 V-2s were fired, and most either exploded prematurely, fell in open

sea and countryside or were destroyed by British defences. The quantity of explosive they carried was tiny – a mere 0.77 per cent of the total tonnage dropped by the Allies on Germany in 1944. Concentration on the V-weapons also distorted Germany's technical capabilities. Weapons like the ground-to-air *Wasserfall* missile, or the Me-262 jet fighter, promised much greater strategic dividends, but the technical effort required to bring them to operational maturity and to produce them in large quantities was squandered on the V-weapons.

Bombing, then, not only diverted German military effort to home defence on a large scale, but also encouraged desperate solutions from Hitler that further undermined economic capacity and postponed the introduction of military technologies that might have had a decisive effect. The ramifications of the bombing campaign were many. The critical question is not so much 'What did bombing do to Germany?', but 'What could Germany have achieved if there had been no bombing?'. The answer is hypothetical, but it would not be bending historical probability too much to argue that if Germany had been free to mobilise its economy, science and manpower, and that of occupied

Bombers crashed all over occupied Europe and in neutral Sweden and Switzerland. This cutting is from a Dutch newspaper and shows the wreckage of a Lancaster brought down over Holland by a Messerschmitt Bf 110 night-fighter.

PHOTO OF YOUR CRASHED LANCASTER TAKEN ON 28th AUGUST 1944

Nr. 198   Mandag den 28. August 1944

Resterne af det ene Plan.

Britisk Maskine skudt ned ved Vejle

Dramatisk A
af Børnelam
Table Forken

Billedet her blev bragt i Vejle Amts Folkeblad, mandag den 28. august 1944. Det viser det ene plan fra den Lancaster III bombeflyet, som blev skudt ned af en Messerschmitt ME 110 jager ved Høgsholt.

Europe, entirely free from the bombing threat, the German war effort would have been potentially too formidable to contemplate a western invasion of Europe. The war would then have unravelled in a very different way.

Of course the bombing campaign was not conducted without a heavy price for both sides. It has often been argued that the material cost for Britain far outweighed the strategic gain. The resources that were mortgaged for the bombing effort could have been used instead to produce more warships or tanks or tactical aircraft. This argument assumes that the proportion of Britain's productive and training effort devoted to bombing was exceptionally high. The figure was in reality surprisingly modest. Post-war calculations based on man-hours devoted to production, maintenance and training showed that the heavy bomber programme absorbed 3.25 million man-years out of a total of 27 million, or 12 per cent. Measured against the totals for the entire war effort (production and fighting) bombing absorbed 7 per cent, rising to 12 per cent in 1944-45. Since at least a proportion of bomber production went to other theatres of war, the aggregate figures for the direct

bombing of Germany were certainly smaller than this. Seven per cent of Britain's war effort can hardly be regarded as an unreasonable allocation of resources. Nor is it clear that Britain would have gained significantly more from diverting the resources devoted to bombing to some other branch of production. The British Army and air forces were not conspicuously short of weapons by 1943-44, and were backed by extensive American production. More tactical aircraft could have been produced between 1941 and 1944, but the RAF had no shortage of them, and little for them to do except wait until Germany was weakened enough to allow the invasion of the Continent. This weakening relied a good deal on bombing in the first place.

As well as the overall cost of the campaign, much of the criticism of bombing has focused on the exceptionally heavy loss rates suffered by the Command on operations of questionable value. There is no argument but that survival rates were poor in the Command, but the issue of manpower losses must also be put into perspective. The losses were sustained over a whole six-year period and not in a single battle. The loss rate declined steadily over the

Just bad luck

'Bombing civilians? Let's put it this way. A factory that makes aeroplanes or makes guns or submarines has got to be staffed by blood and guts men that make them, and if you are going to win a total war there is no way you can do that job without killing civilians. A lot of our innocent civilians were killed in the bombing. I never cringed from the fact or the knowledge, but when you are dropping bombs you have no idea what's underneath you.

When I was in Hamburg in the war, having been brought

down from Denmark on a stretcher, I was at the railway station while an air raid was going on. I was taken down into the cellar on the station and there were numbers of little German girls with fair hair plaited down their backs playing 'Ring a ring of roses'. When you saw that you realised they were the kind of people you were bombing. You didn't have a very good feeling, I must admit. But when you were actually flying you were only concentrating on the target you were bombing and that was all. If there were civilians in the area it was just bad luck.'

Jim Verran, Bomber Command pilot

An absolute necessity

'If you start a major world war you expect to get a bloody nose. Any country that was faced with Nazi Germany did everything it could to make sure that they lost. It's always unfortunate when people get killed, particularly civilians and children, but you should not start wars. We did what was absolutely necessary. We did a great deal in shortening the length of that war. I don't think any one of those young men who died would have felt any differently. I didn't expect to survive, not in any morbid way, but because I felt I was

doing something that had to be done in order to save this country from a fate worse than death.

War is horrible; war is immoral. But you fight it the way you can. Look what happens to innocent civilians when armies roll across great territories and take cities. How many civilians died at Stalingrad? Outside Moscow? Or Leningrad? We were fighting one of the most immoral entities on the planet, and we had to fight it the best way we could. I just cannot and will never accept that bombing Germany was immoral.'

Sir John Curtiss, Bomber Command navigator

Moral judgements

'Bomber Command was the only weapon we possessed. People forget that the British Army for four years did nothing. They stayed in England training, equipping and preparing for the eventual invasion. Bomber Command was available and had to be used every day and every night, weather permitting. Had that force been available and Churchill had got up and said, in the House of Commons, "Well, we have this large bomber force available, but I'm afraid we mustn't use it because as it operates at night we can't be sure of hitting specific targets, and a lot of women and children will get killed", the British people would have been outraged and they would have said, "Not attack them because civilians might get killed? Have you gone mad, Hitler's been killing civilians all over Europe, including England." If Churchill had said that he wouldn't have survived as Prime Minister.

Morality is a thing you can indulge in an environment of peace and security, but you can't make moral judgements in war, when it's a question of national survival.'

Charles Patterson, Bomber Command pilot

A group of RAF prisoners of war, some of the 10,000 that fell into German hands during the war. An estimated 2,800 British and Commonwealth airmen escaped or evaded capture during the war.

war; the early years were much more dangerous. In 1942 the average loss rate was 4.1 per cent of sorties. By 1944 it was 1.7 per cent, and in 1945 0.9 per cent. The losses were also spread across the whole Commonwealth, and were not just 'British' losses, as is often suggested. Of the 55,000 dead, 32,890 were British; 9,856 were Canadian, 1,668 New Zealanders and 4,029 Australians. Of the rest, almost 1,000 Poles serving with Bomber Command lost their lives, and almost 500 from among volunteers from other Allied states.

The losses were not all sustained in bombing raids against German cities. Some 8,090 deaths were recorded from accidents in training and in non-operational flying, a reflection of the dangerous nature of the activity using crews with limited experience. Of the 47,000 combat deaths it is not clear what number occurred in attacks on German targets, and how many were casualties in the tactical battles of 1940 and 1944-5, or in the support for the war at sea. Over 400 bomber aircraft were lost in the mining campaign alone, which suggests that several thousand crew must have lost their lives in the supporting operations for the mining, anti-submarine and anti-shipping roles. The US 8th Air Force and Bomber Command both devoted approximately half their effort to bombing Germany, which was a more hazardous occupation than bombing in France or Italy. This suggests that a figure of rather less than half the casualties can be attributed to operations other than the direct attack of German targets unconnected with the surface battle.

Bomber Command losses need also to be put into another perspective. They are seldom compared with the losses in other services; those sustained by the spearhead divisions of the ground army were also exceptionally high. In North Africa the first American combat divisions suffered 25 per cent casualty rates in a matter of days. In the invasion of France loss rates were disguised by the rapid forward movement of reserves, but the losses in the British and Canadian armies facing Caen were very high. Of course, as a proportion of the whole army, these losses were small; similarly Bomber Command losses as a proportion of all those who worked in the Command, or as a proportion of RAF strength, become much less conspicuous.

What perhaps made bomber crew losses difficult to bear, and has given them a special notoriety since 1945, was their very visibility. A heavily mauled division in the field, or a sunken battleship, had higher casualty rates than Bomber Command, but they occurred all at once, in a single disaster, far from the public gaze. The slow attrition of bomber crews was evident to everyone who saw the limping planes return to base, and the rapid change of faces in the local bars. Losses were high, but they were spread over time and between operations of different types, and were not so much higher than losses in other areas of combat at the sharp end of war.

There were heavy losses on the other side. The best German estimate of the dead from bombing is 410,000, though in addition there were more than 60,000 Italian bomb victims. The German figure may well be higher than this since accurate statistics were difficult to obtain in the last stages of the war. This loss of life, predominantly among women, children and older men, has occasioned the most bitter recriminations of all against the bombing strategy. It is something that Bomber Command survivors take seriously and have thought about deeply. Some of their responses are recorded here, not to justify or to condemn, but to show that in war there are no easy answers. The British authorities believed that after the German bombardment of Rotterdam and Warsaw they were no longer obliged to act in self-restraint. The death of 42,000 Britons in the Blitz of 1940-41 made redundant any further discussion about the rights or wrongs of bombing targets with the risk of civilian casualty. The circumstances of the war explain why the policy was pursued and it can only be understood in that context. It was Air Marshal Harris, in one of his most famous newsreel speeches, who reminded his audience that the enemy had sown the wind, 'and they will reap the whirlwind'. In the middle of the war there were very few dissenting voices.

The balance sheet for bombing has come a long way from Galbraith's dismal judgement. Bomber Command played an important part in every area of Britain's war effort. It contributed to a major dislocation of German strategy, and the eventual loss of the initiative in the air. It made possible a safer re-entry to the Continent of Europe. It held down the pace of German economic mobilisation and technological development to a point where the Allies could be more certain of victory. It did all this with comparatively small losses, and at a cost to Britain's war effort of approximately 7 per cent of the whole. It is difficult to think of any strategy the British Empire might have pursued that could have extracted such a high cost to the enemy with the use of the same resources.

Bombing was a blunt instrument. It was a strategy that had a long and painful learning curve. But for all its deficiencies the 125,000 men and women of Bomber Command made a larger contribution to victory in Europe than any other element in Britain's armed services.

Appendix 1

Bomber Command statistics

Principal aircraft in Bomber Command, 1939-45

Type and Mark	Engine(s)	No of crew	Wing span (ft)	Gross wing area (sq ft)	Length (ft)	Height (tail down) (ft)	Maximum weight (lb)
Wellington 1A and 1C	2 Pegasus XVIII	6	86	830	60.8	18.75	30,000
Wellington II	2 Merlin X	6	86	830	60.8	18.75	32,000
Wellington III	2 Hercules XI	5/6	86	830	60.8	18.75	34,500
Wellington IV	2 Twin Wasp S3C4-G	5/6	86	830	60.8	18.75	31,600
Wellington V	2 Hercules VIII	3	86.2	840	62.6	17.4	32,000
Wellington VI	2 Merlin 60	3	86.2	840	62.6	17.4	31,600
Wellington X	2 Hercules VI	6	86	830	60.8	18.75	36,500
Whitley V	2 Merlin X	5	84	1,232	69.3	12.75	33,500
Hampden	2 Pegasus XVIII	4	69.3	737	53.3	14.9	22,500
Blenheim IV	2 Mercury XV	3	56	469	40	9.2	15,800
Stirling I	4 Hercules XI	7	99	1,460	87	22.75	70,000
Stirling III	4 Hercules VI	7	99	1,460	87	22.75	70,000
Halifax I	4 Merlin X	7	98	1,250	70.1	20.75	59,000
Halifax II and V	4 Merlin XX	6	98	1,250	70.1	20.75	60,000
Halifax III	4 Hercules XVI	7	104	1,275	70.1	20.75	65,000
Manchester	2 Vulture II	5	90.1	1,130	68.8	19.5	50,000
Lancaster I and III	4 Merlin 22, 28 or 38	7	102	1,297	68.9	19.5	68,000
Mosquito IV	Merlin 21	2	54.17	454	40.5	12.5	21,462
	Merlin 23	2	54.17	454	40.5	12.5	21,462
Mosquito IX	Merlin 72	2	54.17	454	44.5	12.5	22,475
Mosquito XVI*	Merlin 72 or 73	2	54.17	454	44.5	12.5	23,000
Mosquito XX	Packard Merlin 31 or 33	2	54.17	454	40.5	12.5	21,462
Fortress I	4 Cyclone R.1820-73	6	104	1,420	66	15.5	53,200
Ventura I	2 Double Wasp S1A4-G	4	65.5	551	52.6	14.2	26,000
Boston III	2 Cyclone G.R.2600-23	4	61.33	465	48.0	15.8	23,000

* Pressure cabin

Bomber Command sorties and losses 1939-45

Grand totals

Total despatched, 1939-45:   Night, 297,663; Day, 66,851
Total missing 1939-1945:   Night, 7,449; Day, 876
Total damaged, Feb 1942-May 1945   Night, 13,778
Estimated cause of loss, July 1942-May 1945   Night, 2,278 by fighters; 1,345 by flak; 112 not by enemy action (mainly collisions);
                                               2,072 from unknown causes
Estimated cause of damage, Feb 1942-May 1945: Night, 1,728 fighters (163 wrecked, 1,565 repairable);
                                               8,848 by flak (151 wrecked, 8,697 repairable);
                                               3,159 not by enemy action (876 wrecked, 2,283 repairable);
                                               43 from unknown causes (37 wrecked, 6 repairable)

Annual totals

Year	Total despatched		Total missing	
	By night	By day	By night	By day
1939	170	163	4	29
1940	17,493	3,316	342	152
1941	27,101	3,507	701	213
1942	32,737	2,303	1,291	109
1943	62,736	1,792	2,255	59
1944	113,352	35,096	2,349	224
1945	44,074	20,664	507	90

Bomber Command casualties, September 3rd 1939-May 8th 1945

	3.9.39 to 2.9.40	3.9.40 to 2.9.41	3.9.41 to 2.9.42	3.9.42 to 2.9.43	3.9.43 to 2.9.44	3.9.44 to 8.5.45	Total 3.9.39 to 8.5.45
RAF, WAAF, Dominion and Allied personnel at RAF posting disposal							
Aircrew							
1. Operational							
Killed	216	659	727	820	1,550	1,610	5,582
Presumed dead	1,150	2,786	5,819	11,302	14,933	5,549	41,548
Died POW	6	15	31	31	43	12	138
Missing now safe	43	38	186	496	1,178	927	2,868
POW now safe	419	906	1,437	2,466	3,596	960	9,784
Wounded	269	600	786	871	1,030	644	4,200
2. Non-operational							
Killed	383	774	1,382	1,933	2,413	1,205	8,090
Wounded	217	535	786	1,112	1,070	483	4,203
Died other causes	15	26	39	36	58	41	215
Missing now safe	8	12	14	21	19	9	83
POW now safe	4	20	12	8	6	4	54
Ground staff							
Killed	157	111	90	108	52	12	530
Wounded	96	162	121	156	150	74	759
Died other causes	93	176	188	211	204	168	1,040
Missing now safe	15	2	7	2			26
POW now safe	30	7	2	11	2		52

		3.9.39 to 2.9.40	3.9.40 to 2.9.41	3.9.41 to 2.9.42	3.9.42 to 2.9.43	3.9.43 to 2.9.44	3.9.44 to 8.5.45	Total 3.9.39 to 8.5.45
RAF and WAAF								
Aircrew								
1. Operational								
Killed		216	565	478	536	1,031	900	3,726
Presumed dead		1,128	2,487	3,958	7,970	10,343	3,278	29,164
Died POW		6	12	22	19	25	6	90
Missing now safe		43	32	113	343	652	463	1,646
POW now safe		418	767	957	1,718	2,397	504	6,761
Wounded		269	531	501	589	669	376	2,935
2. Non-operational								
Killed		378	633	915	1,294	1,400	705	5,325
Wounded		216	442	520	763	654	317	2,912
Died other causes		15	26	28	23	37	28	157
Missing now safe		8	12	13	21	16	9	79
POW now safe		4	14	5	5	4		32
Ground staff								
Killed	RAF	156	109	77	83	43	9	477
	WAAF	1		1		6	2	10
Wounded	RAF	94	158	108	137	116	58	671
	WAAF	1	1	12	10	19	6	49
Died other causes	RAF	90	171	160	178	156	131	886
	WAAF	1	3	15	22	29	11	81
Missing now safe	RAF	14	2	6	1	23		
POW now safe	RAF	30	7	1	4	1		43
Royal Canadian Air Force								
Aircrew								
1. Operational								
Killed			24	124	164	270	392	974
Presumed dead			99	888	2,091	2,752	1,405	7,235
Died POW				3	10	13	5	31
Missing now safe			2	17	97	375	297	788
POW now safe			39	201	515	819	269	1,843
Wounded			22	122	164	219	146	673
2. Non-operational								
Killed			66	254	359	675	293	1,647
Wounded			39	126	176	227	91	659
Died other causes				4	9	13	6	32
Missing now safe				1		2		3
POW now safe			4	1		1		6
Ground staff								
Killed				10	14	2		26
Wounded			1		6	11	7	25
Died other causes				4	4	12	15	35
Missing now safe					1			1
POW now safe								0

	3.9.39 to 2.9.40	3.9.40 to 2.9.41	3.9.41 to 2.9.42	3.9.42 to 2.9.43	3.9.43 to 2.9.44	3.9.44 to 8.5.45	Total 3.9.39 to 8.5.45
Royal New Zealand Air Force							
Aircrew							
1. Operational							
Killed		16	36	37	20	37	146
Presumed dead	5	87	300	439	352	104	1,287
Died POW		1	2	1	2		6
Missing now safe			3	19	23	28	73
POW now safe		31	90	92	69	17	299
Wounded		12	43	40	19	18	132
2. Non-operational							
Killed	3	13	59	63	56	41	235
Wounded	1	9	38	41	40	16	145
Died other causes				2	1	2	5
Missing now safe							0
POW now safe			4		1		5
Ground staff							
Killed		1		1			2
Wounded				1	1		2
Died other causes	1	1			1		3
Missing now safe							0
POW now safe				6			6
Royal Australian Air Force							
Aircrew							
1. Operational							
Killed		6	41	66	194	218	525
Presumed dead		28	394	580	1,305	580	2,887
Died POW			1		3	1	5
Missing now safe		1	22	18	112	115	268
POW now safe		8	72	105	285	114	584
Wounded		6	36	41	96	67	246
2. Non-operational							
Killed		11	103	146	225	132	617
Wounded		13	53	98	111	43	318
Died other causes			5	1	6	4	16
Missing now safe					1		1
POW now safe		1	1	3			5
Ground staff							
Killed			1	2			3
Wounded		1	1	1	3		6
Died other causes	1			2	2	1	6
Missing now safe			1				1
POW now safe			1	1	1		3

	3.9.39 to 2.9.40	3.9.40 to 2.9.41	3.9.41 to 2.9.42	3.9.42 to 2.9.43	3.9.43 to 2.9.44	3.9.44 to 8.5.45	Total 3.9.39 to 8.5.45
South African Air Force							
Aircrew							
1. Operational							
Killed						4	4
Presumed dead				1	5	9	15
Died POW		1					1
Missing now safe					2	2	4
POW now safe		1			1	8	10
Wounded				1	1	3	5
2. Non-operational							
Killed					6	1	7
Wounded					2		2
Died other causes							0
Missing now safe							0
POW now safe							0
Ground staff							
Killed							0
Wounded							0
Died other causes							0
Missing now safe	1						1
POW now safe							0
Other dominions (Rhodesia, India, etc)							
Aircrew							
1. Operational							
Killed					1	2	3
Presumed dead			4	1	11	10	26
Died POW							0
Missing now safe					2	3	5
POW now safe				2	1		3
Wounded			1		2		3
2. Non-Operational							
Killed		2	1			2	5
Wounded		1			1		2
Died other causes							0
Missing now safe							0
POW now safe		1					1
Ground staff							
Killed							0
Wounded							0
Died other causes							0
Missing now safe							0
POW now safe							0

	3.9.39 to 2.9.40	3.9.40 to 2.9.41	3.9.41 to 2.9.42	3.9.42 to 2.9.43	3.9.43 to 2.9.44	3.9.44 to 8.5.45	Total 3.9.39 to 8.5.45
Poles							
Aircrew							
1. Operational							
Killed		32	37	16	10	18	113
Presumed dead	26	52	219	197	103	39	636
Died POW			3	1			4
Missing now safe		2	25	14	5	7	53
POW now safe		42	101	31	12	11	197
Wounded		22	72	24	15	2	135
2. Non-operational							
Killed	1	38	40	42	33	17	171
Wounded		21	39	24	22		106
Died other causes			2	1	1	1	5
Missing now safe							0
POW now safe			1			4	5
Ground staff							
Killed			1	2	1		4
Wounded		1		1			2
Died other causes		1	7	4	2	1	15
Missing now safe							0
POW now safe							0
Allies (other than Poles)							
Aircrew							
1. Operational							
Killed		11	16	1	24	39	91
Presumed dead		33	56	23	62	124	298
Died POW		1					1
Missing now safe		1	6	5	7	12	31
POW now safe	1	18	16	3	12	37	87
Wounded		7	11	12	9	32	71
2. Non-operational							
Killed	1	11	10	29	18	14	83
Wounded		10	10	10	13	16	59
Died other causes							0
Missing now safe							0
POW now safe							0
Ground staff							
Killed		1		6		1	8
Wounded	1					3	4
Died other causes			2	1	2	9	14
Missing now safe							0
POW now safe							0

Territorial distribution of bomb tonnage (cumulative totals month by month)

	Targets at sea	Germany	Italy	Enemy occupied territory	Total from start of war
1942					
Up to February	500	31,714	259	15,598	48,071
March	502	33,611		16,374	50,746
April	505	36,708	272	17,694	55,179
May	524	39,446		18,171	58,413
June	531	45,920		18,535	65,258
July	542	52,128		18,684	71,626
August	553	56,078		18,885	75,788
September	562	61,564		18,985	81,383
October	567	64,556	846	19,223	85,192
November	579	65,386	2,358	19,292	87,615
December	580	67,221	3,098	19,430	90,329
1943					
January	582	70,189		20,805	94,674
February	584	75,927	3,734	25,388	105,633
March	594	84,663		27,233	116,224
April	597	94,575	4,683	27,836	127,691
May	610	107,170		28,148	140,611
June	614	121,394	4,803	29,071	155,882
July	620	136,752	5,804	29,536	172,712
August		153,420	9,086	29,735	192,861
September		165,690		32,320	207,716
October		179,370		32,413	221,489
November		192,296		33,982	235,984
December		203,654		34,426	247,786
1944					
January	622	220,495		36,011	266,214
February	626	232,286		36,270	278,268
March		251,996		44,258	305,966
April	627	266,011	9,089	63,735	339,462
May	628	274,558		92,439	376,714
June		279,460		144,804	433,981
July	628	292,682		189,197	491,596
August	633	307,121		240,608	557,451
September		328,167		272,149	610,038
October		379,700		281,820	671,242
November		432,561		281,981	724,264
December		479,213		284,369	773,304
1945					
January		509,933		286,572	806,227
February		555,333		287,061	852,116
March	634	622,960		287,070	919,753
April		657,420		287,564	954,707
May	634	657,674	9,089	287,647	955,044
% distribution	0.07%	68.8%	0.94%	30.19%	

Estimated average available bomblift, February 1942-April 1945 (tons)

	Light	Medium	Heavy	All types
1942				
February	33	340	137	510
March	39	391	199	629
April	43	311	229	583
May	51	273	381	705
June	58	241	424	723
July	51	287	471	809
August	44	215	538	797
September	39	152	486	677
October	42	187	552	781
November	52	118	469	639
December	63	94	667	824
1943				
January	72	159	915	1,146
February	91	203	1,074	1,368
March	66	254	1,180	1,500
April	61	182	1,325	1,568
May	77	201	1,864	2,142
June	14	153	2,179	2,346
July	17	113	2,225	2,355
August	24	88	2,082	2,194
September	24	59	2,229	2,312
October	28	36	2,542	2,606
November	42	-	2,864	2,906
December	36	-	2,930	2,966
1944				
January	34	-	3,013	3,047
February	37	-	2,682	2,719
March	60	-	3,837	3,897
April	78	-	4,393	4,471
May	92	-	4,768	4,860
June	95	-	4,986	5,081
July	108	-	5,116	5,224
August	101	-	5,086	5,187
September	107	-	5,832	5,939
October	139	-	6,315	6,454
November	167	-	6,354	6,521
December	169	-	6,132	6,301
1945				
January	167	-	5,097	5,264
February	185	-	5,031	5,216
March	198	-	5,356	5,554
April	232	-	6,004	6,236

Distribution of bombing tonnage
(cumulative weight of attack on various types of target)

	Industrial towns	Troops and defences	Transport-ation	Naval targets	Oil targets	Airfields and aircraft industries	Specific industries	Military install-ations	Miscella-neous	Sea mining	Totals
1942											
Up to February	13,614		8,317	13,365	2,295	3,315	2,418		2,881	1,464	49,535
March	15,325	1,866	8,387	13,663		3,347	2,928		3,005	1,702	52,448
April	17,992		8,398	14,510		3,590	3,325		3,214	2,083	57,262
May	20,375			14,741		3,894	3,536		3,308	2,767	61,180
June	26,462		8,409	14,964	2,306	4,284	3,572		3,406	3,549	68,807
July	31,708			15,860		4,383	3,594		3,500	4,150	75,776
August	35,536	1,927		15,970		4,417	3,609		3,614	4,798	80,586
September	40,792			16,073		4,542	3,625		3,709	5,535	86,918
October	43,916			16,467	2,307	4,725	3,662		3,779	6,176	91,368
November	45,616		8,418	17,129		4,733	3,671		3,814	6,936	94,551
December	48,113		8,452	17,153		4,740	3,759		3,878	7,584	97,913
1943											
January	51,038		8,482	18,367		4,806	3,808		3,941	8,445	103,119
February	57,367		8,488	22,768		4,822	3,935		4,019	9,193	114,826
March	63,973		8,561	24,436	2,331	4,837	6,007		4,152	9,964	126,188
April	73,070		8,669	25,771		5,587	6,048		4,288	11,180	138,871
May	84,974		8,782	25,803	2,352	6,187	6,127		4,459	11,931	152,542
June	98,922		8,838	25,927		6,376	6,878		4,612	12,708	168,590
July	115,021		9,094	25,933	2,355	6,380	7,269		4,733	13,322	186,034
August	130,695		9,099			6,382	9,099	2,072	5,299	14,058	206,919
September	142,761	2,597	9,874			6,400	10,125	2,225	5,446	14,843	222,559
October	155,862			25,938	2,361	6,417	10,462		5,753	15,563	236,952
November	168,399		11,330	25,940		6,424	10,681		6,027	16,213	252,197
December	179,599					6,431	10,778	2,571	6,201	16,720	264,506

Bomber Command airfields in use, 1942-45

Group	1	3	4	5	6	8	100	91	92	93	7	Total
February 1942	8	15	10	11		1		22	12			79
January 1943	11	13	12	14	6	4		17	17	11		105
January 1944	14	15	14	15	11	8	4	18	16	13		128
January 1945	12	12	11	12	7	9	8	13	14	1	22	121
May 1945	10	10	9	12	8	9	8	14	14		17	111

Bomber Command strength, 1942-45

	Operational			Training			Miscellaneous established types Medium, Light and Fighter	Grand total
	Heavy	Light or Medium	Total	Heavy	Light or Medium	Total		
February 1942	224	702	926					
January 1943	654	313	1,247	291	1,091	1,382	449	3,078
January 1944	1,298	167	1,465	583	1,277	1,860	479	3,804
January 1945	1,873	371	2,244	531	970	1,501	617	4,362
May 1945	1,994	422	2,416	468	915	1,383	585	4,384

Sea mining statistics, February 23rd 1942-May 8th 1945 (cumulative totals)

	Aircraft despatched	Aircraft missing	No of mines laid
1942			
Up to February	2,761	57	2,185
March	3,027	68	2,541
April	3,771	78	3,110
May	3,821	94	4,133
June	4,337	103	5,300
July	4,771	114	6,197
August	5,153	130	7,165
September	5,621	147	8,266
October	6,082	161	9,248
November	6,664	176	10,404
December	7,085	183	11,391
1943			
January	7,681	199	12,676
February	8,221	208	13,805
March	8,732	226	14,964
April	9,423	259	16,833
May	9,791	267	17,981
June	10,217	274	19,155
July	10,530	280	20,082
August	11,032	290	21,185
September	11,429	293	22,373
October	11,796	298	23,449
November	12,148	306	24,425
December	12,404	311	25,225
1944			
January	12,777	314	26,326
February	13,547	323	27,987
March	14,065	326	29,459
April	14,919	345	32,102
May	15,745	354	34,862
June	16,205	355	36,640
July	16,389	357	37,348
August	16,803	369	38,934
September	16,988	373	39,682
October	17,245	381	40,815
November	17,415	382	41,565
December	17,675	385	42,725
1945			
January	17,834	391	43,393
February	18,126	400	44,747
March	18,402	405	45,945
April	18,682	408	47,307
May	19,025	408	47,307

German estimate of bomb damage to cities, May 1944

| | Percentage of seriously damaged buildings | | | All buildings | | Percentage of seriously damaged housing |
| | | | | | | |
Town	All buildings	Industrial buildings	Non-industrial buildings	Within Zones 1 & 2	Within Zones 4 & 5	
Damage exceeding 50%						
Kassel	54	37	62	78	39	54
Remscheid	53	38	59	96	40	51
Hamburg	51	32	60	73	33	56
Damage 25% to 50%						
Hannover	44	24	52	63	27	48
Frankfurt	42	35	44	57	36	40
Dusseldorf	41	32	46	68	26	36
Augsburg	40	38	41	49	38	39
Cologne	40	27	46	52	29	32
Munchen Gladbach	37	22	46	72	20	47
Munchen Ludwigshafen	37	39	35	38	46	32
Aachen	33	23	39	50	14	42
Wuppertal-Barmen	33	16	41	66	21	37
Wuppertal-Elberfeld	32	24	35	66	23	35
Leipzig	28	15	34	36	28	28
Krefeld	25	16	29	48	8	30
Damage 10% to 25%						
Mulheim	23	14	27	76	15	23
Essen	20	28	16	27	41	24
Schweinfurt	20	18	21	21	25	17
Stettin	20	20	21	19	27	18
Dortmund	19	22	17	36	18	20
Berlin	18	11	21	26	18	25
Bochum	17	13	20	48	16	19
Hagen	15	9	20	37	8	16
Nurnberg	12	9	13	11	13	13
Stuttgart	12	13	12	17	16	11
Oberhausen	10	5	14	2	3	15
Damage less than 10%						
Duisburg	8	6	10	14	5	9
Brunswick	6	2	8	9	2	7
Munich	5	8	4	7	9	5
Munster	5	6	5	5	9	4
Magdeburg	2	4	0	0	5	0

German anti-aircraft personnel, 1940-45

1940	255,200
1941	344,400
1942	439,500
1943	642,700
1944	889,000
1945	842,200

Germany's underground factory programme (square feet of floorspace)

	Planned	In progress	Completed
Aircraft industry	48,150,900	21,933,971	8,371,320
Tanks	2,109,000	1,818,400	290,500
Vehicles	2,808,360	2,711,500	96,800
V-weapons	1,538,700	387,400	1,151,300
Ships	1,775,400	1,248,200	527,200
Weapons	2,173,500	2,119,720	53,800
Machine tools	7,101,600	6,079,400	1,022,200
Other supplies	16,839,400	10,512,500	
SS projects	11,298,000	8,651,100	1,883,000
Totals	93,794,900	71,318,000	13,396,200

Bombing as a 'second front': the diversion of resources to combat the bombing of Germany at its peak in 1944

Air defence manpower	803,000
Heavy AA guns	14,489
Light AA guns	41,937
Aircraft in Reich	68% of the German fighter force, Jan 1st 1944
	81% of German fighter force, Oct 1944
Manpower employed for civil decence, repair etc	1,200,000 (approx)

Total tonnage of bombs dropped on U-boat construction targets, 1939-45

Precision targets	Tonnage (short tons)	Area targets	Tonnage (short tons)
Nordseewerke, Emden	508.6	Emden	8,320.1
Kriegsmarine Werft, Wilhelmshaven	1,019.1	Wilhelmshaven	10,815.3
Deschimag, Wesermunde	Nil	Wesermunde	328.5
Bremer Vulkan, Vegesack	424.1	Vegesack	5.6
'Valentin', Farge	777.1	Bremen	8,004.5
Deschimag, Bremen	4,322.9		
Blohm und Voss, Hamburg	6,381.0	Hamburg	20,209.1
Deutsche Werft, Hamburg	250.0		
Howaldts Werke, Hamburg	126.3		
Stülcken Sohn, Hamburg	Nil		
Flensbürger Schiffbau Gesellschaft, Flensburg	150.1	Flensburg	7.4
Germania Werft, Kiel	3,264.2	Kiel	17,208.8
Deutsche Werke, Kiel	7,830.6		
Howaldts Werke, Kiel	1,315.9		
Walter Werke, Kiel	106.0		
Lübecker Flenderwerke, Lübeck	1.0	Lübeck	442.5
Neptunwerft, Rostock	27.0	Rostock	825.5
Stettiner Oderwerke, Stettin	2.8	Stettin	5,913.8
Stettiner Vulkan, Stettin	Nil		
Deutsche Werke Kiel, Gdynia	Nil	Gdynia	308.0
Danziger Werft, Danzig	306.3	Danzig	63.1
Schichau, Danzig	Nil		
Total	26,813.0		72,452.2

Annual tonnages of bombs dropped on U-boat construction targets

Year	Precision attacks		Area attacks		Total	
1939						
1940	610.5	(7.8%)	7.5	(0.1%)	618.0	(7.8%)
1941	1,700.3	(6.6%)	6,287.9	(24.4%)	7,988.2	(31.0%)
1942			10,936.1	(26.2%)	10,936.1	(26.2%)
1943	3,399.4	(1.9%)	23,502.7	(13.0%)	26,902.1	(14.8%)
1944	1,386.0	(0.2%)	27,838.2	(4.0%)	29,224.2	(4.2%)
1945	19,716.8	(3.4%)	3,879.8	(0.7%)	23,596.6	(4.1%)
Total	26,813.0	(1.7%)	72,452.2	(4.7%)	99,265.2	(6.5%)

The percentages in parentheses are the proportions of the total tonnages dropped on Germany in the same periods.

German aircraft production, 1939-44

	1939		1940		1941		1942		1943		1944	
	No	%	No	%	No	%	No	%	No	%	No	%
Single-engine fighters	1,541	18.6	1,870	17.3	2,852	24.2	4,542	29.2	9,626	37.7	25,860	65.0
Twin-engine fighters	1,050	12.5	1,840	17.0	1,880	16.0	2,422	15.6	4,100	16.0	5,025	12.7
Dive bomber and ground attack	557	6.7	611	5.6	476	4.0	917	5.9	1,844	7.2	909	2.3
Twin-engine bombers	1,579	19.1	2,744	25.3	2,816	24.0	3,620	23.3	4,266	16.8	3,063	7.7
Four-engine bombers	6	0.1	38	0.4	58	0.5	251	1.6	491	1.9	518	1.3
Total combat	4,733	57.1	7,103	65.6	8,082	68.7	11,752	75.6	20,327	79.6	35,394	89.0
Transports	1,037	12.5	763	7.1	969	8.2	1,265	8.1	2,033	8.0	1,002	2.5
Trainers	877	10.6	1,132	10.5	889	7.6	1,170	7.5	2,076	8.1	3,063	7.7
Not elsewhere classified	1,648	19.8	1,828	16.8	1,836	15.5	1,369	8.8	1,091	4.3	348	0.8
Totals	8,295	100.0	10,826	100.0	11,776	100.0	15,556	100.0	25,527	100.0	39,807	100.0

German oil production, January 1944-December 1944, in thousand metric tonnes

| Year and month | Synthetic production | | Domestic refining of crude oil | Production in occupied territories | Imports | Total |
	Hydrogenation and Fischer-Tropsch process	Other synthetic production				
1944						
January	336	162	175	48	179	900
February	306	172	160	48	200	886
March	341	201	191	49	186	968
April	348	153	157	48	104	810
May	285	151	170	47	81	734
June	145	153	129	44	40	511
July	86	143	115	38	56	438
August	47	137	134	16	11	345
September	26	126	113	5	11	281
October	38	117	124	3	34	316
November	78	107	105	10	37	337
December	56	108	108	9	22	303

Major RAF strategic bombing attacks on Italy, 1940-43

Target	Date	Operational base
Turin, Genoa	June 1940	East Anglia
Naples	Oct 1940	Malta
Brindisi	Nov 1940	Malta
Brindisi	Nov 1941	Malta
Naples	Oct 1941	Malta
Taranto	Jun 1942	Malta
Genoa	Oct 1942	East Anglia
Milan	Oct 1942	East Anglia
Genoa, Turin	Nov 1942	East Anglia
Turin	Feb 1943	East Anglia
Milan	Feb 1943	East Anglia
Livorno	May 1943	North Africa
Turin, Milan	July 1943	East Anglia
Rome	July 1943	North Africa
Milan	Aug 1943	East Anglia

Appendix 2
Maps

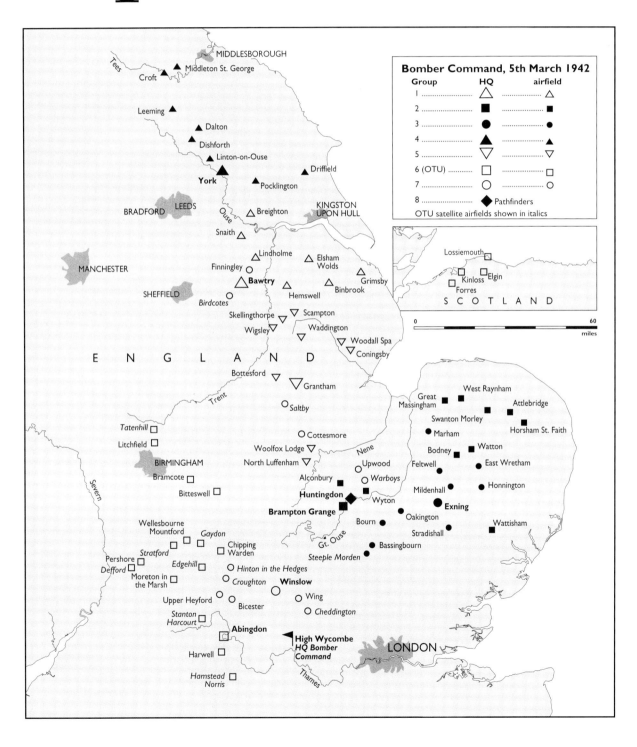

Bomber Command, 5th March 1942

Group	HQ	airfield
1	△	△
2	■	■
3	●	●
4	▲	▲
5	▽	▽
6 (OTU)	□	□
7	○	○
8	◆ Pathfinders	

OTU satellite airfields shown in italics

Tees

MIDDLESBOROUGH

Croft
Middleton St. George

Leeming

Dalton
Dishforth
Linton-on-Ouse
York
Driffield
Pocklington

BRADFORD LEEDS

Ouse

Breighton
KINGSTON UPON HULL

Snaith

MANCHESTER

Lindholme
Elsham Wolds
Finningley
Grimsby
Bawtry
Binbrook
SHEFFIELD
Hemswell
Birdcotes

Skellingthorpe
Scampton
Wigsley
Waddington
Woodall Spa
Coningsby

E N G L A N D

Bottesford

Trent
Grantham

Saltby

Cottesmore

Tatenhill
Litchfield
Woolfox Lodge
Nene
North Luffenham
BIRMINGHAM
Upwood
Bramcote
Alconbury
Warboys
Bitteswell
Huntingdon
Wyton
Brampton Grange
Bourn

Wellesbourne Mountford
Gaydon
Chipping Warden
Gt. Ouse
Bassingbourn
Pershore
Stratford
Edgehill
Steeple Morden
Defford
Moreton in the Marsh
Hinton in the Hedges
Croughton
Winslow
Upper Heyford
Wing
Bicester
Cheddington
Stanton Harcourt
Abingdon
High Wycombe HQ Bomber Command
LONDON
Harwell
Hamstead Norris
Thames

Lossiemouth
Kinloss
Elgin
Forres
S C O T L A N D

0 ————— 60
miles

West Raynham
Great Massingham
Attlebridge
Swanton Morley
Horsham St. Faith
Marham
Bodney
Watton
Feltwell
East Wretham
Mildenhall
Honnington
Exning
Oakington
Wattisham
Stradishall

Severn

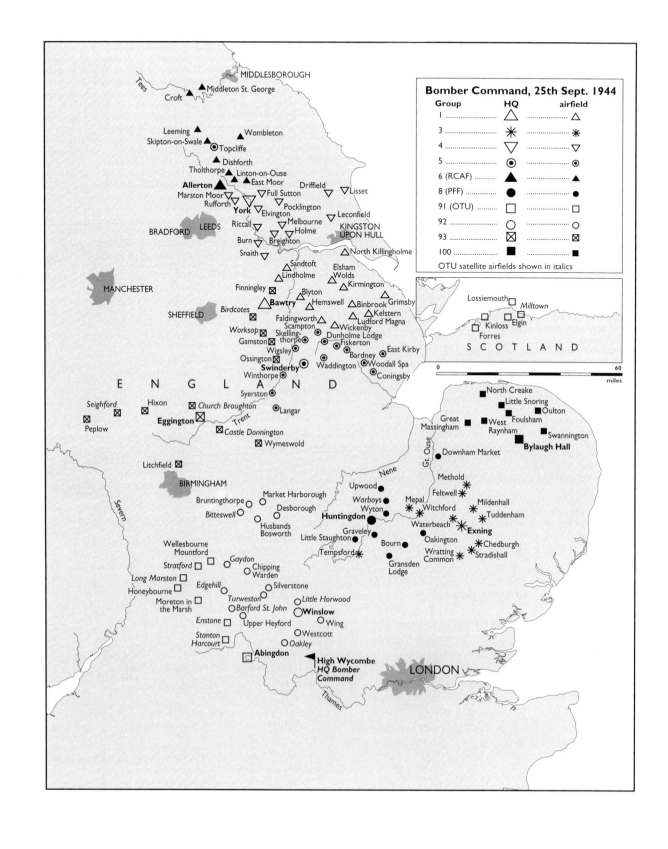

Bomber Command, 25th Sept. 1944

Group	HQ	airfield
1	△	△
3	✳	✳
4	▽	▽
5	◉	◉
6 (RCAF)	▲	▲
8 (PFF)	●	●
91 (OTU)	□	□
92	○	○
93	⊠	⊠
100	■	■

OTU satellite airfields shown in italics

MIDDLESBOROUGH

Tees

Croft
Middleton St. George

Leeming
Wombleton
Skipton-on-Swale
Topcliffe
Dishforth
Tholthorpe
Linton-on-Ouse
Allerton
East Moor
Driffield
Lisset
Marston Moor
Full Sutton
Rufforth
York
Pocklington
Elvington
Leconfield
Riccall
Melbourne
KINGSTON
UPON HULL
BRADFORD
LEEDS
Holme
Burn
Breighton
Snaith
North Killingholme
MANCHESTER
Sandtoft
Elsham
Lindholme
Wolds
Finningley
Kirmington
Blyton
Grimsby
Bawtry
Hemswell
Binbrook
SHEFFIELD
Birdcotes
Faldingworth
Kelstern
Scampton
Ludford Magna
Worksop
Skelling-
Wickenby
thorpe
Dunholme Lodge
Gamston
Fiskerton
Wigsley
Bardney
East Kirby
Ossington
Woodall Spa
ENGLAND
Swinderby
Waddington
Winthorpe
Coningsby
Syerston
Seighford
Hixon
Church Broughton
Langar
Peplow
Eggington
Trent
Castle Donnington
Wymeswold
Litchfield
BIRMINGHAM
Market Harborough
Bruntingthorpe
Bitteswell
Desborough
Husbands
Bosworth
Wellesbourne
Mountford
Stratford
Gaydon
Long Marston
Chipping
Warden
Honeybourne
Edgehill
Silverstone
Moreton in
the Marsh
Turweston
Little Horwood
Barford St. John
Winslow
Enstone
Upper Heyford
Wing
Stanton
Harcourt
Westcott
Oakley
[c] **Abingdon**
Severn

North Creake
Little Snoring
Oulton
Great
West
Foulsham
Massingham
Raynham
Swannington
Bylaugh Hall
Downham Market
Methold
Upwood
Feltwell
Warboys
Mepal
Mildenhall
Wyton
Witchford
Tuddenham
Huntingdon
Waterbeach
Exning
Graveley
Oakington
Chedburgh
Little Staughton
Bourn
Wratting
Stradishall
Tempsford
Gransden
Common
Lodge

Gt. Ouse
Nene

Lossiemouth
Milltown
Kinloss
Elgin
Forres
SCOTLAND

◀ **High Wycombe**
HQ Bomber
Command

LONDON

Thames

0 ————————— 60
miles

Bibliography

Extensive use has been made of air records in the Public Record Office, Kew. The principal materials used are to be found in classes AIR 1, AIR 2, AIR 8, AIR 9, AIR 10, AIR 14, AIR 20.

Air Ministry *The Rise and Fall of the German Air Force 1933–1945* (issued in 1947, reprinted London, 1987)

R. Beaumont 'The Bomber Offensive as a Second Front', *Journal of Contemporary History, 22* (1987)

E. Beck *Under the Bombs: the German Home Front 1942–1945* (Lexington, Kentucky, 1988)

U. Bialer *The Shadow of the Bomber: the fear of air attack and British politics 1932–1939* (London, 1980)

H. Boog (ed.) *The Conduct of the Air War in the Second World War* (Oxford, 1992)

D. Busch *Der Luftkrieg im Raum Mainz wahrend des Zweiten Weltkrieges* (Mainz, 1988)

R. Chisholm *Cover of Darkness* (London, 1953)

R. Cooke, R. Nesbit *Target: Hitler's Oil Allied attacks on German oil supplies 1939–1945* (London, 1985)

C.C. Crane *Bombs, Cities and Civilians: American Airpower Strategy in World War II* (Lawrence, Kansas, 1993)

W.F. Craven,
J.L. Cate *The Army Air Forces in World War II* (6 vols., Chicago, 1948–55)

M. Dean *The Royal Air Force in Two World Wars* (London, 1979)

R.A. Freeman *The American Airmen in Europe* (London, 1991)

J.K. Galbraith *A Life in Our Times: Memoirs* (London, 1981)

S.A. Garrett *Ethics and Airpower in World War II* (New York, 1993)

N. Gibbs *Grand Strategy: Vol I, Rearmament Policy* (London, 1976)

F. Golucke *Schweinfurt und der strategische Luftkrieg 1943* (Paderborn, 1980)

J. Gooch (ed) *Airpower: Theory and Practice* (London, 1995)

O. Groehler *Bombenkrieg gegen Deutschland* (Berlin, 1990)

H. Hansell *The Strategic Air War against Germany and Japan* (Washington DC, 1986)

A.T. Harris *Bomber Offensive* (London, 1947)

A.T. Harris *Despatch on War Operations 23 Feb 1942–8 May 1945* (Introdution by S. Cox, London, 1995)

S. Harvey 'The Italian War Effort and the Strategic Bombing of Italy', *History, 70* (1983)

M. Hastings *Bomber Command* (London, 1979)

M.P. Hiller *Stuttgart im Zweiten Weltkrieg* (Gerlingen, 1989)

P. Johnson *The Withered Garland: reflections and doubts of a bomber* (London, 1995)

N. Jones *The Origins of Strategic Bombing: as study of the development of British air strategic thought and practice up to 1918* (London, 1973)

R.V. Jones *Most Secret War: British Scientific Intelligence 1939–1945* (London, 1978)

A.J. Levine *The Strategic Bombing of Germany 1940–1945* (London, 1992)

R.A. Mason *Air Power: a Centennial Appraisal* (London, 1994)

S.L. McFarland 'The Evolution of the Strategic Fighter in Europe', *Journal of Contemporary History, 10* (1987)

C. Messenger *'Bomber Harris' and the Strategic Bombing Offensive* (London, 1984)

M. Middlebrook *The Berlin Raids* (London, 1988)

M. Middlebrook *The Nuremberg Raid* (London, 1986)

M. Middlebrook, C. Everitt (eds) *The Bomber Command War Diaries: an operational reference book* (London, 1985)

A.C. Mierzejewski *The Collapse of the German War Economy 1944–1945: Allied air power and the German National Railway* (Chapel Hill, NC, 1988)

W. Murray *Luftwaffe* (London, 1985)

R.J. Overy *The Air War 1939–1945* (London, 1980)

H. Penrose *British Aviation: Ominous Skies 1935–1939* (London, 1980)

M.M. Postan *British War Production* (London, 1952)

B.D. Powers *Strategy without Slide Rule: British Air Strategy 1914–1939* (London, 1976)

D. Richards *Portal of Hungerford: the Life of Marshal of the Royal Air Force Viscount Portal of Hungerford* (London, 1977)

D. Richards,
H. Saunders *The Royal Air Force 1939–1945* (3 vols, London, 1953)

D. Saward *'Victory Denied: The Rise of Air Power and the Defeat of Germany 1920–1945* (London, 1985)

J. Slessor *The Central Blue* (London, 1956)

M. Smith *British Air Strategy between the Wars* (Oxford, 1984)

E. Smithies *War in the Air* (London, 1990)

A. Speer *Inside the Third Reich* (London, 1970)

A. Stephens (ed) *The War in the Air* (Canberra, 1994)

J. Stern *The Hidden Damage* (London, 1990)

J. Terraine *The Right of the Line: The Royal Air Force and the European War 1939–1945* (London, 1985)

United States Strategic Bombing Survey (USSBS)
Report 3, The Effects of Strategic Bombing on the German War Economy (Washington, 1945)
Report 4, Aircraft Division Industry Report, (Washington, 1945)
Report 64B, The Effects of Strategic Bombing on German Morale (2 vols, Washington, 1945)
Report 60, V Weapons (Crossbow) Washington, 1945)
Report 109, Oil Division Final Report (Washington, 1945)
Report 200, The Effects of Strategic Bombing on German Transportation (Washington, 1945)

A. Verrier *The Bomber Offensive* (London, 1964)

C. Webster, N. Frankland *The Strategic Air Offensive against Germany* (4 vols, London, 1961)

M.K. Wells *Courage and Air Warfare: The Allied Aircrew Experience in the Second World War* (London, 1995)

Acknowledgements

The Publishers would like to thank the following individuals and organisations for the supplying photographs for use in this book.

Back cover: Bruce Robertson. 2: Bruce Robertson. 9: Jackie Assheton. 10: Jackie Assheton. 14: Bruce Robertson (two). 15: Bruce Robertson (two). 16: RAF Museum. 18: Bruce Robertson. 19: Bruce Robertson. 20: John Gee. 21: Bruce Robertson. 22: Bruce Robertson. 23: Bruce Robertson/RAF Museum. 24: Bruce Robertson. 25: Bruce Robertson. 26: Bruce Robertson (two). 31: RAF Museum/Greg Gregson. 34: Bruce Robertson/RAF Museum. 35: Bruce Robertson. 36: Bruce Robertson/Charles Patterson. 37: Bruce Robertson. 38: Bruce Robertson. 39: Bruce Robertson. 40: Bruce Robertson/Harry Jones. 41: RAF Museum. 42: Bruce Robertson/RAF Museum. 45: Bruce Robertson/RAF Museum. 46: RAF Museum. 47: RAF Museum/Bruce Robertson. 48: RAF Museum/Bruce Robertson. 49: RAF Museum/Bruce Robertson. 50: Bill Jacobs/Don Elliott. 51: Bruce Robertson. 53: Bruce Robertson. 55: Bruce Robertson (two). 56: RAF Museum. 57: Bruce Robertson/RAF Museum. 58: Bruce Robertson/Alex Kerr. 59: Arnold Derrington/Bruce Robertson. 60: Bruce Robertson. 62: Jackie Assheton. 64: RAF Museum. 65: RAF Museum. 66: Jim Verran. 67: RAF Museum/Jackie Assheton. 68: John Gee. 71: RAF Museum (two). 73: Popperfoto/Bruce Robertson. 74: RAF Museum. 75: RAF Museum. 76: RAF Museum (two). 77: Bruce Robertson/RAF Museum. 78: Howard Lees. 79: Howard Lees. 81: Bruce Robertson/RAF Museum. 82: RAF Museum. 83: Bruce Robertson/RAF Museum. 84: RAF Museum/RAF Museum. 85: RAF Museum. 88: Howard Lees. 89: RAF Museum (three). 91: Bruce Robertson. 92: RAF Museum (three). 93: RAF Museum. 96: RAF Museum. 97: RAF Museum. 98: Bruce Robertson. 100: Bruce Robertson. 103: Howard Lees. 106: Howard Lees. 107: Howard Lees. 109: RAF Museum. 110: Ivor Broom. 112: Ivor Broom/Norman Daly/RAF Museum. 113: RAF Museum (two)/Pip Brimson. 114: RAF Museum. 116: RAF Museum (two). 117: RAF Museum (two). 118: Bruce Robertson/RAF Museum. 119: RAF Museum (two). 120: RAF Museum/ps. 121: RAF Museum/Harry Jones. 122: RAF Museum. 123: RAF Museum. 125: RAF Museum. 126: RAF Museum (two). 127: Howard Lees. 128: Howard Lees. 131: John Gee. 132: Howard Lees/RAF Museum. 134: Bruce Robertson. 135: Bruce Robertson. 136: Bruce Robertson. 137: Bruce Robertson. 138: RAF Museum. 140: RAF Museum. 141: RAF Museum/Ted Sismore. 142: Arnold Derrington. 144: RAF Museum (three). 145: RAF Museum/Bruce Robertson. 146: Jim Verran. 147: Pip Brimson (two). 148: Larry Donnelly. 149: Jim Verran. 150: Howard Lees/RAF Museum. 151: Pip Brimson/RAF Museum. 152: RAF Museum. 153: Pip Brimson (two). 154: RAF Museum (two). 155: RAF Museum (two). 156: RAF Museum/John Gee. 157: RAF Museum (two). 158: RAF Museum/Bruce Robertson. 159: RAF Museum/Bruce Robertson. 160: Bruce Robertson/Pip Brimson. 161: Ted Sismore/Bruce Robertson. 162: Pip Brimson/Bruce Robertson. 163: Bruce Robertson. 164: Bruce Robertson. 165: RAF Museum (three). 166: RAF Museum/Bruce Robertson. 167: Norman Daly. 168: John Curtiss. 169: Norman Daly. 170: RAF Museum. 171: Norman Berryman. 172: RAF Museum (two). 173: Maurice Chick. 174: RAF Museum. 175: Pip Brimson/Bruce Robertson. 176: RAF Museum. 177: Bruce Robertson. 178: Bruce Robertson. 179: Charles Patterson. 180: F. Moss. 186: RAF Museum (two). 187: RAF Museum (two). 188: Charles Patterson/Ivor Broom. 189: RAF Museum. 190: RAF Museum (two). 191: RAF Museum. 192 Howard Lees. 193: Howard Lees/H.S./Harry Jones. 194: Harry Jones. 195: Harry Jones. 196: Harry Jones/RAF Museum. 199: Jim Verran. 201: RAF Museum.

Index